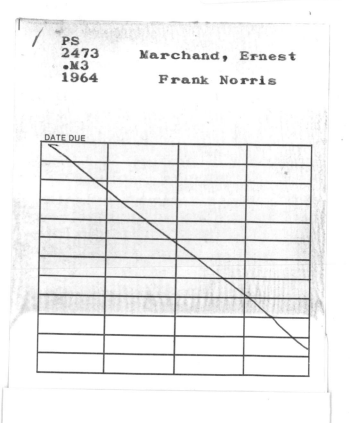

FRANK NORRIS
A Study

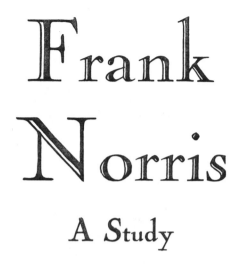

Frank Norris

A Study

By
ERNEST MARCHAND

1971

OCTAGON BOOKS

New York

Reprinted 1964
by special arrangement with Stanford University Press

Second Octagon printing 1971

OCTAGON BOOKS
A DIVISION OF FARRAR, STRAUS & GIROUX, INC.
19 Union Square West
New York, N. Y. 10003

LIBRARY OF CONGRESS CATALOG CARD NUMBER: 64-16376

Printed in U.S.A. by
NOBLE OFFSET PRINTERS, INC.
NEW YORK 3, N. Y.

". . . . though one ought to feel affection for his theme, he should never flatter anybody."—HIPPOLYTE ADOLPHE TAINE, Special "Introduction" (1871) to the English translation of the *History of English Literature*

Preface

Following his death, Frank Norris remained without a biography for thirty years; Professor Franklin Walker's *Frank Norris: A Biography* appeared in 1932. In 1933 M. Marius Biencourt published in Paris his *Une Influence du Naturalisme Français en Amérique: Frank Norris,* exhibiting the influence of the work of Zola on that of his American admirer. Here, in this first extensive study of one of our chief novelists, I have endeavored to place Norris against the wider background of his period—social and intellectual as well as purely literary—to examine the several aspects of his thought and of his work, and to take stock of critical opinion about him from his own day to the present.

To Professor Harry Hayden Clark of the University of Wisconsin, who from the beginning has faithfully stood godfather to this study, my obligations are very great. At every stage I have profited by his sound advice, patient and kindly criticism, and wide and scholarly knowledge. Professor Franklin Walker has very kindly loaned me his extensive bibliography of Frank Norris and his transcripts of Norris' letters. My indebtedness to his life of Norris is evident throughout this work. Professor Sophus Keith Winther of the University of Washington long ago increased my pleasure in Frank Norris by sharing it with me. I have also to thank him for reading the manuscript and for making several useful suggestions. To Mr. Charles G. Norris, who read the completed manuscript, I am especially grateful for generous encouragement, for allowing me to see Frank Norris' notes for *The Octopus,* and for other marked kindnesses. I wish to record here my sense of obligation to the late Mrs. Kate Felton Elkins, founder of the George Loomis Fellowship in American Literature, by whose benefaction I have profited with the award to me of the Fellowship in 1935–36 and again in 1936–37, during which time I was engaged on this study. I wish also to signify my appreciation to Dr. Nathan van Patten, Director of Stanford University Libraries, for his part in awarding me the Fellowship.

I am indebted to Mrs. Janet Black, widow of Frank Norris, for permission to quote from *Moran of the Lady Letty, A Man's Woman,* and *Collected Writings Hitherto Unpublished in Book Form;* to Miss Mildred Howells for permission to quote from William Dean Howells' review of *McTeague* in *Literature* (March 24, 1899) and from other writings of Howells; to Mr. John D. Barry for the use of passages from his review of *McTeague* in the *Literary World* (March 18, 1899); to Mr. Harry Robertson for permission to quote from Ambrose Bierce's *The Shadow on the Dial and Other Essays;* and to Mr. Gustavus Myers for lines from the Preface to the revised edition of his *History of the Great American Fortunes.*

E. M.

Palo Alto, California
August 12, 1942

Contents

ix

FRANK NORRIS
A Study

Chapter I

The Ends & Purposes of the Novel

Fiction may keep pace with the Great March, but it will not be by dint of amusing the people. The muse is a teacher, not a trickster.—FRANK NORRIS*

IN THE closing years of the last century, when the ormolu glitter of the Gilded Age was melting into the aesthetic tints of the Mauve Decade and when Frank Norris was meditating his first novel, a strange disproportion existed between American letters and American life. The curious citizen of a distant realm who had only American poetry and novels to guide him would have formed but the vaguest, most confused, and inaccurate conceptions of the life led by more than sixty millions of people. Above all he would have been struck by the disposition of writers to ignore American life altogether.

Everywhere he would have found the main business of

---

* From "The Novel with a 'Purpose'," in *The Responsibilities of the Novelist* (copyright 1901, 1902, 1903, by Doubleday, Doran & Company, Inc.), p. 33.

existence, whether pictured abroad or at home, to be romantic love. The story of that love was often enacted in remote times and far places by men and women garbed in the appropriate costumes and addressing each other in an antique tongue filled with "thou" and "thee." Or, again, the union of hearts would occur in imagined principalities of Europe where gallant officers in uniforms of scarlet and gold wooed incredibly beautiful heroines on moonlit marbled terraces. He would have found poets longing to stroll through the bazaars of Samarkand, or to gallop across deserts on stallions shod with fire. Or, if the scene were America, it was no less idyllic. The fragrance of new-mown hay was the all-sufficing symbol of country life; or, in the South, magnolias half-concealing white-columned verandas. The time-tried Alger formula of the poor boy who marries the boss's daughter and is taken into the firm embraced all that imaginative literature need present of the life of the industrial city.

But scarcely anywhere would our supposed investigator have seen that the main business of life is the hard struggle to live, in which romantic love must be but an incident; or that for the middle classes, raised in varying degrees above the struggle in its crudest form, the main business of life is getting on in the world, the sharp competition of outdoing one's neighbor in the effort to acquire a better house on a better street, to display more of the accepted evidences of worth. Very little would our hypothetical reader have found of grinding poverty, dirt, squalor, disease; of futility, defeat, despair; of bitter and ironic injustice; of the pressure of inescapable circumstance. The cynical and ruthless or ignorant and self-deluded lords of industry and finance, in their true characters, would have been absent. The sense of manifold activity, the tumult and confusion attendant upon the exploitation of a continent by an energetic people would have been lacking. The very appearance of the land in other than its picturesque natural features would not have arisen before the imagination of the reader. He would not have seen the flame-shot smoke arising from the deep valley where the Monongahela joins the Alleghany, the long freights laden with squealing pigs trundling across the flat expanses of Illinois toward Chicago, the mechanical reapers creeping around the diminishing squares of wheat in Kansas or the Dakotas, the black ore dumps of Butte, the devastated mountainsides in Oregon and Washington—brown wastes of bark and shattered branches after the passage of the logging crews. Nor would he have seen the sprawled corpses along the river in Homestead, or the charred carcasses in Mississippi and Georgia by means of which the inferior race is kept in awe. These things were absent from the record, not because they did not exist or rarely occurred, but because by an almost universal tacit agreement they were considered unfit for literary representation. Theodore Dreiser, recalling his early days as a struggling journalist in New York, thus records his sense of the failure of contemporary literature to deal faithfully with American life:

. . . . in a kind of ferment or fever due to my necessities and desperation, I set to examining the current magazines and the fiction and articles to be found therein: *Century, Scribner's, Harper's.* I was never more confounded than by the discrepancy existing between my own observations and those displayed here, the beauty and peace and charm to be found in everything, the almost complete absence of any reference to the coarse and the vulgar and the cruel and the terrible. How did it happen that these remarkable persons—geniuses of course, one and all—saw life in this happy roseate way? Was it so, and was I all wrong? . . . . They seemed to deal with phases of sweetness and beauty and success and goodness such as I rarely encountered.[1]

Howells, it is true, in a long series of novels practiced what he called realism and held close to American scenes and subjects; but his realism was of a mild and denatured sort, in conformity with his well-known dictum that "the more smiling aspects of life are the more American"[2]—a sentiment which might have been taken as the official gospel for all who would interpret America to herself. Here the grosser, more violent passions slumbered; tragedy belonged to ruder ages or to the half-barbaric peoples of the East, failure and frustration to the effete and crowded nations of Europe. A few hardy spirits like H. H. Boyesen attempted to introduce Zola, Maupassant, Flaubert, Tolstoy, and other Continental realists to the American reading public and to recommend their methods to American writers. A ferocious battle of the books ensued, with the magazines as the field of combat. Maurice Thompson, Charles Dudley Warner, Francis Marion Crawford, and William Roscoe Thayer, supported by a swarm of indignant criticasters, were among the leading champions of what they called romance, as opposed to realism.

The objections to realism, as formulated by this company, may be boiled down to three: (1) It was indecent. Literature, Crawford wrote, must be "suited to maiden ears and eyes."[3] There must be no suggestion that human

---

[1] Theodore Dreiser, *A Book About Myself* (Constable & Co., London, 1929), p. 490. Quoted by permission of G. P. Putnam's Sons.

[2] William Dean Howells, *Criticism and Fiction* (New York: Harper and Brothers, 1891), p. 128.

[3] F. Marion Crawford, *The Novel: What It Is* (By permission of The Macmillan Company, publishers, 1893), p. 29. Howells, though a defender of realism, also believed fiction should accommodate itself to the innocence of

beings know physical passion, which, presumably, is indecent even when experienced under the sanction of law and religion. There must be no more of the "disposition, which may well be called alarming, to trifle with the marriage relation," declared R. O. Beard, warning in *The Dial* (October 1882) against "A Certain Dangerous Tendency in Novels."

(2) Realism was not art. It was a mere photographic presentation of facts untouched by the creative imagination. Thus William Roscoe Thayer, discussing "The Bases of Fiction" in *The Open Court* (July 17, 1890): "M. Zola and Mr. Howells are inferior because they lack imagination, and content themselves with photographing the transitory surfaces of life."

(3) Realism was pessimistic, depressing, and degrading. "The Purpose novel," wrote Margaret Deland in *The Independent* (April 20, 1899), "is too apt to leave, not hope and buoyancy in the reader's mind, but a miserable feeling of helplessness . . . . truth is not true unless it holds hope! . . . . nobody has a right to make this beautiful, puzzling, sad world any more mournful than it is for anybody else."

But these objections often served to cover another yet more serious: the presence in the new realistic literature of certain critical and revolutionary ideas touching contemporary society. It was Maurice Thompson, in an article on Tolstoy in *The Literary World* (August 20, 1887), who

the young girls who formed the greater part of its audience. For his part he would not by any frankness on sexual matters cut himself off from the "high and sweet" pleasure of appealing to his young girl readers (*Criticism and Fiction* [New York: Harper and Brothers, 1891], p. 149). But H. H. Boyesen refused to submit so tamely. The female reader, he declared, "is the Iron Madonna who strangles in her fond embrace the American novelist" ("Why We Have No Great Novelists," *The Forum*, February 1887).

let the cat out of the bag: "All this hacking at wealth and all this apostrophizing of poverty is not in the spirit of Christ; it is in the spirit of communism, socialism and anarchy . . . ."

Any literature, however, which designs itself primarily for "maiden ears and eyes" and which shuns anything remotely resembling an idea is doomed to impotence and sterility. Is it any wonder that as long as these attitudes prevailed among readers and writers American literature should have been, with a few notable exceptions, thin, pale, bloodless, sentimental, insipid, or that the grand theme of American life which embraced nearly all the rest—namely, the triumphant advance of a middle-class culture founded on industrial exploitation—should have been so little or so inadequately dealt with by the literary artist?

The social and economic development of the United States since the Civil War, together with the disparity during the 'seventies, 'eighties, and 'nineties between that development and its reflection in the national letters, has become a familiar story to all. The American scene of those decades has been painted again and again in all its aspects with both skill and artistry, and from varied points of view, by such men as Van Wyck Brooks, Lewis Mumford, Thomas Beer, V. L. Parrington, V. F. Calverton, Ludwig Lewisohn, Granville Hicks, John Chamberlain, Walter Millis, and Matthew Josephson.

Upon that scene there stepped, about the year 1894, an elegantly dressed young man, then a senior in the University of California and lately from the studio of Julien in Paris. Frank Norris, then twenty-four years old, was at that moment revolving a novel (the first chapters of which he had probably already written) destined to sound a new note in American fiction, for he found himself in opposition to some of the current literary tendencies.

But in estimating his work and the thought from which it arose it must always be remembered that if Norris was not the son of the Gilded Age he was its grandson, and hence never able to sever himself completely from its notions and prejudices. His family was almost fabulously representative of the American middle class in its ideal of success and of the appropriate roles of husband and wife. His father, as a poor Michigan farm boy, had begun his rise to fortune as a jeweler's apprentice; he had become successively an itinerant mender of clocks and a purveyor of jewelry, Chicago representative of a New York firm, and at length owner of a prosperous wholesale jewelry business. He could now indulge a certain taste for display which satisfied itself with a many-roomed house on Michigan Avenue, a cockaded coachman, monogrammed carriages, and massive walnut furniture. A vulgarian in his tastes, he was content to leave culture where he thought it belonged—in the hands of the women. Frank's mother, accordingly, was left in sole charge of what are called the higher things of life. Her husband submitted with a tolerable grace when she read Meredith to him and when, later, she became the founder and leading spirit of the San Francisco Browning Club.[4] It was out of this domestic environment that Frank Norris emerged to write a series of novels several of which were to be more than faintly repugnant to his mother.

[4] In the 'eighties and 'nineties Browning appears to have been one of the chief lures by which women enticed men to culture and, incidentally, as not infrequently happened, to the parson as well. Page Dearborn, sister of Laura, the heroine of Norris' last novel, *The Pit* (p. 225), is interested in a certain young broker's clerk, Landry Court; "he wants to cultivate his mind and understand art and literature and that," she gushes to Laura. "I'm going to read

But Norris did very little theorizing on the subject of literature till after he had written nearly all the fiction that he was to live to write, and till after he had secured something of a reputation for himself. His observations then, as so often happens, were frequently rationalizations of what he had already done, rather than carefully wrought theories to be put subsequently to the test. His literary essays nevertheless form a chapter in the critical debate of their decade which cannot be ignored; and for the illumination which they cast on his own work they are of the first importance.

What, in his view, is the function of the novel in the modern world, with its enormous reading public, eager for the ever flooding products of the press, played upon by a thousand appeals to its passions and its prejudices? That function is a high and serious one, imposing grave responsibilities upon the man who would address that audience through the medium of the novel:

> The Pulpit, the Press and the Novel—these indisputably are the greatest moulders of public opinion and public morals to-day. But the Pulpit speaks but once a week; the Press is read with lightning haste and the morning news is waste-paper by noon. But the novel goes into the home to stay. It is read word for word; is talked about, discussed; its influence penetrates every chink and corner of the family.

> Right or wrong, the People turn to [the novelist] the moment he speaks, and what he says they believe.[5]

In thus coming to his problem by way of the relation between author and the great public, Norris betrays a strong sociological bias; he never, indeed, viewed litera-

---

to him. We're going to begin with the 'Ring and the Book.' " (Copyright 1903, 1921, by Doubleday, Doran & Company, Inc.)

[5] Norris, *The Responsibilities of the Novelist* (copyright 1901, 1902, 1903, by Doubleday, Doran & Co., Inc.), pp. 10, 9.

ture in the light of any abstract ideal of pure art, nor yet as the product of an almost holy imperative toward self-expression, nor, again, as the preoccupation of an esoteric cult. The novel for him was the theater in which all the vital concerns of life were to be exhibited in action, not for the momentary distraction of waiting customers in barber shops or of commuters on suburban trains, but for the enlargment of understanding and the enrichment of experience—to provoke thought rather than suspend it, to raise doubts rather than proclaim the obvious, to put questions rather than confirm complacencies. Hence to him the first obligation of the novelist was to tell the truth (p. 11):

The People have a right to the Truth as they have a right to life, liberty and the pursuit of happiness. It is *not* right that they be exploited and deceived with false views of life, false characters, false sentiment, false morality, false history, false philosophy, false emotions, false heroism, false notions of self-sacrifice, false views of religion, of duty, of conduct and of manners.

Or, to make the idea concrete: They are not to be told that every boy who is honest and industrious and saves his pennies may achieve fortune; it is also possible that his honesty and industry will be rewarded by the loss of his accumulated pennies through the financial jugglery of some great and much-admired prince of capital. They are not to be told that for every virtuous and modest maid awaits a rich and gallant lover, that all uncertainties cease at the altar, and that romance endures to the edge of the grave; it is quite as likely that her virtue will be rewarded with a dull husband, narrow circumstances, wrinkles, forty years of dishwashing, and an obscure death. They are not to be taught that, though hitherto all civilizations have been founded, as Anatole France says, on two great principles—respect for the rich and contempt for the poor—

those principles are immutable; that morals forbid shop-lifting, extra-marital dalliance, or murdering one's rival in love, but are perfectly consistent with buying a public servant, falsifying one's tax statement, and paying one's employees six dollars a week; that God is solicitous about the fall of a sparrow; and that the man who dips his soup toward him is a menace to civilization.

But what if this is the kind of pabulum for which the people clamor? What if they are indifferent to truth or unable to recognize or appreciate it when it is placed before them? Is the novelist then absolved from his duty? May he give the people what they want? By no means. Giving the public what it wants, Norris would say, is one of the most vicious sophisms of the irresponsible. The public is given trash in books, in music, in art because that is what it wants, and wants it because that is what it gets (pp. 10–11).

. . . . these gentlemen who are "in literature for their own pocket every time" have discovered that for the moment the People have confounded the Wrong with the Right, and prefer that which is a lie to that which is true. "Very well, then," say these gentlemen. "If they want a lie they shall have it . . . ."

"For the moment," says Norris; but he had faith that in the long run the people would judge aright (p. 7):

It is all very well to jeer at the People and at the People's mis-understanding of the arts, but the fact is indisputable that no art that is not in the end understood by the People can live or ever did live a single generation. . . . . in the last analysis, the People pronounce the final judgment. The People, despised of the artist, hooted, caricatured and vilified, are after all, and in the main, the real seekers after Truth.

Here, with his democratic theory of art, he enters on doubtful and controversial ground wherein he displays, perhaps, something of naïveté. Aesthetic critics believe that they have long since disposed of the problem, that literature on its highest levels must ever be caviar to the general. But the issues raised will not down, and are sure to rise anew in every generation. Certainly the boundary between the two realms—that of the cultivated elect and that of the general reader—has never been established with the precision which as a rule marks an international frontier. And a few works, at least, seem to have the freedom of both; if *The Shepherd of the Hills* has sold its half-million copies, so has *Of Human Bondage,* with its austere naturalism. Unfortunately, social statistics fail us here, and we cannot be sure that the half-million readers were the same for each book. It may well be that *Of Human Bondage* was ignored by the half-million admirers of *The Shepherd of the Hills,* and we are back at our starting point. Further, such works as have just been named may not be valued in the two regions for the same reasons. Norris would grant this, but would put the non-aesthetic motives first. "Who is it, after all," he inquires, "whose interest is liveliest in any given work of art?" and he replies thus to his query (pp. 7–8):

It is not now a question of *esthetic* interest—that is, the artist's, the amateur's, the *cognoscente's*. It is a question of *vital* interest. Say what you will, Maggie Tulliver—for instance—is far more a living being for Mrs. Jones across the street than she is for your sensitive, fastidious, keenly critical artist, litterateur, or critic. . . . . The cult consider [fictitious characters] almost solely from their artistic sides. The People take them into their innermost lives.

For Norris those qualities in a literary work which are capable of arousing this vital interest are always more important than what he calls mere aesthetic qualities.

Tolstoy's *What Is Art?* appeared in 1898 and was soon translated into the chief European languages. Wherever it was read it wrung cries of anguish from the aesthetic critics. Norris nowhere makes a reference to the work, but that he was familiar with Tolstoy as novelist we know. There is no room to doubt, however, that the great Russian had made a complete convert of the American writer.

It will be necessary only to compare a few statements of the two men in order to make clear the likeness of their views. If upper-class art "never can be the art of the whole people," as Tolstoy was ready to grant, the fault lies not with the people but with the art:

if art is an important matter, a spiritual blessing, essential for all men ("like religion," as the devotees of art are fond of saying), then it should be accessible to every one. And if, as in our day, it is not accessible to all men, then one of two things: either art is not the vital matter it is represented to be, or that art which we call art is not the real thing.[6]

Norris wrote: "A literature that cannot be vulgarized is no literature at all and will perish just as surely as rivers run to the sea. The things that last are the understandable things—understandable to the common minds, the Plain People . . . . Is the 'Marseillaise' a thing of subtlety or refinement? Are the Pyramids complex?"[7]

Tolstoy continues with his defense of popular taste (p. 88):

Moreover, it cannot be said that the majority of people lack the taste to esteem the highest works of art. The majority always have understood, and still understand, what we also recognize as being the very best art: the epic of Genesis, the gospel parables, folk legends, fairy-tales, and folk-songs, are understood by all.

Norris wrote on another occasion: "For say what you will, the People, the Plain People who Read, do appreciate good

[6] Tolstoi, *What Is Art?* (translated by Aylmer Maud) in *Works* [Vol. XIII], New York: Thomas Y. Crowell Company, [1899], pp. 61–62.

[7] *The Responsibilities of the Novelist* (Doubleday, Doran & Co., Inc.), pp. 280–81.

literature in the end (p. 296)." In the future, Tolstoy believed, "the appraisement of art in general will devolve, not, as is now the case, on a separate class of rich people, but on the whole people . . . ." (p. 167). *"In the last analysis,"* declared Norris (p. 297), emphasizing his words, *"the People are always right."*

What Tolstoy says—and what Norris says after him—is true: Some art provides a common human ground on which all may stand. All men may understand, be moved by, and love "Swing Low Sweet Chariot"; all may find a true pleasure in the tale of Ali Baba and the forty thieves. But when they are confronted by a composition of Debussy or a Bach fugue or a novel of Meredith (to cite Norris' chief aversion) or a poem of Verlaine, they begin to part company. Does it follow, however, that what Debussy, Bach, Meredith, and Verlaine have created is not art, or is not the best art? Is it not an entirely gratuitous and needless sacrifice to part with them because all cannot find their account in them?

It follows as a necessary corollary of Norris' views that the novelist must himself be a man of the people in the sense that he mingles freely in the affairs of the world and takes the most lively interest in them. He can no longer be a man of the study; formerly the writer was aloof (p. 280):

> One shut oneself in the study; one wore a velvet coat; one read a great deal and quoted Latin; one knew the classics; one kept apart from the vulgar profane and never, never, never read the newspapers.

Now he cannot know too much of what is going on in the world—politics, science, religious controversy, diplomacy, socialism are all useful to him. "No piece of information—mere downright acquisition of fact—need be considered worthless. Nothing is too trivial to be neglected." And he instances a famous novelist who valued higher than his honorary Harvard degree several scraps of information he had picked up he knew not where— namely, "That great cities tend to grow to the westward; that race-horses are shod with a long and narrow shoe; and that the usual price charged by an electrician for winding an armature is four dollars" (p. 283).

Norris went farther. Not only must the novelist be a man of the people, address himself to the people, and tell the people the truth; he must himself be a good man. The "contention that the personal morality of the artist . . . . has nothing to do with his work, and that a great rascal may be a good painter, good musician, good novelist"—this contention he stoutly opposed. He admitted some doubt about painters and musicians; but about novelists, he thought, there could be none. He proceeds (p. 292):

the mind capable of theft, of immorality, of cruelty, of foulness, or falseness of any kind is incapable, under any circumstances, or by any degree of stimulation, of producing one single important, artistic or useful piece of fiction.

As examples of good men whose work was great because "like the Arab philosopher of the poem, they, first of all, have 'loved their fellow-men,'" he cites Tolstoy, Hugo, Scott, Stevenson, and Howells, "our own 'Dean.'"

Unfortunately for these admirable sentiments, they are not borne out by experience. One thinks of Cellini and Villon, who could hardly be called good men in any usual sense of the term but who have left something behind them that the world would not willingly part with. Lapses from virtue are about as frequent among artists as among other men, and the roll of writers and painters can show nearly every variety of scamp from liars to wife-deserters and drunkards. As for mere selfishness, pettiness, and vanity, the tribe of artists could furnish out the rest of mankind altogether. Even Ruskin, with his peculiar ideas on the relation of morality and art, was less exigent than Norris concerning the character of the artist. He was a little puzzled and disturbed by what he saw in the lives of the men he admired, but he would not deny the facts of his own observation:

Certainly it seems intended that strong and frank animality, rejecting all tendency to asceticism, monachism, pietism, and so on, should be connected with the strongest intellects . . . . Homer, Shakespeare, Tintoret, Veronese, Titian, Michael Angelo, Sir Joshua, Rubens, Velasquez, Correggio, Turner, are all of them boldly Animal. Francia and Angelico, and all the purists, however beautiful, are poor weak creatures in comparison. I don't understand it; one would have thought purity gave strength, but it doesn't. A good, stout, self-commanding, magnificent Animality is the make for poets and artists, it seems to me . . . .[8]

If the modern novelist, then, must address himself to a great audience—if the novel, as Norris puts it, is the bow of Ulysses in the hands of the writer, at what are its arrows to be launched? What is that truth which it is the obligation of the novelist to deliver? With what does it concern itself and where is it best sought for? In a middle-class society engaged in the business of exploitation of both human and natural resources, and where the endless reiteration of a fatuous optimism is looked upon as a necessity, the most congenial theory of literature is that propounded by F. Marion Crawford: "The novel . . . . is an intellectual artistic luxury . . . . We [novelists]

[8] Ruskin, *Works* (Library Edition, edited by E. T. Cook and Alexander Wedderburn) (London: George Allen; New York: Longmans, Green and Co., 1905, VII, xl.

are nothing more than public amusers."[9] The more the novel can be emptied of ideas, the better. If it have any purpose beyond amusement, it may be permitted to inculcate morals—private morals. There is no harm in recommending to people through fiction not to get drunk, beat their wives, or hold up the mail coach; or, on the positive side, to be kind to animals, help old ladies across crowded streets, and attend church. But when the novel begins to suggest that there is fundamental injustice in the organization of society itself or, less sweepingly, that particular institutions or practices are corrupt, then it soon becomes a nuisance if it stirs up doubt or discontent, or even an actual danger if it tends to threaten the privileges or profits of specific individuals or classes.

But an instrument for pricking the social conscience is precisely what Norris would make it:

It is the complaint of the coward, this cry against the novel with a purpose, because it brings the tragedies and griefs of others to notice. . . . . [The modern novel] may be a flippant paper-covered thing of swords and cloaks, to be carried on a railway journey and to be thrown out the window when read, together with the sucked oranges and peanut shells. Or it may be a great force, that works together with the pulpit and the universities for the good of the people, fearlessly proving that power is abused, that the strong grind the faces of the weak, that an evil tree is still growing in the midst of the garden . . . .[10]

This belief in the social function of literature he had already exhibited in *The Octopus*. Presley, who plays something of the role of *raisonneur* in that novel, has written with intense emotion and conviction a poem, "The

[9] Crawford, *The Novel: What It Is*, pp. 9, 22. Quoted by permission of The Macmillan Company, publishers.

[10] Norris, *The Responsibilities of the Novelist* (Doubleday, Doran & Company, Inc.), p. 32.

Toilers." "It is Truth . . . . you have seen clearly," his friend Vanamee the shepherd tells him, and continues:

> "Now . . . . I presume you will rush it into print. To have formulated a great thought, simply to have accomplished, is not enough."
>
> "I think I am sincere," objected Presley. "If it is good it will do good to others. You said yourself it was a Message. If it has any value, I do not think it would be right to keep it back . . . ."[11]

Novels, Norris believed, fall into three classes: those that tell something, the novel of adventure like *The Three Musketeers;* those that show something, that deal primarily with the minds and characters of people, of which *Romola* is the type; and, the highest type of all, those that prove something, of which *Les Misérables* is an example. Such a novel as the last-named "draws conclusions from a whole congeries of forces, social tendencies, race impulses, devotes itself not to a study of men but of man."[12] It is the highest type because in the nature of things it includes the others, for "Fiction can find expression only in the concrete." Hence it must have action like type one, and it must study character like type two. The combination reveals the purpose, makes the demonstration.

Is the novelist then a mere propagandist? Norris denies it. The purpose must be accomplished subtly, by indirection, must be implicit in the story itself. "The moment, however, that the writer becomes really and vitally interested in his purpose his novel fails." This he admits is a "strange anomaly." To explain it he asserts that the writer has a double personality, "himself as a man, and himself as an artist." The man may be passionately

[11] Norris, *The Octopus* (Doubleday, Doran & Company, Inc., 1901, 1929), p. 376.

[12] *The Responsibilities of the Novelist*, p. 26.

moved by some spectacle of injustice; but the artist must remain calm, detached. He sets up a hypothetical case:

Let us suppose that Hardy, say, should be engaged upon a story which had for purpose to show the injustices under which the miners of Wales were suffering. It is conceivable that he could write a story that would make the blood boil with indignation. But he himself, if he is to remain an artist . . . . will, as a novelist, care very little about the iniquitous labour system of the Welsh coal-mines. It will be to him as impersonal a thing as the key is to the composer of a sonata.[18]

Mrs. Stowe must have been greatly more interested in the writing of *Uncle Tom's Cabin* than in "all the Negroes that were ever whipped or sold. Had it not been so that great purpose-novel never would have succeeded."

But Norris fails a little here in perception. The success of Mrs. Stowe in *Uncle Tom's Cabin* is owing directly to her passionate concern over her whipped Negroes, not to the suppression and denial of it. If her book has defects— some conventional devices, sentimentality—they are such as may be found in novels written with or without passion, with or without social purpose. "The novel with a purpose *is* . . . . a preaching novel," Norris insists. "But it preaches by telling things and showing things . . . . not [by] direct appeal by the writer" (pp. 27–28). If Mrs. Stowe failed, it was here, by resorting to direct appeal, not because she was passionately moved by her theme. The question resolves itself, then, in respect to any particular novel into whether that novel is a good workmanlike job or a bungling one. As long as the artist does not allow his purpose to run away with him, all will be well. Resort to Norris' theory of double personality is unnecessary. The sympathy of the man and that of the artist are one. Let the passion of the man by all means be under the due

[18] *Ibid.*, pp. 28–29.

control of the artist, lest he indulge merely in a fit of hysterics. But purely "literary" emotions not rooted in the truest feelings of the man are as spurious as they are ineffective.

The question of "purpose" in fiction has risen again in our day to enliven talk about books, appearing this time in the angry debate of the nineteen-thirties over the proletarian novel.[14] The controversy has not been free of disingenuousness. In the case of any given critic it is not always possible to tell whether his cry of bad art is a rationalization of his objection to a novelist's ideas or, on the other hand, whether his defense of the artistically indefensible is in reality dictated by the warmth of his feeling for some social or economic doctrine.

Now, the "novel of purpose" in Norris' day was almost invariably the realistic or naturalistic novel, and its enemies found one of their greatest objections to it in the fact that it commonly ended unhappily. Norris recognized this and saw very well the falsity and hollowness of the complaint, always made in the same trite terms. "Ah," people say, "we see so much suffering in the world, why put it into novels?"

Do they? Is this really true? The people who buy novels are the well-to-do people. They belong to a class whose whole scheme of life is concerned solely with an aim to avoid the unpleasant. Suffering, the great catastrophes, the social throes, that annihilate whole communities, or that crush even isolated individuals—all these are as far removed from them as earthquakes and tidal-waves. Or, even if it were so, suppose that by some miracle these blind eyes were opened and the sufferings of the poor, the tragedies of the house around the corner, really were laid bare. If there is much pain in life, all the more reason that it should appear in a class of

[14] See, for example, Joseph Freeman's "Introduction" to the anthology, *Proletarian Literature in the United States*, 1935.

literature which, in its highest form, is a sincere transcription of life.[15]

If the purpose of the serious novel is to lay bare "the sufferings of the poor," its writer will of necessity find himself exploring mean streets. Moreover, it is here that the student of human nature finds his best opportunity. Thus young Strelitz of the short story, "His Sister," in search of literary material, "roamed idly from street to street. Now in the theater district, now in the slums and now in the Bowery. As a rule he avoided the aristocratic and formal neighborhoods, knowing by instinct that he would be more apt to find undisguised human nature along the poorer unconventional thoroughfares."[16]

Always and everywhere Norris is the enemy of convention, of over-refinement, of aestheticism, of the genteel, of the academic. In fact, in drawing away from what he conceived to be these enfeebling influences in American life and literature he leaned over backward. Walter Pater became for him the symbol of flight from reality. The wife of Magnus Derrick in *The Octopus* is a shrinking, timid woman, an ex-teacher of writing in a young ladies' seminary. The vast spaces, the boundless horizons, the brilliant crude sunlight, the titanic labor of sowing and harvest on Derrick's great ranch in the San Joaquin valley

[15] *The Responsibilities of the Novelist*, pp. 31–32. The same attitude against which Norris protested, illustrating the uncongeniality of the middle-class mind and tragedy, or the realism of misfortune, was common a century and a half ago, as may be seen in Mrs. Hannah Webster Foster's popular novel, *The Coquette* (1797, Letter LII): "Are there not real woes . . . . sufficient to exercise our sympathy and pity, without introducing fictitious ones into our very diversions?" The occasion of this remark was *Romeo and Juliet*. The self-made Silas Lapham of Howells' novel echoes the familiar words: "I want something that'll make me laugh. I don't believe in tragedy. I think there's enough of that in real life . . . ." (William Dean Howells, *The Rise of Silas Lapham*, Boston: Houghton Mifflin Company, 1912 [1884], p. 122.)

[16] *Frank Norris of "The Wave": Stories and Sketches from the San Francisco Weekly, 1893 to 1897* (San Francisco: The Westgate Press, 1931), p. 38.

terrified her. "The direct brutality of ten thousand acres of wheat, nothing but wheat as far as the eye could see, stunned her a little. . . . . She did not want to look at so much wheat." She preferred instead to dream "of Italy, Rome, Naples, and the world's great 'art centres.'" At our first glimpse of her she is seated at breakfast on the porch of the ranch house, "stirring her coffee with one hand [and holding] open with the other the pages of Walter Pater's 'Marius.'"[17] Norris delights to satirize the world of pseudo-art and has a genuine talent for reducing the business to absurdity. Mrs. Cedarquist, wife of the San Francisco manufacturer, loves to gather around her a curious assortment of Russian countesses, Japanese poets, tenors, mandolin players, Mohammedan ladies, female elocutionists, university professors, Christian Scientists. In her salon she puts them through their paces, asking always solemnly of each one, "How long have you known you had this power?"

The university professor put on a full dress suit and lisle thread gloves at three in the afternoon and before literary clubs and circles bellowed extracts from Goethe and Schiller in the German, shaking his fists, purple with vehemence. The Cherokee, arrayed in fringed buckskin and blue beads, rented from a costumer, intoned folk songs of his people in the vernacular. The elocutionist in cheese-cloth toga and tin bracelets, rendered "The Isles of Greece, where burning Sappho loved and sung."[18]

Overbeck of "Dying Fires" (who is Norris himself up to a point) has written honestly and well of the rough California life he knows, of freighters and "biscuit shooters" and gamblers of the mining camps. His work attracts attention in the East and he is invited to join the editorial staff of a magazine in New York. There he falls

[17] *The Octopus*, pp. 60, 59, 58.
[18] *Ibid.*, pp. 313–14.

among a parcel of Bohemians who write sonnets with such titles as "A Cryptogram Is Stella's Soul," translate novels from the Italian and Hungarian, gabble about "tendencies," "influences," "tones," and "notes," and have lines from Pater, Ruskin, and Arnold forever on their tongues.

"Not so much *faroucherie,* you dear young Lochinvar!" they said . . . . The passions of a waitress in a railway eating-house—how sordid the subject! Dear boy, look for the soul, strive to rise to higher planes![19]

These literary Delilahs shear Overbeck completely of his strength and leave him impotent ever again to write anything of worth. It is to be feared that Norris was not a close reader of Arnold, Ruskin, and Pater but had formed his impressions rather from the unfortunate company in which these writers were frequently found.

His deep distaste for aestheticism, which indeed in the 'nineties had been pushed to absurd extremes following the activities of Wilde and the group around the *Yellow Book,* caused him to set up an irreconcilable opposition between literature and life, commonly with a large "L." He extends his suspicion from literature to thought in general, and like most anti-intellectuals employs a good deal of intellection in demonstrating the inferiority of thought to sensation, to spontaneous response to experience, to "action." Thus Ross Wilbur, the product of civilization, and the girl Moran, the untamed Viking's daughter, in the intervals of cutting the livers out of still-live sharks (in which enterprise they have been thrown together by a series of strange chances), hold a little conversation on the sun-blistered beach of Magdalena Bay:

[19] Norris, *The Third Circle,* p. 227. Quoted by permission of the publishers, Dodd, Mead & Company, Inc.

"I suppose you think it's a queer kind of life for a girl," said Moran. "I've lived by doing things, not by thinking things, or reading about what other people have done or thought; and I guess it's what you do that counts, rather than what you think or read about."[20] Under her tutelage Ross comes to believe that civilized life is indeed a sham.

Norris' characters are most pleasing to their creator when their brains are "almost as empty of thought . . . . as those of . . . . fine, clean animals," like Condy Rivers and Blix, the "good chum" lovers of his third published novel, *Blix,* or like Lloyd Searight, the robust heroine of *A Man's Woman,* who exults that it is her way "to do things, not to think them . . . . not to read them."[21]

Of Presley, poet and dreamer of *The Octopus,* we are told that his "refinement had been gained only by a certain loss of strength . . . . his mental life was not at all the result of impressions and sensations that came to him from without, but rather of thoughts and reflections germinating from within." Presley himself, groping for his epic theme in the varied fresh life of the West, feels the handicap of too much culture:

Ah [he exclaims], to get back to that first clear-eyed view of things, to see as Homer saw, as Beowulf saw, as the Nibelungen poets saw. The life is here, the same as then; the Poem is here; . . . . the primeval, epic life is here . . . . It is the man who is lacking, the poet; we have been educated away from it all. We are out of touch.[22]

A bit later, under the influence of the tremendous panorama of nature exposed to his view from one of the foot-

[20] Norris, *Moran of the Lady Letty: A Story of Adventure off the California Coast* (New York, 1898), p. 114.

[21] Frank Norris, *Blix* (New York: Doubleday, Doran & Company, Inc., 1899, 1928), p. 237; *A Man's Woman* (New York, 1900), p. 57.

[22] *The Octopus,* pp. 8, 41.

hills of the Sierra, he sinks into a state more elemental, more nearly favorable to the production of literature.

> By degrees, the sense of his own personality became blunted, the little wheels and cogs of thought moved slower and slower; consciousness dwindled to a point, the animal in him stretched itself, purring.[23]

Again and again Norris returns to the theme in the series of essays which were collected after his death to form the volume called *The Responsibilities of the Novelist.* Yet it is well, he concedes, that the writer should learn what he can of the technique of his craft from those who have gone before him. On one occasion he so far relaxed his rule for the writer that books "have no place in his equipment" as to assert, "The more one reads the easier one writes."[24] But let him be on his guard lest his admiration for some great storyteller betray him into borrowing from that man his ideas and his very personality. In this, Norris is doing penance for his own early aping of Kipling, a weakness which he ridicules amiably in *Blix.*

Only a simple untutored fellow was Frank Norris, one who drew his knowledge and his strength direct from life, and one who had read nothing—nothing, that is, except Scott, Cooper, Dickens, Thackeray, Hugo, Zola, Balzac, Flaubert, Tolstoy, George Eliot, Hardy, Stevenson, Howells, Hawthorne, Defoe, Froissart, the Icelandic sagas, Homer, and several score other writers.[25] Great and valuable as is the truth that he wishes to drive home—that the

---

[23] *Ibid.,* p. 44.

[24] *The Responsibilities of the Novelist,* pp. 282, 233.

[25] He mentions from first to last one hundred and two writers great and small, mostly of the nineteenth century. It is not to be supposed that he had a close knowledge of all of them, but to speak of his "limited reading," as does his biographer Franklin Walker (*Frank Norris: A Biography,* p. 283), is a little misleading.

proper thing for the writer is firsthand observation of life rather than the more remote knowledge of it to be drawn from books—in his zeal he tends to lose sight of a corresponding truth, one well expressed by John Macy:

Literature is a succession of books from books. Artistic expression springs from life ultimately but not immediately. It may be likened to a river which is swollen throughout its course by new tributaries . . . . ; it reflects the life through which it flows, taking colour from the shores; the shores modify it, but its power and volume descend from distant headwaters and affluents far up stream. . . . .

The literary mind is strengthened and nurtured, is influenced and mastered, by the accumulated riches of literature.[26]

Norris' almost shouted insistence that "life is better than literature" is to be understood in relation to the conditions that prevailed at the time. It is a mark of his revulsion from the sickly pallor of the genteel which had crept over the face of American fiction, of his desire to restore something like solid content to the novel and bring it to grips with American life.

In his remarks on the technique of fiction he reveals a natural enough prejudice in favor of the kind of novels he himself wrote. For him the novel without action, "plot" in the conventional sense, was a contradiction in terms. Hence prose fiction was the product of two kinds of workmen—those with the storyteller's gift and those without it, "novelists of composition," who, however admirable their art in other respects, lack the storytelling quality. The first write by "spontaneous improvisation"; the second must bring to bear all the resources of intellect, learning, and acquired skill to compensate for the absence of the genuine native "sense of fiction." In the possession of this sense Dumas, he believed, is superior to George

[26] John Macy, *The Spirit of American Literature* (New York: Doubleday, Doran & Company, Inc., 1913), pp. 3–4, 5.

Eliot, and Conan Doyle to Tolstoy. Eliot's novels are "character studies, are portraits, are portrayals of emotions of pictures of certain times and certain events, are everything you choose, but they are not stories . . . ." *Anna Karenina,* great as are its merits, is altogether deficient in the final merit of being a "story." "The power was all [Tolstoy's], the wonderful intellectual grip, but not the fiction spirit—the child's knack and love of 'making up stories'."[27] For Norris held that the storytelling imagination is the natural property of every child; if it is not blunted or destroyed that child may become a writer of tales. In this he describes his own character and history, since we know with what effortless fecundity he invented exploits for his lead soldiers and with what precocity he wrote endless yarns for the amusement of himself and his younger brother.

He disclaims any wish to assert that one of the two types of fiction which he distinguishes is better than the other; but it is plain where his preference lies. And that preference suggests, perhaps, a weakness in his own work; for, universal and legitimate as is the love of sheer narrative for its own sake, to make it the ground of subtraction from the merit of great fiction is an error. Norris himself allows his preoccupation with it to betray him more than once into melodrama. "Effects" had for him an irresistible fascination; and one phrase, he thought, summed up "the whole system of fiction-mechanics—preparations of effect." There must, moreover, be a pivotal event—"All good novels have one."

Putting aside for the moment the plain fact that not every good novel has one, it is evident that he knew the time-honored tricks of the craft; his conception of the

²⁷ *The Responsibilities of the Novelist,* pp. 43, 44.

novel is essentially dramatic. In the building up of the whole, each chapter is to be considered as a unit, "distinct, separate, having a definite beginning, rise, height and end, the action continuous, containing no break in time, the locality unchanged throughout . . . ."[28] He thus insists, whether he was aware of it or not, on the three classical unities; and following these principles his best novels, despite some lapses, are admirable pieces of literary architecture. But in technique he had nothing new to offer. He could never have been greatly sympathetic with that development of the novel so prominent in the last thirty years in which plot has well-nigh vanished; it is impossible to imagine him wishing, like Maurice Hewlett, that he could write a novel wherein "as mostly in life, thank goodness, nothing happens."[29] But his further ideas on the art of the writer will be best reserved for the discussion of his realistic method, in a later chapter.

When Norris was a student at Harvard in 1895, working on his first novel, *McTeague,* and laying it aside to write *Vandover and the Brute,* the best sellers of the year were *Trilby, The Prisoner of Zenda, Beside the Bonnie Briar Bush,* and *The Manxman,* not one of them by an American author. F. Marion Crawford, in conformity with his theory that the novel was meant to amuse, published his twenty-fifth literary bonbon, *Casa Braccio.* The next year saw the outbreak, with Charles Major's *When Knighthood Was in Flower,* of that epidemic of cloak-and-sword romance which was to ravage American fiction for a full decade. Readers were carried through

[28] *Ibid.,* pp. 152, 148, 153.
[29] Maurice Henry Hewlett, "The Crystal Vase," in *In a Green Shade.*

every epoch of European history, and the American past as well was ransacked for picturesque characters and episodes. A spirit of tender romance breathed from the pages. Booth Tarkington opened *The Two Vanrevels*,[30] whose scene is an Indiana town just before the Mexican War, with these words:

It was long ago in the days when men sighed when they fell in love; . . . . in that mellow time so long ago, when the young were romantic and summer was roses and wine, old Carewe brought his lovely daughter home from the convent to wreck the hearts of the youth of Rouen.

And Mary Johnston at the end of her tale of colonial Virginia, *To Have and to Hold,* allows her hero to say with a perfection of banality that taxes belief:

she came to my arms like a tired bird to its nest. I bent my head, and kissed her upon the brow, the blue-veined eyelids, the perfect lips. "I love thee," I said. "The song is old, but it is sweet. See! I wear thy color, my lady" (Boston: Houghton Mifflin Company, 1900), p. 399.

It is no wonder that Norris would later make Corthell the artist (in *The Pit*) declare, no doubt in response more to his hope than to his conviction, that the novel of the future would be without a love story.

Norris himself had but recently passed through a phase of absorption in the Middle Ages. Sent to Paris by his reluctant bourgeois father to study art, he had spent his time frequenting the museums and curio shops in order to make himself master of the fine points of medieval armor, the subject which indeed first drew him into print with an article in the *San Francisco Chronicle* (March 31, 1889). He steeped himself in Froissart and wrote an interminable romance concerning the exploits of one Gaston le Fox, of

[30] Copyright 1902, 1930, by Doubleday, Doran and Company, Inc.

the time of Charles the Bold of Burgundy. But though certain emotional and temperamental needs satisfied by the romantic mood never left him, by the time of the writing of *McTeague* he was nearly cured. The popular historical romance of the day filled him with impatience— it was "the literature of chambermaids." With the completion of *The Octopus* (1900) he had arrived at some pretty definite ideas as to the state of American literature and as to what was needed to cure it of its anemia and send it forward in lusty health.

The first necessity was to throw off the overlordship of New England:

The New England school for too long dominated the entire range of American fiction—limiting it, specializing it, polishing, refining and embellishing it, narrowing it down to a veritable cult, a thing to be safeguarded by the elect, the few, the aristocracy.[31]

The fact of that overlordship will hardly be denied, though that any should resent it was perhaps a little shocking, even in 1903, when Norris' defiance was published. Where but to Boston and Cambridge, during two generations, did young American writers look for approval? They went to New England to live, to study, to write, like Howells, Mark Twain, and Hamlin Garland, from their Western prairies; they sat at the feet of the New England worthies; they courted Boston publishers and Boston editors. Young Howells from his Ohio backwoods made the pilgrimage to Cambridge with the reverential awe of a pious Mussulman from the steppes of Turkestan setting

---

[31] *The Responsibilities of the Novelist,* p. 140. Norris makes Laura Dearborn (heroine of *The Pit,* who has fled from her native Massachusetts to Chicago) reflect thus on the social life of New England (p. 44): "The life was barren, the 'New England spirit' prevailed in all its severity; and this spirit seemed to her a veritable cult, a sort of religion, wherein the Old Maid was the priestess, the Spinster the officiating devotee, the thing worshipped the Great Unbeautiful . . . ."

out for the city of the Prophet. It was because of this domination, Norris believed, that America had neglected her true literary resources; at the very time when the great epic drama of the westward movement was being enacted, in which "The prairie schooner is as large a figure . . . . as the black ship that bore Ulysses homeward from Troy," literature was (pp. 62–63)

a cult indulged in by certain well-bred gentlemen in New England who looked eastward to the Old World, to the legends of England and Norway and Germany and Italy for their inspiration, and left the great, strong, honest, fearless, resolute deeds of their own countrymen to be defamed and defaced by the nameless hacks of the "yellow back" libraries.

When Norris began to write, the regionalism that had been launched in the early 'seventies had nearly exhausted itself, and was ending in futility. Every corner of the country had been combed again and again for what it might yield in quaint speech and homely or picturesque custom. But the regionalists in the main had been too much obsessed by the picturesque; they had tried less to paint their respective sections as they were then being modified by the expansion of industry, the growth of the cities, the influx of new races, than to preserve customs and manners already vanished.[32] Nevertheless there had been a sound principle in their work: that an author will write best of that which he knows best, and that he can know best his own heath, wherever it be. Norris believed that principle to be still valid, for the reason that we were still a nation of distinct and divers sections, each of different origin and different social pattern:

There is no homogeneousness among us as yet. The Westerner thinks along different lines from the Easterner and arrives at differ-

[32] In this I but follow Granville Hicks in his *The Great Tradition* (New York, 1933), pp. 57–67.

ent conclusions. What is true of California is false of New York. Mr. Cable's picture of life is a far different thing than that of Mr. Howells. . . . .

The school of fiction American in thought, in purpose and in treatment will come in time, inevitably. Meanwhile the . . . . cultivation of one's own vine is quite sufficient for all energy.[33]

For this reason the search for the great American novelist and his long-wished-for product, "the great American novel," was illusory and had better be abandoned. When a novelist, he points out, becomes universally admitted to be the great French or English or Russian novelist, he no longer belongs exclusively to his own country but becomes the property of the whole world, like Tolstoy. On the other hand, "the possibility of *A*—note the indefinite article—*A* Great American Novel is not too remote for discussion. But such a novel will be sectional."[34]

Of all the regions of the country the West seemed to him to be least exploited and to offer the greatest possibilities. His own seven novels all belong to the West and, with the exception of *The Pit* and the early chapters of *A Man's Woman,* to California, although in his grandly conceived epic trilogy of the wheat his vision had surely leaped sectional, and even national, boundaries. In many of his short stories he ranged afield; but the best of them are placed, like the novels, in the West. Presley, in *The Octopus,* brilliant graduate and postgraduate of an Eastern college, had come out to California determined to be the poet of the West.

The few sporadic attempts, thus he told himself, had only touched the keynote. He strove for the diapason, the great song that should embrace in itself a whole epoch, a complete era, the voice of an entire people . . . . their legends, their folk lore, their fightings, their

[33] *The Responsibilities of the Novelist,* pp. 199, 200.
[34] *Ibid.,* p. 87.

loves and their lusts, their blunt, grim humour, their stoicism under stress . . . . their direct, crude speech, their generosity and cruelty, their heroism and bestiality, their religion and profanity, their self-sacrifice and obscenity—a true and fearless setting forth of a passing phase of history, uncompromising, sincere; . . . . swept together, welded and riven together in one single, mighty song, the Song of the West.[35]

How Norris himself handled some aspects of Western life and in what terms he conceived that life will be the concern of the next chapter.

[35] *The Octopus,* pp. 9–10.

Chapter II

Romance: Realism: Naturalism

> *As much romance on Michigan Avenue as there is realism in King Arthur's court.*
>
> *Romance and Realism are constant qualities of every age, day and hour. They are here to-day. They existed in the time of Job. They will continue to exist till the end of time, not so much in things as in point of view of the people who see things.**

W<small>HEN</small> William Dean Howells reviewed Norris' first novel, *McTeague* (in *Literature,* March 24, 1899), he was obliged to point out among many and great merits—its "touches of character at once fine and free," its "little miracles of observation"—one folly, as he called it: "the insistence on the love-making of those silly elders, which is apparently introduced as an offset to the misery of the other love-making . . . ." From that day to this critics have been puzzled to account for the presence of incongruous elements of romanticism and realism in Norris' work. Was he a romanticist turned realist, or a realist striving to free himself from the trammels of his drab craft? To add to the puzzlement he shows no consistent movement from one to the other; his progress is erratic and subject to retrogressions. Beginning with *Yvernelle*

---

* Frank Norris, "The True Reward of the Novelist," in *The Responsibilities of the Novelist* (copyright 1901, 1902, 1903, by Doubleday, Doran & Company, Inc.), pp. 19, 20.

(his first published volume, 1891), a medieval tale of superstition, love, and revenge, written in the meter of Scott's verse romances, he proceeds to the masterly picture of the little world of San Francisco's Polk Street in *McTeague,* with its small shops, saloons, and "coffee joints," its plumbers' apprentices, cash girls, and car conductors, moving in a fixed daily rhythm of life, ebbing and flowing through the street, the same with every rise and set of sun. Here the only lingering romance is the idyl of the belated love of old Grannis and Miss Baker, the retired dressmaker, the more striking by reason of the sordid background against which it is placed. Before *McTeague* was finished Norris laid it aside to write *Vandover and the Brute,*[1] a piece of unrelieved naturalism. But his next three books are a return to romance—*Moran of the Lady Letty,* a tale of sea adventure; *Blix,* a love story, a slight work mainly interesting today for its autobiographical passages; and *A Man's Woman,* a two-fisted celebration of primitive strength and the struggle with nature. With *The Octopus,* realism is once more the ostensible pattern; but, not content to leave the tale without romantic adornment, he wove through it the bright-colored strand of Vanamee's strange love and mystic yearning. His last novel, *The Pit* (second

[1] This novel narrowly escaped total loss. Norris, believing quite justly that it was too bitter a dose for the delicate public stomach of the 'nineties, refused after one or two rebuffs to offer it to a publisher during his lifetime. After his death certain of his effects were stored in San Francisco in a warehouse which burned in the fire following the earthquake of 1906. It was believed by the few who knew of its existence that the manuscript of *Vandover* perished on this occasion, unhappily at the very moment when a publisher was negotiating for it. But seven years later Charles G. Norris, younger brother of Frank, learned from the storage company that several crates had been removed to safety shortly before the destruction of the warehouse. Thus the manuscript was recovered and *Vandover and the Brute* was published by Doubleday, Page & Company early in 1914. (See Charles G. Norris' foreword to the volume.)

34

volume of his unfinished epic trilogy), is without the bizarre or contrasting episodes of the Vanamee-Grannis order, though its force is weakened by the overprominence of the love story of Laura Dearborn and Jadwin, their marriage, subsequent estrangement, and reconciliation.

A reader thoroughly acquainted with the thirteen volumes of Norris' published work carries away the conviction that he is the same Frank Norris from first to last. Romance and realism were coexistent in him from the beginning. There was no development of one to the exclusion of the other. His development lay rather in the enlargement of his experience, some deepening of thought, a better grasp of the social significance of the novel; but it still remains true that his first work, *McTeague,* is a better than his last, *The Pit.* Whether or not he would ever have been satisfied with a straight realistic or naturalistic formula is a matter of speculation. At the time of his death he was projecting an epic trilogy on the Battle of Gettysburg, a volume for each day of the conflict. It is not impossible to imagine what certain features of the work would have been like: some colossal battle scenes in the grand manner, with an eye to Hugo's Waterloo in *Les Misérables* and Zola in *La Débâcle*; by way of contrast with carnage and death, some tender love episode, enacted, let us say, in a farmhouse marooned in the midst of the contending armies and miraculously preserved from destruction. The little drama would rise to its climax on the second day and terminate sweetly on the third just as Pickett's brigade broke and rolled down the slope of Cemetery Ridge.

It was not by accident or inadvertence that Norris inserted romantic interludes in *McTeague* and *The Octopus* but in response to a deliberate theory. Presley's experience in this particular can be taken for Norris' own. His imagi-

nation has been set on fire by the West; but he conceives
it in essentially romantic terms:

the sunsets behind the altar-like mesas, the baking desolation of
the deserts; the strenuous, fierce life of forgotten towns, down there,
far off, lost below the horizons of the southwest; the sonorous music of unfamiliar names—Quijotoa, Uintah, Sonora, Laredo, Un-
compahgre . . . . the Mission, with its cracked bells, its decaying
walls, its venerable sun dial, its fountain and old garden . . . .[2]

In Guadalajara he listens to a tale told by an ancient Mexican who remembered the old days before the American
conquest—a tale of De la Cuesta, the lord of boundless
acres, with the power of life and death over his depend-
ents—how on seeing the miniature portrait of a girl he had
never met he determined to marry her; how he sent a
horse for the girl to ride, "white, pure white; and the
saddle was of red leather; the head-stall, the bit, and
buckles . . . . of virgin silver"; how the town feasted for
a week in celebration of the marriage, and De la Cuesta
gave to each of his chief tenants a horse, a barrel of tallow,
an ounce of silver, and half an ounce of gold dust. " 'Ah,
those were days,' " concludes the ancient. " 'This'—he
made a comprehensive gesture with his left hand—'this
is stupid.' "

But Presley is continually groping and suffers from a
sense of bafflement. Just when he is about to grasp his
theme, some dissonant note intrudes to shatter its harmony, some prosaic, or harsh, or ugly material fact. The
ranchers of the San Joaquin are engaged in a conflict with
the octopus, the great Pacific & Southwestern Railroad.
They can talk of nothing but the predatory policy of the
road, whose subtle ramifications reach into the smallest
concerns of their lives. "He searched for the True Ro-

[2] Frank Norris, *The Octopus* (copyright 1901, 1929, by Doubleday, Doran
& Company, Inc.), p. 48.

mance, and, in the end, found grain rates and unjust freight tariffs. 'But the stuff is *here,*' he muttered . . . . 'I'll get hold of it yet.' " Or he meets Hooven, the garrulous little German tenant of Magnus Derrick, overalled and dusty. How make romance of such material? "These uncouth brutes of farmhands . . . . grimed with the soil they worked upon, were odious to him beyond words. Never could he feel in sympathy with them, nor with their lives, their ways, their marriages, deaths, bickerings, and all the monotonous round of their sordid existence."[3] Yet Presley wants above all to tell the truth. But when the old Mexican has finished his yarn he is again overcome by doubt (pp. 22–23):

Never would he grasp the subject of his great poem. To-day, the life was colourless. Romance was dead. He had lived too late. To write of the past was not what he desired. Reality was what he longed for . . . . Yet how to make this compatible with romance.

Then toward the close of his long somnolent afternoon on the hilltop overlooking the great valley, under the influence of the scene's immensity and his own musings, the solution comes to him (pp. 48–49): "The beauty of his poem, its idyl, came to him like a caress; that alone had been lacking . . . . At last he was to grasp his song in all its entity." The idyl! It is that which Norris sought. To reconcile romance and reality. And so we have the Vanamee episode of *The Octopus* as counterpoint to the economic struggle of ranchers and railroad, with its accompaniments of intrigue and corruption—Vanamee, the bearded ascetic with the burning eyes, the wanderer of the deserts and mountains, gifted with the power of halting a man in his tracks at the distance of a mile by the sheer force of thinking his name; Vanamee, who spent

[3] *Ibid.*, pp. 22, 13, 5.

whole nights of vigil under the stars in the garden of the Mission San Juan, with its moss-rimmed fountain, its graves, its crumbling sundial, and its magnolia; Vanamee, the intensity of whose love triumphed over the grave and who by the power of his yearning reincarnated, as it were, in the person of her daughter, the exotic Angéle, who is described in the following lush terms, almost Biblical, of the Song of Solomon:

> She came to him from out of the flowers, the smell of the roses in her hair of gold, that hung in two straight plaits on either side of her face; the reflection of the violets in the profound dark blue of her eyes, perplexing, heavy-lidded, almond-shaped, oriental; the aroma and the imperial red of the carnations in her lips, with their almost Egyptian fulness; the whiteness of the lilies, the perfume of the lilies, and the lilies' slender balancing grace in her neck. Her hands disengaged the odour of the heliotropes. The folds of her dress gave off the enervating scent of poppies. Her feet were redolent of hyacinths.[4]

There is something in Norris strongly reminiscent of the method of Victor Hugo, whom he so warmly admired.[5] There is the same desire to mingle the genres, the same love of brilliant light and color accentuated by its immediate juxtaposition with the deepest shadow. Poetry, says Hugo in the preface to *Cromwell,* "se mettra à faire comme la nature, à mêler dans ses créations, sans pourtant les confondre, l'ombre à la lumière, le grotesque au sublime ... la bête à l'esprit ..." Contrast and incongruity are of the very essence of Norris' style, as of Hugo's. Like Hugo he delights to startle the imagination and the senses into activity by a sharp prod. In *Notre-Dame de Paris,* while Esmeralda is doing penance before the doors

---

[4] *The Octopus,* p. 142.

[5] He saw plainly the resemblances between the arch-romantic Hugo and the naturalistic Zola; see his "Zola as a Romantic Writer," San Francisco *Wave,* June 21, 1896, quoted by Walker, pp. 83–84.

of the cathedral in preparation for her hanging, Captain Phoebus, who has been her lover, courts a girl of the gentles in the house a few yards distant. In *The Octopus* at the precise moment when Presley, returning after dusk to the Derrick ranch house from his excursion in the hills, is at the highest pitch of his exalted and spiritualized mood, that mood is abruptly broken by the terrible incident of the slaughter of the sheep (symbol of the ruthlessness of the corporation). With a heart-stopping clamor a locomotive of the Pacific & Southwestern shoots by as Presley is about to cross the tracks. As the noise of its passing dies away in the distance, he becomes aware of a new sound, "Prolonged cries of agony, sobbing wails of infinite pain . . . ." The engine had plowed through Vanamee's flock:

To the right and left, all the width of the right of way, the little bodies had been flung; backs were snapped against the fence posts; brains knocked out. Caught in the barbs of the wire, wedged in, the bodies hung suspended. Under foot it was terrible. The black blood, winking in the starlight, seeped down into the clinkers between the ties with a prolonged sucking murmur.[6]

Elsewhere, emotional crises occur in circumstances absurd in their homeliness. McTeague has asked Trina to marry him, has kissed her; she is swept as by a storm of unknown passion; she flies home to break the news:

Trina burst in upon her mother while the latter was setting a mousetrap in the kitchen.
"Oh, mamma!"
"Eh, Trina? Ach, what has happun?"
Trina told her in a breath.
"Soh soon?" was Mrs. Sieppe's first comment. "Eh, well, what you cry for, then?"
"I don't know," wailed Trina, plucking at the end of her handkerchief.

[6] *Ibid.*, p. 50.

"You loaf der younge doktor?"

"I don't know" . . . .

"You don' know, you don' know? Where haf your sensus gone, Trina? You kiss der doktor. You cry, and you don' know . . . ."

Mrs. Sieppe set down the mousetrap with such violence that it sprung with a sharp snap.[7]

And the chapter ends, with the trap a symbol of Trina's marriage.

In "A Salvation Boom in Matabeleland," a little tale inspired by his sojourn in South Africa in 1895–96, we have the curious spectacle of Otto Marks, Salvation Army sergeant, seated at a parlor organ mounted on a bullock wagon in the midst of the South African veldt. Otto is playing and singing for dear life "I am so glad that Jesus loves me," to soothe an impi of savage Zulus which by evil chance the expedition has encountered. The natives are crazed with drink—"Cape Smoke"—and hypnotized by the rhythm of their dance. As long as he plays they will continue; but he breaks under the strain and leaps to his feet, mad with terror. At that moment an

assegai struck him . . . . full on the face, and he spun about twice, gripping at the air, and then went over sideways upon the keyboard of the organ, his blood splashing the dazzling white of the celluloid keys.[8]

---

[7] *McTeague* (by Frank Norris, copyright 1899, 1927, by Doubleday, Doran & Company, Inc.), p. 86. The same spirit animates the concluding scene of *La Faute de l'Abbé Mouret* of Zola, Norris' master. The Abbé Mouret, serene of soul because he has at length freed himself from the longings of the flesh, is conducting the funeral of the girl Albine, with whom he had grievously sinned. As the coffin settles upon the bottom of the grave, the Abbé's sister Désirée thrusts her head above the wall which divides the cemetery from the neighboring farmyard and utters a joyous shout: "Serge! Serge! cria-t-elle . . . . en tapant des mains, la vache a fait un veau!"

[8] *Collected Writings Hitherto Unpublished in Book Form* (Vol. X of *Works,* New York, 1928), p. 26. Norris was so pleased with the image of the blood on the white keys that he returned to it a year later, placing it in an episode of the Franco-Prussian war (*ibid.,* p. 79).

Or he pictures a great stupid brute of a man, a laborer, returning from a day's work amidst massive machines and ponderous materials—pig iron, granite: "At a street crossing he picked up a white violet, very fresh, not yet trampled into the mud. It was a beautiful thing, redolent with the scent of the woods . . . . It lay very light in the hollow of his immense calloused palm." He is vaguely stirred but knows no means of expression for the unaccustomed feeling that troubles him. He stares at the fragile flower for some moments; "then instinctively his hand carried it to his mouth; he ground it between his huge teeth and slowly ate it. It was the only way he knew."[9] Condy Rivers and Blix, too, are alive to these picturesque incongruities. They revel in Captain Jack's tales in which oaths mingle with sonnets and "spilled wine with spilled blood."[10] And there is Father Sarria of the Mission San Juan, in *The Octopus,* who tenderly nurses every sick or injured beast of the neighborhood, and who in secret keeps fighting cocks and enjoys their murderous conflict.

The serene beauty of the night torn across by the agonized cries of mangled sheep—love and mousetraps—a fine splash of crimson blood against the white of ivory—a violet in the mud—pity and cruelty beneath the same cassock—it is such things as these, startlingly, violently, thrust upon the senses, that impart to existence its savor for such temperaments as that of Frank Norris.

He was apparently never entirely comfortable under the denomination of realist, and when *McTeague* and *The Octopus* had got him something of a reputation as a purveyor of muscular fiction, he was at pains to remove what

<hr />

[9] "Brute," *ibid.,* p. 81.

[10] Norris, *Blix* (copyright 1899, 1928, by Doubleday, Doran & Company, Inc.), p. 226.

he considered some popular misconceptions concerning realism and romance. He has, he asserts in "A Plea for Romantic Fiction," no quarrel with genuine romance, but the term has been confused and needs redefinition. Moreover, certain impostors are masquerading under the name romance: sentimentalism, which ought to be "handed down the scullery stairs"; and the "cut-and-thrust" historical novel. True romance concerns itself, not with the far away and long ago, but with the living present, and with life not alone of Fifth Avenue: "this very day, in this very hour, she is sitting among the rags and wretchedness, the dirt and despair of the tenements of the East Side of New York." Romance penetrates the surface of this life, reveals the hidden passions, hopes, fears, tragedies, lusts. Realism, by Norris' definition, "is the kind of fiction that confines itself to the type of normal life." Hence it sees only the outside of things, the obvious. It loses itself, he thought, in the trivial. Native realism in his day had become almost completely identified with the work of Howells and James, the realism of the genteel, of the drawing room, where every character that counts wears a good coat, shows a decent respect for the proprieties of speech, and could never conceivably have had manure on his boots or machine oil on his hands. It is at Howells that Norris is pointing when he writes: "Realism is minute; it is the drama of a broken teacup, the tragedy of a walk down the block, the excitement of an afternoon call, the adventure of an invitation to dinner." Romance, on the other hand, "is the kind of fiction that takes cognizance of variations from the type of normal life." Very revealing of Norris is this definition. It explains his indefatigable search for the bizarre and the striking, his conceiving existence in dramatic terms, his effort to squeeze out of common experience some essence of the uncommon, some drop of the picturesque. Hence his peregrinations about San Francisco in quest of "Little Dramas of the Curbstone"[11]—an old woman with her blind idiot son in the empty windy street outside the clinic; a youth in the clutches of a policeman, preferring arrest to returning home with his mother, whose pleas he stoutly resists. "It was a veritable situation," writes Norris with relish. "It should have occurred behind footlights . . . ." There is romance in the familiar, he felt, if only we have eyes to see it. It is true he did not arrive at this view immediately. During his two years (April 1896–February 1898) as editorial assistant on the San Francisco *Wave* he subscribed to the notion that only three big cities in the United States are "story cities"—New York, New Orleans, and San Francisco, "best of the lot."[12] Chicago, he thought—or Buffalo, or Nashville—was impossible. But a few years later he had come to believe that romance, as well as realism, exists eternally, not in things or places, but in the eye of the beholder. The issue, then, is not an irreconcilable conflict between romance and realism; the only issue is "which formula is the best to help you grip the Real Life of this or any other age."[13] Only let the writer go direct to life for his material and let him be sincere, with a proper regard for the truth and a proper sense of the responsibility that rests upon him as a man who speaks to many, predisposed to receive what he says. "Go out into the street," he commands, "and stand where the ways cross and hear

[11] Title of a series of sketches contributed to the San Francisco *Wave*, later collected in *The Third Circle*.

[12] "The House with the Blinds," in *The Third Circle*, p. 31. Quoted by permission of the publisher, Dodd, Mead & Company, Inc.

[13] "The True Reward of the Novelist," in *The Responsibilities of the Novelist*, pp. 19–20.

the machinery of life work clashing in its grooves. Can the utmost resort of your ingenuity evolve a better story than any one of the millions that jog your elbow?"[14]

But what is truth in fiction? By what means does the literary artist transfer that stuff, that "real life" (about which critics and writers agitate themselves so much and the great mass of those who, presumably, live the "real life" agitate themselves so little), to the printed page? Literary truth, avers Norris, is not an abstraction; it is (p. 51)

as concrete as the lamp-post on the corner, as practical as a cable-car, as . . . . commonplace as a bootjack . . . . It is the thing that is one's own, the discovery of a subject suitable for fictitious narration that has never yet been treated, and the conscientious study of that subject and the fair presentation of results.

Emphasis on two things may be noted in this description: originality of subject, and close observation of the material. The first is the natural reaction to a time when the novel seemed to be doing little but rethreshing old straw and to be leaving out of account large and important areas of American life. The second brings Norris into relation with the methods of observation, documentation, and verification of certain of the Continental realists and naturalists. But the fruits of observation, he holds, must be submitted to the operation of invention and imagination and be ripened by sympathy; for, by a curious paradox, an exact copy of reality will belie itself and seem not true but false. The test is not whether the thing actually happened, was actually observed by the writer, but solely: does it *seem* true? It may be rendered with complete accuracy and yet *seem* utterly false: "life is not always true to life—from the point of view of the artist." He gives an example from his

14 "The Need of a Literary Conscience," *ibid.*, p. 52.

own experience; he had once to tell a man of the violent death of his only brother. The man "threw up both hands and staggered back, precisely as they do in melodrama, exclaiming all in a breath: 'Oh, my God! This is terrible! What will mother say?'"

Conversely, a thing may violate actuality and yet create the illusion of truth. Norris illustrates by reference to a picture of a French cuirassier by Detaille, and to the scene in *Ivanhoe* where Rebecca at her window describes to the wounded knight the storming of the castle walls. In the picture a spot of light blue appears on the trooper's horse; and Rebecca's language is too studiously attentive to the dramatic climaxes of the action she is witnessing. Yet in each instance the effect is true. "Paint the horse pea-green if it suits your purpose," is Norris' injunction; "fill the mouth of Rebecca with gasconades and rhodomontades interminable . . . . the point is whether the daubs of pea-green will look like horseflesh and the mouth-filling words create the impression of actual battle."[15]

He himself occasionally puts words in the mouth of a character with unhappy results. A conspicuous instance occurs in *Moran of the Lady Letty*. Moran is a blonde giantess who has been born and reared on the sea and whose only real companion has been her father, a Norwegian ship's captain. She is immensely strong; raw whiskey goes down her throat like water, and apparently with no more effect; the picturesque and sometimes blood-freezing curses of the forecastle roll off her tongue with the ease and fluency of lifelong usage. In the rough and tumble combat which is no infrequent occurrence in the life she has led, she becomes blind with fury and is as

[15] "A Problem in Fiction," in *The Responsibilities of the Novelist*, pp. 224, 228.

likely to strike friend as foe. And so in the skirmish with the beachcombers. She rushes upon Wilbur oblivious of everything but the lust of battle. It is only after a terrific struggle that he subdues her and she comes again to her senses. So far so good. But by proving himself her master he has won her love; she trusts herself entirely to him, in token whereof she says to him some time later (p. 238): "you must be good to me now . . . . I'm just a woman now, dear—just a woman that loves you with a heart she's just found." Now it may be that women have made, and do make, such speeches, though when they do they are probably unconsciously echoing what they have read it is appropriate to say under the circumstances; but, coming from such a woman as Moran is painted, her words are not "true to life," are the very depth of bathos, banal and ridiculous to the last degree.

But lapses of this sort are to be noticed only in contrast to the general faithfulness and truthfulness of Norris' renderings of experience, filled as they are with "little miracles of observation," as Howells so justly says. A passion for exactness and minuteness of detail marked him from the first. And it is to be noted that he indulged it before he ever thought of applying it to the depiction of contemporary American life, when he was still engrossed in Froissart and the pageantry of the Middle Ages. His biographer records that in Paris he spent hours in the Musée d'Artillerie of the Hôtel des Invalides and in the Musée de Cluny, taking measurements of armor, making sketches of the various pieces, and taking copious notes. The thing that delighted him in Kipling was the verisimilitude that author gains by his skillful use of technical terms. Condy Rivers, in *Blix,* whose career as newspaper man and writer closely parallels Norris' own, reads "The

Strange Ride of Morrowbie Jukes" to Blix. It is a triumph of realism, he thinks, when Kipling makes Jukes—a civil engineer—notice that the slope of the sides of the sand pit into which he has fallen is about forty-five degrees. Norris formed the habit of collecting assiduously, in a notebook which he carried, everything that might conceivably be of use to him. "This book," writes his brother, "was his greatest treasure. Years afterward he told me that keeping it taught him the difference between seeing life subjectively and objectively. No one, he believed, could become a writer, until he could regard life and people, and the world in general, from the objective point-of-view . . . ."[16] In preparation for the writing of *McTeague* he read Thomas Fillebrown's *Text-book of Operative Dentistry*,[17] learned the names of the instruments used, the types of dental architecture, and something of the anatomy of the mouth and jaws—all in order to describe with fidelity the crowning of a tooth. Like the historian Parkman, who visited and tramped over the scenes of the battles he was to describe, whenever possible he must see for himself. When he had conceived the idea of his trilogy of the wheat, his first care was to spend two months on a ten-thousand-acre rancho in San Benito County, California, where he took his geographical bearings, got the "feel" of the land, watched the growth of the grain, and took part in the harvest. When the scene was to be transferred to Chicago for the second volume he moved to that city, haunted the board of trade, observed the life of the business district, and watched the operations of the wheat pit.

---

16 Charles G. Norris, *Frank Norris, 1870–1902: An Intimate Sketch* . . . . ([28-page pamphlet], New York: D[oubleday], P[age] & Co. [1914?]), pp. 7–8.

17 See Willard E. Martin, Jr., "Frank Norris's Reading at Harvard College," *American Literature*, May 1935.

Later he secured the services of a broker of his acquaintance to explain to him the intricacies of market gambling. The locale of all of his novels, with the single exception of the first part of *A Man's Woman,* which deals with Arctic exploration, was familiar to him by personal observation.

Such was Norris' method. It has been disparaged by writers of another sort and by some critics as prosy, unimaginative, and fruitless of the best results. It must not be thought, however, that Norris was ever the slave of his notebook. This gathering of facts was merely to provide the imagination with raw material. A literal transcription of what he observed was never his way. The proper training of the novelist, he wrote, is the "achieving less of an aggressive faculty of research than of an attitude of mind —a receptivity, an acute sensitiveness."[18] What was his own experience in the actual labor of composition may be learned from that of two writers who figure in the novels—Condy Rivers of *Blix* and Presley of *The Octopus.* There were times when every word must be dragged forth by a painful effort. Condy "must shut his eyes to the end of his novel . . . . driving his pen from line to line, hating the effort, happy only with the termination of each chapter. . . . ."[19] According to his biographer, *A Man's Woman* was such a task for Norris. But when he had a theme which engaged all his faculties, which interested him profoundly, there is no doubt that he was seized by the tremendous excitement of creation, like Presley when he writes the final stanzas of his poem "The Toilers." Presley has been stirred to burning indignation by the cynical injustice of the railroad toward the ranchers.

[18] "Novelists of the Future," in *The Responsibilities of the Novelist,* p. 208.
[19] *Blix* (Doubleday, Doran & Company, Inc.), p. 261.

He went up to his little room and paced the floor with clenched fists and burning face, till at last, the repression of his contending thoughts all but suffocated him, and he flung himself before his table and began to write. For a time, his pen seemed to travel by itself; words came to him without searching, shaping themselves into phrases,—the phrases building themselves up to great, forcible sentences, full of eloquence, of fire, of passion. As his prose grew more exalted, it passed easily into the domain of poetry . . . .

Presley laid down his pen and leaned back in his chair, with the certainty that for one moment he had touched untrod heights. His hands were cold, his head on fire, his heart leaping tumultuous in his breast.[20]

The net result of Norris' documentation, his care for technical accuracy, his responsiveness to all the impressions of sense, his occasional experience of the fusing power of what is called "inspiration" is much realism of a high excellence. His great strength lies in the skillful and completely satisfying re-creation for the senses of his reader of human material surroundings—houses, furnishings, theaters, streets, railway stations—wherever people live and move. It is not alone the physical aspect of these things— their form and color, the sounds and smells that are associated with them—that he conveys so successfully, but the atmosphere that clings to them as well, whether of comfort, of shabby gentility, of vulgarity, of squalor, of stagnation, of pretentiousness, of animation, of repose—every subtle, surely sensed, but not easily explained feeling that human living imparts to its habitual environment. In this he resembles Balzac. The famous respectable bourgeois pension of Madame Vauquer in *Père Goriot* or the house of old Grandet in *Eugénie Grandet* are not more authentic than the combined dental "parlor"-bedroom of McTeague with its second-hand chairs, the steel engraving of the court of Lorenzo de' Medici "bought because there were a great

[20] *The Octopus*, pp. 371–72.

many figures in it for the money," the bookshelves bearing the seven volumes of "Allen's Practical Dentist," the stone pug dog before the stove, the whole saturated with a "mingled odor of bedding, creosote, and ether."[21]

The late Victorian living room of the middle-class home, both on its upper and its lower levels, he has observed with a relentless eye. Every detail is there to evidence every popular notion of what constituted the ornamental, the "artistic," the correct in taste: the "enlarged" portraits on brass easels, the steel engravings of Priscilla and John Alden, the bisque figurines, the pianos that nobody ever played, the clocks set in red plush palettes, the gilded cattails tied with pink ribbon; a copy of the *Chautauquan* on the center table to represent culture, the mottled marble mantelpieces, Alaskan baskets filled with photographs; the whatnots bearing seashells, Chinese coins, lacquer boxes, and sawfish bills. All these things are described with an air of solemn objectivity which only enhances a lurking intention of humor and satire. It has since become a part of the stock-in-trade of novelists to entertain their readers at the expense of the ways of last century; but Norris' satire in this kind marks the beginning in this country of the revulsion from Victorian taste.

The realism of *McTeague* laid bare a section of American life where the fiction writer had scarcely ever thought to probe, and in a spirit and manner altogether new—the spirit and manner of the anatomist. Stephen Crane's *Maggie: A Girl of the Streets,* which belongs to the same genre, preceded *McTeague* by six years, but went almost completely unnoticed. Some earlier sporadic and isolated attempts there had been to deal with the life of the industrial worker or of the city poor—efforts like Rebecca

[21] *McTeague,* p. 4.

Blaine Harding's "Life in the Iron Mills" (*Atlantic Monthly,* April, 1861), or Elizabeth Stuart Phelps's *Hedged In* (1870). But such studies were not consonant with the expansive mood of post–Civil War national growth. Such as appeared were usually marked by sentimentalism and a pallid piety. They were apt to be patronizing. Here, their authors seemed to say, are souls to be saved, sin to be purged away; here is a God-sent opportunity for the exercise of Christian charity. There is nothing of this in Norris' study of the denizens of Polk Street.[22]

Norris' realism has the further character which makes it what has come to be designated naturalism. Realism becomes naturalism at the moment when it adopts a philosophy of materialistic determinism. Man was the last object of the phenomenal universe to be brought under the laws that rule all the forms of matter. This service was performed by the nineteenth-century biology for a world which received it at first with a surly ingratitude, rising at times to ferocious resentment. But the scientific view of human origins and human behavior was destined to influence profoundly every department of thought.

To apply the spirit of experimental science and even the methods of the laboratory to imaginative literature was a step easy and inevitable. Sainte-Beuve, commenting on the materialistic and scientific spirit which was making ever deeper incursions into the literature of his time, concluded his review of *Madame Bovary* with the apostrophe, "Anatomists and physiologists, I find you everywhere." The main lines of naturalism were drawn by

---

22 It should be noted that the people of *McTeague* do not represent the victims of abject poverty. Poverty, however, is but one short remove from them and is the inevitable result of any derangement of the economic routine. Poverty it is that rots away the character of McTeague.

the Goncourts in *Renée Mauperin* (1864) and *Germinie Lacerteux* (1865); "aujourd'hui," they wrote in the preface to the latter, "le Roman s'est imposé les études et les devoirs de la science." At the same time, by a deliberate choice of subject from "ce qu'on appelle 'les basses classes,'" they reveal a tendency of the naturalists to forsake the more genteel social levels. It was Zola, however, who wrote the handbook of the movement, *Le Roman Expérimental* (1880), and who became the chief practitioner of the naturalistic novel.

Naturalism was to explain man as the product of two things—heredity and environment. Its material was to be drawn from the facts of experience; it was to treat that material by the method of science; that is, it was to be objective and experimental. Given characters of such and such heredity, placed in such and such a milieu, played upon by such and such forces: problem, to find the resultant behavior. "Il ne faut admettre," said Zola, quoting with approval the physiologist Claude Bernard, "rien d'occulte; il n'y a que des phénomènes et des conditions des phénomènes." Taine, in the Introduction to his *History of English Literature* (1863), had already issued his famous dictum, "Vice and virtue are products, like vitriol and sugar." Zola closed *Le Roman Expérimental* with these words:

L'homme métaphysique est mort, tout notre terrain se transforme avec l'homme physiologique. Sans doute la colère d'Achille, l'amour de Didon, resteront des peintures éternellement belles; mais, voilà que le besoin nous prend d'analyser la colère et l'amour, et de voir au juste comment fonctionnent ces passions dans l'être humain ... la méthode expérimentale, aussi bien dans les lettres que dans les sciences, est en train de déterminer les phénomènes naturels, individuels et sociaux, dont la métaphysique n'avait donné jusqu'ici que des explications irrationelles et surnaturelles.

In the light of a deterministic philosophy the swelling ego of man, which had strutted and postured up and down the stage of the world for so many centuries, appeared but a poor thing. To the naturalist the universe had lost its once benign character and had become impersonal, indifferent to man. The point of view is well exemplified in Norris' contemporary, Stephen Crane, who wrote:

> A man said to the universe:
> "Sir, I exist!"
> "However," replied the universe,
> "The fact has not created in me
> A sense of obligation."[23]

The impersonality of the universe was, of course, not the invention of the naturalists. For a long time, parallel with the development of science, the idea had been everywhere gaining ground. In 1844 Alfred de Vigny, for example, imagined nature to speak thus to humankind:

> "Je n'entends ni vos cris ni vos soupirs; à peine
> Je sens passer sur moi la comédie humaine
> Qui cherche en vain au ciel ses muets spectateurs."[24]

The intrusion of this concept is indeed the source of the cosmic bellyache which filled the literature of the nineteenth century with so many cries of pain.

Since the naturalist was to treat his material objectively, he was to maintain toward it a strictly amoral attitude. He was not to extend his hands in benediction over the good, the true, and the beautiful; neither was he to inveigh against wickedness. He was merely to record and lay down the pen without comment.

Now a deterministic philosophy is ill sorted to a land where the appearance, and in great part the actuality, of

[23] Stephen Crane, *War Is Kind, and Other Lines*, in *Works*, Vol. VI (New York: Alfred A. Knopf, 1926), p. 131.

[24] Alfred de Vigny, *La Maison du Berger*, lines 285–87.

unrestricted individual opportunity generates feelings of hope and optimism and the confidence that every man can carve out his own destiny according to his own specifications. Emerson testified to the existence of these feelings when he wrote: "There is in America a general conviction in the minds of all mature men, that every young man of good faculty and good habits can by perseverance attain to an adequate estate . . . ."[25] But the rapid economic expansion which seemed to justify optimism and a romantic exuberance contained within itself potentialities destined in time to weaken seriously the sanguine feelings it at first excited. The 'seventies and 'eighties saw the birth of all the great monopolies—railroads, oil, steel, meatpacking, farm implements—whose growth inevitably encroached on the field of individual enterprise. The enormous flood of immigration made the pressure of population felt in the great industrial centers and tended to depress the condition of labor. By about 1890 the public lands were gone, closing another avenue of individual opportunity. The efforts at governmental control of big business and the opposed efforts of big business itself to control government in its own interest had the same result—a greater centralization of political power. Machine products, advertising on a national scale, improved communication, introduced an element of standardization which would increase as time went on. Industrial conflict became a more prominent feature of the economic life. Centralization, standardization, depersonalization—such was the process. In this scheme of things the individual began to count for less and less, became more and more a cog in a vast machine.

[25] Ralph Waldo Emerson, "Social Aims," in *Works* (Centenary Edition, Boston: Houghton Mifflin Company, 1903), VIII, 100.

As a result of these developments the national mood was sure to undergo some change. But of course the change did not occur suddenly, nor did it affect uniformly all classes of the population. The old mood would persist after the conditions that gave rise to it had nearly passed away. Thus, although our social environment and many details of our material circumstances justified in some part the deterministic philosophy of the naturalists, our habitual optimism and our romantic conceptions rejected it. The time nevertheless was ripe for its appearance when Norris published *McTeague* in 1899. Zola and the French naturalists had been made accessible through translation, and the controversy in the magazines over their work had created a wide popular interest.[26]

No one knows just when or under what circumstances Norris first encountered Zola. The logical time was during his two years in Paris beginning with 1887, the very year of the publication of *La Terre,* which set all France, all Europe, by the ears. It seems incredible that even the most indifferent could at that moment fail to hear the name of the pugnacious Provençal uttered on every hand; but he appears to have been so completely absorbed in his study of medieval armor that he was entirely unconscious of his literary surroundings.[27] It was only after his return to San Francisco that he made the great discovery under the stimulus of which he was to see with new eyes the streets, the wharves, the swarming various life of the Western metropolis. He was now never seen without a

[26] See Herbert Edwards, "Zola and the American Critics," *American Literature,* May 1932.

[27] Charles Norris once states that Frank "brought back with him from France a keen interest in the novels of Émile Zola" (Introduction to *Collected Writings Hitherto Unpublished,* p. ix); but Professor Franklin Walker finds no evidence in support of this statement.

yellow paper-covered volume of Zola under his arm as he strolled about the campus of the University of California. During his first term at the university he was finishing his medieval poem *Yvernelle,* but by his senior year he was already at work on *McTeague.* Somewhere in the interval he experienced the new impulse. With the foregoing brief outline of the theory of naturalism as a guide, we may turn to the application of the formula in Norris' novels, leaving till later a more detailed consideration of the influence of Zola.

If naturalism concerns human action as determined by the two forces of heredity and environment, there is no reason why some men of good heredity and fortunate surroundings should not occasionally be brought as a result to positions of success or power. But this is seldom the way of the naturalistic novel. Its characters contain some defect of blood; they are surrounded by adverse circumstance; they suffer mischance; an evil fate hounds them, and in the end they are destroyed. As Norris himself conceived it,

Terrible things must happen to the characters of the naturalistic tale. They must be . . . . flung into the throes of a . . . . terrible drama that works itself out in unleashed passions, in blood, and in sudden death.[28]

And terrible things happen to McTeague and to Trina his wife.

McTeague's father, a shift boss in one of the mines of the Sierra, drinks himself to death. His mother is an ignorant woman coarsened by hard work but ambitious

[28] "Zola as a Romantic Writer," San Francisco *Wave,* June 27, 1896; quoted from *Frank Norris: A Biography,* by Franklin Walker (copyright 1932; reprinted by permission of Doubleday, Doran & Company, Inc.), p. 83.

for her son, whom she apprentices to an itinerant quack dentist. In due time McTeague picks up such knowledge as his master has to offer, and when the novel opens he is established in his dental parlors above the branch post office on Polk Street in San Francisco. He is a giant of enormous strength and Gargantuan appetite. On Sundays he varies his weekly routine by gorging himself with an extraordinary quantity of cheap, greasy food in the car-conductors' coffee joint hard by; he then retires to his "parlors" and, seated in his dentist's chair, regales himself with a pitcher of steam beer and a pipe of strong tobacco. Presently he falls into a heavy torpor, like a boa constrictor which has recently swallowed a pig. He has two powerful affections—for his canary and for his concertina, on which he knows how to play six tunes of an incomparable dolor. His wits are bovine, ponderous. He is slow to anger, but when once aroused he is dangerous, blind in fury. "Yet there was nothing vicious about the man. Altogether he suggested the draught horse, immensely strong, stupid, docile, obedient."[29]

Trina Sieppe is the daughter of petty bourgeois German parents. With the exception of Trina, Norris conceives the family in terms of unmistakably Dickensian comedy:[30] Papa Sieppe, who marshals them all with the fierce bluster and gestures of a Prussian drill sergeant; hen-like Mama Sieppe, fluttering and squawking over her brood; little "Owgooste," forever whining, forever

[29] *McTeague*, p. 3.

[30] During Norris' childhood it had been the custom of his mother to read aloud to her family night after night from one or other of the novels of Dickens. With the exception of Scott no other writer was more intimately familiar to him from these early years. His biographer sees in old Grannis and Miss Baker of *McTeague* "eccentrics" modeled on those of Dickens. Mrs. Wessels (Aunt Wess') and Grossman the Jew in *The Pit* and Hooven the comical German farmer in *The Octopus* are also clearly Dickensian figures.

suffering under a hail of prohibitions, threats, and objurgations from his parents.

Chance brings McTeague and Trina together. One day, as his patient, she lies in his dentist's chair unconscious from the ether he has just administered to her. Suddenly he is intoxicated by the feminine odor of her person as he bends over her. He endures a terrific struggle such as he had never in his life experienced: "the blood sang in his ears; his face flushed scarlet; his hands twisted themselves together like the knotting of cables. The fury in him was as the fury of a young bull in the heat of high summer."[31] But he feels that if he yields to the impulse which goads him so mercilessly "her charm for him would vanish in an instant" (curious weakness and paradox of the romantic conception of love, which Norris could never put aside). The ordeal is too great; McTeague kisses her "grossly, full on the mouth." Thenceforth events move steadily and inevitably to the marriage of McTeague and Trina.

The courtship is developed in two or three episodes: First there is the picnic in Schutzen Park, which enables Norris to establish more firmly his milieu, the speech, the habits, the manners of the social class he has elected to study—the class characterized in its amusements by the presence of children and dogs, and by the public munching of peanuts. Then there is the theater party when McTeague escorts Trina, her mother, and "little Owgooste" to a cheap vaudeville. McTeague's agonies of embarrassment, his fears that something may go wrong; the naïve wonder and admiration of the little group at the tawdry glitter, the banal tunes produced by striking glass

[31] *McTeague*, p. 31.

58

bottles, the sentimental songs; their delight in the trite and crude humor of certain "numbers"; the matchless rich vulgarity of the entire performance and of the audience itself—all are given with absolute fidelity.[32]

With the winning by Trina of the $5,000 in the lottery and with McTeague's practice on a sound footing, the way is clear for their marriage. After the wedding supper—one of the finest pieces of genre painting in the book or indeed in American fiction—they settle down in the flat above the branch post office, having added two rooms to McTeague's "parlors." With her neat German housewifely ways Trina is a civilizing influence on McTeague. Under a gentle pressure from her he abandons some of his crudities—he is induced to change his shirt twice a week, to cease eating with his knife, to drink bottled instead of steam beer, to tip his hat to Miss Baker. He begins to read the newspapers and to entertain opinions on public questions. The two of them begin to think of a house of their own. Their lives settle into a routine of comfort and contentment. They know a modest and growing prosperity. So pass three years.

Then one day McTeague sees a large, fat, official-looking envelope come sliding through the mail slot of his "parlors" to fall upon the floor with a heavy slapping sound, as ominous, had he but known, as the knocking on the gate in *Macbeth*. Here is the crisis, the turning of the

[32] The incident should be compared with the opera party of the Cresslers which opens *The Pit;* they are companion pieces, one drawn from low life, the other from "society." Norris is quite aware that the opera offers as much matter for his restrained satire. The audience, with its solemn illusion that it is being cultured, and its sartorial ostentation of wealth; the rumbling basso, and the gesticulating fat tenor—are as banal as their homologues of the Orpheum. Laura, trying to lose herself in an ecstasy of romantic sentiment, in the pauses of the music hears all around her scraps of low-toned talk: "one hundred and six carloads," "paralyzed the bulls," "fifty thousand dollars."

tide in the lives of McTeague and Trina. To this point the movement has been steadily upward; after, it is as relentlessly downward to tragedy and death. The envelope contains a summons from the state board ordering McTeague to cease practice; for he has never attended a dental college and has no diploma. He is stunned, stupefied; he cannot understand. "What had a clerk at the City Hall to do with him? Why couldn't they let him alone? . . . . I ain't going to quit for just a piece of paper (pp. 264–65)." But a second, more threatening, summons obliges him to lay down his tools. It is here that the naturalistic theme of the novel especially asserts itself. To another the incident, serious as it is, would have been merely a temporary setback. A little study, combined with his practical experience, would have enabled McTeague to meet the requirements of the law. But this never once, even remotely, occurs to him. It is impossible that it should. The barrier is insuperable. McTeague can see nothing ahead but ruin. Nor does the simple solution occur to Trina, with her greater intelligence. The deficiencies of her education and of her knowledge of the world forbid it. They are in the grip of forces within and without themselves—forces beyond their comprehension and beyond their control. The powerful impulse of sex had originally joined their lives. No sooner had they met than (p. 89)

Their undoing had already begun. Yet neither of them was to blame. . . . . Chance had brought them face to face, and mysterious instincts as ungovernable as the winds of heaven were at work knitting their lives together. Neither of them had asked that this thing should be . . . . If they could have known, they would have shunned the fearful risk. But they were allowed no voice in the matter.

True, they have Trina's $5,000; but it is her capital and

she will not allow it to be touched. For the acquisition of this money had awakened in her a latent instinct of avarice. Ever since their marriage it has been growing steadily, manifesting itself in a thousand little ways. In the end it becomes a consuming mania and we see her lying naked on her bed, which she has covered with gold pieces, pressing and rolling her body against the cool gleaming metal.

From the moment of the cessation of his practice the degradation of McTeague and Trina proceeds at a pace more and more rapid. They first abandon the apartment, so bright and clean, which had been Trina's joy. They sell most of their effects and take a small single room at the top of the flat. McTeague's grief, his stumbling words at parting with his dentist's equipment, the steel engraving, the stone pug dog—his sense of frustration at abandoning the occupation of twelve years—are of a true and powerful pathos.

Now begin the thousand miseries, the mean little economies, of Trina's self-imposed penury, aggravated by a succession of misfortunes which cannot be here detailed but which in their cumulative effect crush the reader under a sense of intolerable oppression. McTeague, who at first finds a job only to lose it as a consequence of hard times, lapses into sullenness, consoling himself at times with whiskey, which makes him vicious rather than drunk. The habit of idleness grows upon him. He cherishes a mounting resentment against Trina as the source of all his woes. A strain of sadistic brutality appears in him. Sometimes he strikes her in anger, but again gives himself the more deliberate pleasure of lacerating her fingers cruelly between his great strong teeth. At length, having robbed her of the money she has earned and hoarded during a number of years, he deserts her. Her occupation of carving Noah's ark animals, which has enabled them both to live, is made impossible by the amputation of several of her fingers; raw from McTeague's ill-usage, they have been poisoned by the paint she was accustomed to apply to the wooden animal figures. She becomes a frowzy, work-hardened charwoman in a school near by, sleeping in a little room on the premises (pp. 352–53):

> She went about her work from dawn to dark, and often entire days passed when she did not hear the sound of her own voice. She was alone, a solitary, abandoned woman, lost in the lowest eddies of the great city's tide—the tide that always ebbs.

Meanwhile McTeague's sense of wrong and injury has been turned to deadly hatred by her refusal of even so much as a dime on an occasion when he was derelict and starving. Then one night he seeks out Trina for the last time, and we have the terrible scene in the deserted schoolroom. Here Norris shows that he is aware of the value of suggestion and restrained statement. He does not let us see McTeague batter and crush the life out of Trina. After describing the preliminaries of the encounter, in which Trina "fought for her miserable life with the exasperation and strength of a harassed cat," he merely writes the tremendously effective sentence: "Then it became abominable." Our further impressions are gained from the behavior of the cat,[33] crouched behind the coal

---

[33] Norris at first mismanaged this business of the cat, attempting to penetrate the animal's consciousness. But Professor Lewis E. Gates of Harvard, under whom he was studying at the time, pointed out that he should remain objective and confine himself to a description of the cat's acts and appearance. Norris was much gratified, filled with admiration at the improvement thus wrought.

scuttle, "wildly terrified, his eyes bulging like brass knobs." Then, after an interval (pp. 377–78):

> Trina lay unconscious, just as she had fallen under the last of McTeague's blows, her body twitching with an occasional hiccough that stirred the pool of blood in which she lay face downward. Towards morning she died with a rapid series of hiccoughs that sounded like a piece of clockwork running down.

Having brought his novel thus far, Norris was apparently at a loss how to dispose of McTeague. He laid aside his manuscript for two years, and when he returned to it in the autumn of 1897 resolved to give his story a thrilling flight and pursuit conclusion. Accordingly he endowed McTeague with a sixth sense to warn him of the near presence of his pursuers, sent him on a long flight through the mountains, far south into the Panamint Range, and thence into Death Valley. It is quite credible that McTeague, fleeing the law, should turn instinctively to his old haunts in the mountains. This sort of manhunt is common enough in real life, though somewhat trite and elementary as a fictional device. It is also credible that he should be abnormally alert to danger. What is improbable is that every time his sixth sense warned him to move on, his pursuers were actually closing in on him. A sixth sense will do as a figure of speech but not as an infallible instrument of perception.

In Death Valley, McTeague is overtaken by Marcus Schouler, his one-time bosom friend but now his implacable and treacherous enemy, for it was Schouler who had revealed to the authorities McTeague's lack of a diploma. Marcus had been the accepted but lukewarm suitor of Trina. In a burst of magnanimity he had retired in favor of McTeague. But shortly thereafter Trina had won the $5,000, whereupon his former friend had taken on for

Marcus the aspect of a robber who had foully despoiled him of what by right should have been his own.

As the two now confront each other an accident occurs which causes them momentarily to forget their feud in face of a common peril. Schouler has drunk his last drop of water. McTeague's only supply is contained in a canteen hung on the pack-saddle of his mule. But when Marcus reaches for the canteen the animal suddenly bolts. Now follows a desperate chase, mile after mile, the two men stumbling in pursuit, sweating and cursing, the mule keeping ever out of reach. Maddeningly the beast allows them to approach, only to dart away again just when his bridle is nearly within grasp. At length there is nothing left but to kill the mule. Schouler, after firing several times and expending his last bullet, brings the beast down, but in falling it rolls upon the canteen and bursts it open. In a moment the precious water vanishes into the sand. The two enemies stare at each other. " 'We're dead men,' said Marcus." Presently, without hope, they prepare to move on; but when McTeague reaches for the sack containing Trina's gold pieces, Schouler's hatred flares up again. They grapple and roll together upon the ground. After a sharp struggle McTeague kills his foe, but Marcus with his last strength handcuffs their wrists together. McTeague rises to his feet. There he stands under the murderous sun in the midst of a fiery desolation, manacled to a corpse, a hundred miles from the nearest habitation, a hundred miles from the nearest water. It was a "situation" such as Norris loved, one on the invention of which he never ceased to congratulate himself; nor would he ever admit its inharmony with the main theme and mood of the narrative. He wrote to Howells: "I agree in every one of your criticisms always excepting the anticlimax, the 'death in the desert' business. I am sure that has its place."[34] With this death in the desert ends the first important naturalistic novel in American fiction, its pattern somewhat broken by the sentimental love story of old Grannis and Miss Baker, and by the melodramatic close.

But though the end of *McTeague* may be called melodrama, it is undeniably good melodrama. It is not half so improbable as the conclusion of Stendhal's *Le Rouge et le Noir,* which is reckoned a masterpiece of realism and which Taine admired so much that he is reputed to have read it eighty times. At the end of his novel Stendhal treats us to the spectacle of Mathilde de la Mole setting up on a little marble table the severed head of her guillotined lover and kissing the ghastly relic on the forehead. When, in her closed carriage, she follows the corpse of Julien to the tomb, she holds his head on her lap, her strange act of devotion unknown of course to those who form the funeral procession. After all have gone from the graveside she buries the head of her lover with her own hands. This may be realism, though it sounds like "Monk" Lewis or G. W. M. Reynolds.

Before we leave *McTeague,* one remaining feature of the work deserves notice. Norris once told Howells[35] that he first thought of calling his novel *The Golden Tooth.* For like his master Zola he was irresistibly drawn to the use of some powerful symbol which would dominate his books, unify his themes, and drive them into the consciousness of his readers with overwhelming force. In *McTeague* this symbol is gold, as later in *The Octopus* it

[34] *Life in Letters of William Dean Howells* (New York: Doubleday, Doran & Company, 1928; quoted by permission of Miss Mildred Howells), II, 102.

[35] W. D. Howells, "Frank Norris," *North American Review,* December 1902, p. 773.

would be wheat. Gold is the material token of the greed which destroys Trina and McTeague and Schouler and Maria Macapa and old Zerkow. The yellow sheen of gold is seen everywhere. Zerkow, the Jewish junk dealer, has but one passion—gold: "The glint of it was constantly in his eyes; the jangle of it sang forever in his ears . . . ." He makes the half-mad Mexican girl Maria tell over and over the story of the service of gold plate which had once been in her family—"more than a hundred pieces . . . . thick, fat gold . . . . red, shining, pure gold, orange red . . . ."[36] No one knows whether this fabulous treasure exists outside Maria's imagination, but Zerkow comes to believe in its reality. He licks his cat-like lips and contracts his claw-like fingers at the thought of it. The color of gold is suggested by McTeague's yellow canary and its gilt cage. Most striking of all is the Gargantuan tooth—sign of his trade—which hung outside the window of his dental "parlors," shining and beautiful in its coat of French gilt. Trina will have nothing but coins of gold in her hoard. McTeague, after the murder, flees to a gold mine in the Sierra. Later, prospecting with a partner, he discovers a rich vein of gold quartz, though he has to leave it at the urging of that mysterious sixth sense which warns him of pursuit. "The wonder is," writes Professor Parrington, "that [Norris] didn't give Trina gold hair instead of black."[37]

Symbolism is evident also in other parts of the narrative. The story of Zerkow and Maria Macapa is the story in little of McTeague and Trina. Zerkow, in the hope of gaining the service of gold plate, marries Maria and takes

[36] *McTeague*, pp. 43, 46.

[37] Vernon Louis Parrington, *The Beginnings of Critical Realism in America* (New York: Harcourt, Brace and Company, 1930), p. 331.

her to live in his wretched hovel. Exasperated to madness by what he believes her refusal to disclose the hiding place of the treasure, he cuts her throat. It is Trina who finds the dead girl. In a few months she too will die at the hands of a husband, with real instead of imaginary gold as the motive of the crime. The deadly enmity which will spring up between the boon companions McTeague and Marcus is foreshadowed in the perpetual feud of the two dogs—Marcus' setter Alexander and the collie who dwells in the yard of the branch post office. At the very moment when the friendship appears firmest the hint is given that it will not endure. McTeague and Marcus have just returned from the walk during which Marcus has generously offered to leave McTeague a clear field for the courtship of Trina. Suddenly the two dogs, with the fence between, break into a furious quarrel. "By damn!" cried Marcus, "they don't love each other. Just listen; wouldn't that make a fight if the two got together?" With this evil augury the fourth chapter ends.

Vandover and the Brute is conceived on more rigidly naturalistic lines than *McTeague.* Its narrative of moral and physical disintegration is undisturbed by love idyls or "Wild West" episodes. The social level of the characters is higher than that in *McTeague.* Vandover's father (obviously modeled on Norris' own) is a man of considerable wealth. Vandover himself (whose life is parallel at several points with that of his creator) is educated at Harvard. After graduation he returns to San Francisco with the idea of becoming a painter. But from the first his character is weak; he loves physical comfort, is naturally self-indulgent and prone in any situation to take the line of least resistance. Having money and leisure, he becomes a young man about town, a frequenter of fashionable bars and clubs in the society of a pair of his boyhood friends and Harvard classmates. Habits of gambling, drinking, and sexual indulgence, already contracted in college, grow upon him. Gradually he develops symptoms of an obscure and fearful disease, lycanthropy. In this affliction the victim suffers under the delusion that he has become a wolf. In the end we find Vandover in his room, naked, on all fours, padding back and forth, swinging his head from side to side, snarling, growling, and snapping like a beast.

Norris had here a powerful theme, conceived, as has been remarked, on more severely naturalistic lines than *McTeague*; but the execution is less good, for he is unable to hold so well the objective and amoral attitude which the naturalistic writer professes to maintain. The weakness of the book is already hinted in the title, which suggests nothing more nor less than the old Christian dualism of flesh and spirit struggling for mastery. The novel becomes a kind of debate of the soul and body, given a modern setting and deprived of its theology and eschatology. There is nothing either scientific or objective in the body-soul notion, in the beast-man theory of human nature. It is merely a figure of speech, which begs all attempt to determine causes. Norris could never rid himself of the idea of the dual nature of man, nor rid himself of his tendency to personify.

The suicide of the girl Ida Wade (whom he had seduced), followed closely by the death of his father, shocks Vandover momentarily out of his dissipations. He sets himself up comfortably in a studio of his own and imagines that he is done with his old life, that he will henceforth be a changed man. But, Norris reminds us, Vandover here made a "fatal mistake: the brute in him had

68

only been stunned; the snake was only soothed. His better self was as sluggish as the brute, and his desire of art as numb as his desire of vice."[38] We are asked to believe that it is only by an exercise of the will, "an active and energetic arousing and spurring up of those better qualities in him still dormant and inert," that his regeneration can be accomplished. But what determines the will?

The grosser member of this pair—soul and body, man and brute—is almost invariably associated with sex, as was already apparent in *McTeague*. The idea is ineradicably planted in Norris' mind that the sexual impulse is of its very nature evil and to be deplored. Even McTeague reasons dimly in the same fashion. Having kissed Trina as she lay unconscious in the dentist's chair, he asks himself with incomparable banality why he could not always love her "purely, cleanly." After a terrific struggle he masters his feelings. "But for all that," Norris admonishes, "the brute was there. Long dormant, it was now at last alive, awake. From now on he would feel its presence continually; would feel it tugging at its chain, watching its opportunity." But here the cause is the naturalistic one of heredity, and McTeague is absolved from responsibility.

> Below the fine fabric of all that was good in him ran the foul stream of hereditary evil, like a sewer. The vices and sins of his father and of his father's father, to the third and fourth and five hundredth generation, tainted him. . . . . He did not desire it. Was he to blame?[39]

This is good naturalistic doctrine, though it seems hard that desire for a woman should consign a man to the ancestral sewer.

[38] Frank Norris, *Vandover and the Brute* (copyright 1914, 1928, by Doubleday, Doran & Company, Inc.), pp. 179–80.
[39] *McTeague*, p. 32.

In *Vandover and the Brute,* however, determinism and responsibility exist side by side, unreconciled. At one moment it is a passage like the following that seems to strike the key (pp. 230–31):

. . . . Life . . . . the great, mysterious force that spun the wheels of Nature and that sent it onward like some enormous engine, resistless, relentless . . . . driving before it the infinite herd of humanity . . . . at breathless speed through all eternity, driving it no one knew whither, crushing out inexorably all those who lagged behind the herd and who fell from exhaustion, grinding them to dust beneath its myriad iron wheels. . . . .

Now if one of the innumerable manifestations of this "great mysterious force," life (which must bear within itself as well the forces of destruction and death), is lycanthropy, a form of hysteria, a recognized species of insanity, and Vandover is its victim, there is nothing more to be said. We may observe the process of his disintegration with whatever of pity and terror lies in us to feel, and close the book. But Norris gives Vandover moral responsibility and cannot refrain from scolding him throughout for his failure to exercise it. Thus his disease was the punishment for "his vile submission to the brute."

The novel contains some excellent pictures of the futile triviality which marks the lives of leisure-class young men of a certain sort, and (in chapter ix) one memorable scene in the best Zolaesque manner—the wreck of the "Mazatlan," on which Vandover is returning to San Francisco from a vacation at Coronado Beach. As it is a fine example of Norris' descriptive powers, we may pause a moment over it.

A boat bearing Vandover and others has been lowered from the foundering vessel. As it is about to put off, a little greasy Jew, whom Vandover had previously remarked, leaps from the rail, strikes out for the small boat, and, though warned off, succeeds in grasping the gunwale of the already perilously overloaded craft. "Push him away! Save my little girls! Let him drown!" cries one of the women. The ship's engineer obligingly beats the Jew's fingers into a bloody pulp with the stump of an oar. "When his hands were gone," writes Norris casually, "he tried to embrace the oar with his arms." He then sank from sight in a froth of crimson bubbles. " 'Oh, God!' exclaimed Vandover, turning away and vomiting over the side."

The conclusion of *Vandover* is stronger and more consonant with the tone of the whole than perhaps that of any other of Norris' novels. Vandover, a physical ruin, stripped of his last shred of pride or self-respect, and reduced to beggary, is given a job by his old friend, Charley Geary, who has cheated and robbed him of a valuable property, now occupied by a factory. Near by Geary has erected a swarm of cheap houses to rent to the workers. Vandover is provided with soap, scrubbing brush, and pail and instructed to clean one of these dwellings for the reception of new tenants. All afternoon he labors, often on hands and knees, till his head swims and his back seems breaking. As he nears the end of his task, the new tenants come to inspect the result—a pale little straw-colored burnisher from the factory, his wife, her sister, a fat woman "smelling somehow of tallow candles and cooked cabbage," and the burnisher's little boy, solemnly munching a piece of bread and butter. Suddenly there is a clamor from the burnisher's wife. Vandover has overlooked the cubby under the sink (p. 351):

"What's that over in the corner there?" cried the wife, bending down. "I can't see, it's so dark under there—something gray; can't you see, in under there? You'll have to crawl way in to get at it—go way in!" Vandover obeyed. The sink pipes were so close above him that he was obliged to crouch lower and lower; at length he lay flat upon his stomach. Prone in the filth under the sink, in the sour water, the grease, the refuse, he groped about with his hand searching for the something gray that the burnisher's wife had seen. He found it and drew it out. It was an old hambone covered with a greenish fuzz.

When he has removed a further quantity of the foul detritus of squalor, he gathers up his things and prepares to leave. Dusk has fallen over the city and the wretched little house; the tenants have gone. But the little boy lingers, fascinated by every movement as Vandover ties his bundle. Having finished, he looks up. "For an instant the two remained there motionless, looking into each other's eyes, Vandover on the floor . . . . the little boy standing before him eating the last mouthful of his bread and butter." It is our parting glimpse.

Despite every fault *Vandover* is not inferior to *Mc-Teague* in concentrated effect. It has the same absolute authenticity of concrete realization. It roots itself in the mind with a tenacity that nothing can shake.

McTeague and *Vandover and the Brute* are individual studies set in a contracted, narrowly defined frame. The volumes intervening between them and *The Octopus*—namely, *Moran of the Lady Letty, Blix,* and *A Man's Woman*—have little or nothing to do with naturalism except in so far as *Moran* and *A Man's Woman* make much of brute strength and primitive passions; and the early chapters of the last-named, relating how the explorer Ward Bennett brought his expedition down from the Arctic, contain some of Norris' most vigorous description in the style of Zola. With *The Octopus,* however, the scale is enormously magnified till it reaches epic proportions. As Norris himself exclaimed when the conception first dawned upon him, it is a theme "as big as all outdoors." Here the great protagonists are, first, physical nature and, second, impersonal economic forces. In the interplay of these forces, men are but pawns. Uniting in itself the character of a natural and of an economic force, is the wheat, intended in Norris' design to dominate the epic trilogy of which *The Octopus* is but the first part. Here we are to witness the first stage of the process by which the wheat fulfills its function as the appeaser of human hunger, namely, the planting, the growth, and the harvesting of the grain. The scene is the West (more specifically the San Joaquin Valley of California), that region which Norris believed had been neglected and which offered, he thought, the richest and the grandest themes for American fiction. The dramatic action is supplied by the struggle between the ranchers and the powerful Pacific & Southwestern Railroad (by which is intended the Southern Pacific). The road employs all the methods and artifices familiar in the history of American railway economics —extortionate and discriminatory rates, corruption of legislatures, courts, and state railroad commissions. It plants its agents in the national congress. It has thrown open to settlement under fine promises and specious inducements certain areas of the San Joaquin—a gift to it from the public domain. Title to the land remains with the road, with the understanding that the settlers may purchase eventually at a nominal price. When the ranchers have brought the land under cultivation and greatly enhanced its value, the road offers to sell at a ruinous rate. It answers protests by reclaiming the entire region and sending the agents of the law to evict the present occupants. The colossal and spidery brain which sits at the center of this vast web is Shelgrim, modeled directly (though, one suspects, considerably idealized) on Collis P. Huntington, the organizing genius of the Southern Pacific. But, in conformity with Norris' main conception, Shelgrim himself is merely representative of larger issues, one actor in a social-economic drama of national, even of world, scope; he is "a giant figure in the end-of-the-century finance, a product of circumstance, an inevitable result of conditions, characteristic, typical, symbolic of ungovernable forces."[40]

The climax of the action comes when the ranchers, goaded to desperation, make armed resistance to the officers sent to drive them from their homes. There is a skirmish and a general slaughter.[41] Thenceforth we have only to follow the course of the surviving characters to their moral and material ruin to witness the complete triumph of the corporation.

The canvas is crowded with figures—ranchers, sheepherders, cowboys, railroad men—for Norris wished, like the poet Presley, to embrace the whole life of the West in all its color and movement, not omitting the lingering traces of the Spanish regime in the persons of Father Sarria and the ancient Mexican idler of Guadalajara.

Norris has a pronounced taste for the immensities of nature — a taste which is evident in the latter part of *McTeague* but which finds its fullest opportunity in *The Octopus*. He lays in the physical background with large bold strokes fitting the California landscape with its tremendous distances, its startling contrasts of mountain and

[40] *The Octopus,* p. 104.

[41] This was founded on an actual occurrence known as the Mussel Slough affair, which took place (as a result of the same causes described in the novel) on May 11, 1880. Norris "read up" the details in the Mechanics Library, San Francisco, and in the files of the *San Francisco Chronicle* (Walker, *op. cit.,* pp. 246–47).

plain, of the desert and the sown. This overawing vastness is made to do service throughout to the naturalistic theme in dwarfing the human actors. Thus Presley finds Vanamee crouching over his campfire in a remote part of the range: "The bald, bare landscape widened about him to infinity. Vanamee was a spot in it all, a tiny dot, a single atom of human organization, floating endlessly on the ocean of an illimitable nature."[42] Again and again we are reminded of the impersonality and indifference of nature toward man, in the reflections of Presley, in those of the wife of Magnus Derrick (p. 180):

She recognized the colossal indifference of nature, not hostile, even kindly and friendly, so long as the human ant-swarm was submissive . . . . Let, however, the insect rebel . . . . and at once it became relentless . . . . a vast power, huge, terrible; a leviathan with a heart of steel, knowing no compunction, no forgiveness, no tolerance; crushing out the human atom with soundless calm . . . .

The operations of the economic world produce a similar effect. Following the lead of Annixter, Magnus Derrick had installed a stock ticker in the office at the ranch house. During a crisis in the market he and his son Harran had sat up half the night watching the tape with intense excitement (p. 54):

At such moments they no longer felt their individuality. The ranch became merely the part of an enormous whole, a unit in the vast agglomeration of wheat land the whole world round, feeling the effects of causes thousands of miles distant—a drought on the prairies of Dakota, a rain on the plains of India, a frost on the Russian steppes, a hot wind on the llanos of the Argentine.

But, diminished as are the figures of *The Octopus* by their physical background and the economic circumstances in which they are caught, they are not without individual character. Some, it is true, are distinguished in the manner

[42] *The Octopus*, p. 375.

of Dickens by some oddity of feature, speech, manner, or dress, which comes to signify its possessor and which is invariably introduced on his every appearance. Such are Osterman, who is always described as having "the face of a comic actor, with its great slit of mouth and stiff, red ears," and old Broderson, who can never make a positive assertion without immediately qualifying it. S. Behrman is an animated caricature of the "trusts," of the sort which became common in the press during the Populist agitations of the 'nineties. He is paunchy, and joweled like a pig, and the design of interlocked horseshoes which decorates his brown linen vest needs only to be changed to dollar marks in order to complete his likeness to the cartoons.

But Annixter and Hilma Tree and Dyke among others are fully realized individuals. Granville Hicks[43] scoffs at the idea that Annixter should be "capable of a miraculous transformation under the influence of pure love." On the contrary, it is entirely credible. He is a gruff, crochety fellow, truculent, tactless, and irritable; he has an iron digestion but deludes himself with the notion that he is cursed with the crankiest of all stomachs. He is always munching dried prunes from a paper sack and in his moments of leisure reading Dickens, the only novelist, in his opinion, who ever existed. He is frequently guilty of the grossest unreasonableness, as in his discharge of the cowboy, Delaney. He is morbidly suspicious of the wiles of "feemales," toward whom he affects a violent antipathy. He can conceive of but one relation of a woman to a man —that of mistress. Yet this uncouth man is softened and humanized by his love of Hilma Tree, the dairymaid on

---

[43] *The Great Tradition* (The Macmillan Company, 1933), p. 173.

his own ranch. He sees his fellowmen with a new eye; unsuspected depths of pity and sympathy are disclosed in his nature. Norris presents the entire affair of the courtship and marriage, the development of Annixter's character, without a grain of sentimentality; and the unprejudiced reader will see in it nothing "miraculous" or implausible.

Once more, as in *McTeague,* Norris makes full use of a master symbol—this time the wheat, significant of life, ever renewed, exhaustless, and (viewed as a force) imperishable, though its particular vessels may perish. Once again, as in his first novel, he introduces a romantic subplot, this time the story of Vanamee and Angéle Varian. Vanamee and Angéle had been accustomed to meet nightly beneath the ancient pear trees that bounded the Mission garden. But one dark night, arriving at the meeting place, he stumbled upon her body lying unconscious where she had been ravished by some prowler, never discovered. Left half-crazed by her experience, she did not survive the birth of her child, and was buried in the Mission garden. Through eighteen years Vanamee cherished his passion and his grief. He had become a wanderer in the wastes of the Southwest. At long intervals he would reappear mysteriously, no one knew whence, to haunt the grave of Angéle for a time and then to vanish again into the mountains and deserts. When the novel opens he is back once more in the Valley of the San Joaquin. In the dusk of a spring evening he sits with Father Sarria in the cloistered garden of the Mission—the Mission with the beautifully resonant name, San Juan de Guadalajara. At one moment he rebels passionately against the fact of death and spurns the platitudinous consolations of faith offered by the priest. He frightens and horrifies Father Sarria with terrible words: "Ha!" he exclaims bitterly, "your God! . . . . There is no God. There is only the Devil." At the next instant he is exalted, ready to believe, expecting a miracle. God "can give her back to me if he only will," he exclaims. Night after night, when the priest has gone to bed, he keeps vigil in the garden, pouring out his soul in longing, sending the silent cry of his spirit out into the infinite darkness. With the strange power he owns of projecting his thought and his will through space (the power that had brought Presley to a halt at a mile's distance), he almost imagines he can call his lost love back from the grave. Then suddenly occurs a marvel. Vanamee feels that he has had an answer, faint, but unmistakable. He is puzzled, troubled, vaguely excited. Night after night he returns and repeats his telepathic summons. As the spring deepens, stronger and stronger grows his sense of a presence advancing toward him little by little through the exotic profusion of flowers on the neighboring seed ranch where Angéle had once lived. At length on one of these occasions, when dawn is near, he becomes aware that a real being is mounting the slope where he lies on the ground with his head buried in his arm. He can hear little sounds of its approach. It pauses within a few paces. He raises his eyes. There before him stands a young girl.

She was dressed in a gown of scarlet silk, with flowing sleeves, such as Japanese wear, embroidered with flowers and figures of birds worked in gold threads. On either side of her face, making three-cornered her round, white forehead, hung the soft masses of her hair of gold. . . . . from between her parted lips—lips of almost an Egyptian fulness—her breath came slow and regular, and her eyes, heavy lidded, slanting upwards toward the temples, perplexing, oriental, were closed. She was asleep.

It was Angéle—or so Vanamee for the moment believed. Then the girl retreats down the slope and is gone. As he leaps up, exalted as by the sight of a miracle, he finds Father Sarria beside him. " 'I saw her,' said the priest. 'It was Angéle, ... your Angéle's daughter. She is like her mother.' "[44] Vanamee, by his mysterious hypnotic power, had drawn the girl to him in her sleep. It is indeed all "pure romance—oh, even mysticism, if you like," as Norris wrote to Marcosson.[45]

Meantime, half a mile or so distant, Annixter has been sitting on a stone in the open fields, under the stars, wrestling all night long with his soul. Hilma, deeply shocked, has repulsed his suggestion that she become his mistress. He is in torment. He cannot fathom what is the matter with him. It has never entered his cross-grained head that he might marry the girl; it has not once occurred to him that he loves her. But gradually, after much travail of spirit, the realization comes, and he utters the words " 'Why—I—I, I *love* her' .... It was a Memnonian cry, the greeting of the hard, harsh image of man, rough-hewn, flinty, granitic, uttering a note of joy, acclaiming the new risen sun."[46] For now the dawn has come, and as Annixter gazes out over the fields he witnesses another wonder. During the night the wheat has come up. "The winter brownness of the ground was overlaid with a little shimmer of green."

As Vanamee returns to the ranch in the rapidly waxing light of the new day, he too sees the new-sprung wheat.

---

[44] *The Octopus*, pp. 146, 391. An improbability appears in this. Vanamee has been in the neighborhood for some months; yet we are supposed to believe that he is ignorant of the presence of Angéle's daughter at the old home of her mother, a fact which his intimate friend the priest, if no one else, could hardly have failed to mention.

[45] Isaac F. Marcosson, *Adventures in Interviewing* (Dodd, Mead & Company), p. 238.

[46] *The Octopus*, p. 368.

He "flung out his arms with a mighty shout: 'Oh, Death, where is thy sting? Oh, Grave, where is thy victory?' "[47] Thus simultaneously the wheat springs from the earth, love burgeons in the crabbed heart of Annixter, and Angéle emerges as it were from the grave in the person of her daughter, who is so strikingly her image. In this manner Norris brings together and unites momentarily under his symbol three strands of his novel: his epic theme, the Annixter-Hilma story, and the Vanamee-Angéle story.

Whether or no one feels that the presence of Vanamee in *The Octopus* is justified, he does not forget the lean, black-bearded shepherd. Vanamee is not altogether an unreal figure, though his telepathic powers will convince but few. On examination this proves to be because Norris frequently brings him into contact with commonplace realities and thus gets life into him. When we see him, dressed in a gray flannel shirt and brown canvas overalls tucked into laced boots, or see him hitching a team of horses to a gang plow, climbing to the seat, and competently running his furrow; when we see him at noon eating his lunch out of a tin bucket, and again at supper seated with fifty other plowhands at an oilcloth-covered table filling himself with beef, bread, and wine—then it is not hard to believe in him as a real person.

Presley, too, has been thought by some to be a shadowy creation. But one does not forget Presley, and for the same kind of reasons that give substance to Vanamee. One does not, in truth, forget any creature sprung from the imagination of Frank Norris. It is a high tribute to his genius.

Despite, however, its many high excellences, its satis-

---

[47] *The Octopus,* p. 393. "Precisely, despite the bad, shrill rhetoric, where it was before," sourly comments Ludwig Lewisohn (*Expression in America* [New York: Harper & Brothers, 1932], p. 323).

fying amplitude of design, its vitality and movement and color, the rich variety and reality of its characters, the masterly way in which its dozen strands are woven but never tangled, the skillful subordination of a mass of detail to the main action, the memorable scenes (the dance in Annixter's huge new barn, the plowing, the rabbit drive) through which the life of the valley is made vividly real—despite all this *The Octopus* is not a completely successful naturalistic novel. The moral and philosophical issues are not clear-cut. Norris was unable to give up a teleological view of the world, and there lingered in him a notion that good and evil are absolute entities inherent in the nature of the cosmos, instead of human concepts. Hence he wavers between the idea of impersonal force for which good and evil have no meaning and the idea of a triumphant good for which the universe itself stands sponsor. When the final catastrophe has overtaken all his friends, Presley makes his solitary way to an eminence in the foothills of the Sierra for a last look at the great valley.

Men were naught [he reflects], death was naught, life was naught; FORCE only existed—FORCE that brought men into the world, FORCE that crowded them out of it to make way for the succeeding generation, FORCE that made the wheat grow, FORCE that garnered it from the soil to give place to the succeeding crop.[48]

On his return he meets Vanamee and they discourse on the recent calamities. Vanamee disposes of evil and of death itself by assigning to them a merely negative character. His parting words might have been lifted out of Emerson or of Browning. "Evil is short-lived," he assures Presley. "Never judge of the whole round of life by the mere segment you can see. The whole is, in the end, perfect." But all those on whose side stood justice have been

[48] *The Octopus*, p. 634.

crushed. Annixter and Harran Derrick and Osterman and old Broderson and Hooven have been killed. Dyke, the engineer, is in prison. Old Mrs. Hooven has fallen and died of exhaustion and hunger as she tramped the streets of San Francisco. Minna Hooven, starved and desperate, has been tricked into a life of prostitution. Magnus Derrick, whose integrity of character was his dearest possession, is a pitiable, cringing ruin of a man. Yet in view of all this, Presley (and Norris with him) finds comfort in the thought that *"the* WHEAT *remained.* Untouched, unassailable, undefiled, that mighty world-force, that nourisher of nations, wrapped in Nirvanic calm, indifferent to the human swarm, gigantic, resistless, moved onward in its appointed grooves" (p. 651).

But it is a very precarious thing to entrust human good to the operations of the cosmos. Norris tends too much to personify his wheat and make of it an independent entity. The growing of wheat is not a cosmic process, but a purely human activity. No humanity, no cultivation of wheat. Nor is there any necessity that individuals should suffer injustice and death in California in order that "thousands of starving scarecrows on the barren plains of India" may be fed. Such a procedure argues but a bungling sort of efficiency in that process which Norris so complacently believes (in the final words of his novel) to work "inevitably, resistlessly . . . . for good." Even men, "motes in the sunshine" though they be, might conceivably do better.

In *The Pit,* the second novel of the trilogy of the wheat and the last which Norris lived to write, the epic theme is blurred and weakened by the too-close rivalship of the personal love story of Curtis Jadwin and Laura Dearborn. The interest is thus divided and the wheat fails to dominate as it had in *The Octopus*. As Norris' biographer points out, the wheat was never physically present. It was off there somewhere in the hinterlands of the prairies; in Chicago it was represented merely by the insane clamor of the bidders on the floor of the exchange. The best Norris could do (and he leans heavily on exposition to do it) was to show in Jadwin's attempted corner of the market that no individual man or even group of men could successfully interfere with the resistless flow of the wheat toward the hungry millions whose lives it was destined to sustain. Jadwin, at the crisis of his desperate venture, pauses to listen to the tumult of the wheat pit:

It was the Wheat, the Wheat! . . . . Almighty, blood-brother to the earthquake, coeval with the volcano . . . . that gigantic world-force . . . . was swelling and advancing . . . . What were those scattered hundreds of farmers of the Middle West, who because he had put the price so high had planted the grain as never before? What had they to do with it? Why the Wheat had grown itself; demand and supply, these were the two great laws the Wheat obeyed. Almost blasphemous in his effrontery, he had tampered with these laws, and had roused a Titan.[49]

And the Titan crushed him.

Jadwin is again modeled on Norris' father, but magnified and raised to the proportions of one of those colossi of business who so fill the eye and command the admiration of the American public. He is a self-made man and a thoroughgoing Philistine, whose favorite songs are "Daisy Dean" and "Open Thy Lattice to Me," and whose taste for fiction is satisfied by *Mr. Barnes of New York*. "Buy May wheat," he bids Corthell, who is making discreet love to his wife. "It'll beat art all hollow" (p. 255).

Laura Dearborn, Jadwin's wife, has many of the traits

[49] Frank Norris, *The Pit* (copyright 1903, 1921, by Doubleday, Doran & Company, Inc.), pp. 373, 374.

of Norris' mother—her force of character, her histrionic temperament, her longing for the stage, her absorption in a genteel literary culture which deliberately excluded contemporary writers, with a grudging exception for Howells. The relation of Jadwin and Laura is the familiar one of the husband completely absorbed in business and the wife smarting under a sense of neglect, thwarted romance, and starved emotions. Into this situation steps the inevitable consoler in the person of Sheldon Corthell, dilettante artist and aesthete, and one of her former suitors. In his portraits of artists Norris falls in with the popular convention which imagines them as more than a little effeminate, a little alien from the good Anglo-Saxon character of forthrightness and vigor. Corthell is a slight, dark man who wears a small pointed beard and a French-looking moustache. His task with Laura is not easy; for, fascinated as she is by his refined sensibilities, the tact and delicacy of his attentions, she is drawn instinctively to Jadwin (p. 65):

the men to whom the woman in her turned were not those of the studio. Terrible as the Battle of the Street was, it was yet battle. Only the strong and the brave might dare it, and the figure that held her imagination and her sympathy was not the artist, soft of hand and of speech, elaborating graces of sound and color and form . . . . but the fighter, unknown and unknowable to women as he was; hard, rigorous . . . .

After the ruin of Jadwin's fortunes in the collapse of his corner in wheat, he consoles himself with the thought that after all money isn't everything (though we are left with the suggestion that he will lose no time in beginning to amass it once more); he turns anew to his wife, understanding is re-established between them, and we have the happy ending which we had not in *McTeague, Vandover and the Brute,* and *The Octopus.* Thus the mountain labors mightily—and brings forth a mouse. We are invited to witness epic events, the resistless rolling tide of the wheat sweeping over all petty human obstacles toward the million hungry mouths which await it. We see instead the triumph of a vain, self-centered woman who demands an exclusive admiration and who, if she cannot have it from her business-engrossed husband, will have it from the artist and aesthete, Corthell. Only the accident of Jadwin's return to the house at precisely the right moment, defeated and repentant, determined her to remain with him instead of going away with the artist, as she had resolved and promised to do. Now her rival—the thrilling and desperate game which Jadwin has been playing—is removed, and she is content.

It is sentimental and naïve little Page, Laura's younger sister, who sees through her tragic poses, sees her wrapped in self-pity, and forms a true estimate of her character. The crisis of Jadwin's corner in wheat occurs on Laura's birthday. She makes an issue of it. This day must be hers. As he prepares to leave for his office in the morning, she adjures him thus (p. 362):

"It is mine," she said, "if you love me. Do you understand, dear? You will come home at six o'clock, and whatever happens—oh, if all La Salle Street should burn to the ground, and all your millions of bushels of wheat with it—whatever happens, you—will—not—leave—me—nor think of anything else but just me, me."

As well ask Napoleon to quit the field of Waterloo with a kiss for the Empress—if he loves her. All day Laura plays her little drama with herself. Will he telephone? Will he send word? Will he come? But Jadwin gives no sign, and Laura grooms herself for her role of martyred queen. It is at this juncture that Page bursts out passionately at her sister, accusing her of deliberate refusal to take any interest in Jadwin's great battle with the market, and reproaching her for her childish moping. Laura is indignant at this denunciation, but Norris asks us to believe that it planted the seed of change in her character.

View it how one will, the conclusion of *The Pit* is anticlimactic, trivial. Looking back over the two volumes of the trilogy, it is as if the wheat had been grown with much labor far away in California, as if Magnus Derrick had been broken and dishonored, Annixter and Harran and the others killed, as if Hilma had lost her unborn child and Mrs. Hooven had starved to death, as if a gigantic battle of the market had been fought, affecting a million lives, mostly for evil—all in order that an idle egoistic woman might be able to ask, "Do you love me, only me?" and that she might hear the answer, "Yes, only you!"

Some have attempted to excuse the inferiority of *The Pit* to *The Octopus* on the ground that its theme offered Norris less opportunity, that the marketing of wheat is intrinsically less interesting than the growing of wheat. But this is hardly sufficient. He missed his chance to equal his earlier performance from the moment when he allowed the love story to gain the upper hand, from the moment when he refused to conceive the work in terms of sharp, unmitigated, uncompromising tragedy for its principal figures. It is not strange, however, that to this day *The Pit* remains the best known and most read of Norris' novels.[50]

Its merits resolve themselves into some convincing pictures of the domestic and social life of the nouveau riche

[50] Paul H. Bixler ("Frank Norris's Literary Reputation," *American Literature*, May 1934) has gathered statistics of the sale of Norris' novels. Professor Bixler finds that his books all together have sold more than half a million copies, *The Pit* leading with 189,445. Less complete figures are given by Walker, *op. cit.*, p. 286.

and the near-rich in the Chicago of the 'nineties, some animated scenes of the business quarter, and some lyric passages which communicate with an eloquence almost poetic the symbolical significance of the great city in the life and growth of the nation. Of these the best is the following (pp. 62–63):

Here, midmost in the land, beat the Heart of the Nation, whence inevitably must come its immeasurable power, its infinite, infinite, inexhaustible vitality. Here, of all her cities, throbbed the true life —the true power and spirit of America; gigantic, crude with the crudity of youth, disdaining rivalry; sane and healthy and vigorous; brutal in its ambition, arrogant in the new-found knowledge of its giant strength, prodigal of its wealth, infinite in its desires.

In November 1899 Norris wrote to Isaac F. Marcosson of *A Man's Woman:* "It's different from my other books, but it's the last one that will be . . . . I am going back *definitely* now to the style of MacT. and stay with it right along." And he promised that the "Wheat series will be straight naturalism with all the guts I can get into it." Yet nearly a year later he wrote again to Marcosson declaring that *The Octopus* (then nearing completion) was "the most romantic thing I've yet done."[51]

The truth is that Norris never fully understood scientific determinism and hence the full bearings of literary naturalism. He could thus conclude *The Octopus* with the assertion that "all things . . . . work together for good," and at the same time proclaim that the universe was neither benign nor malevolent, that "FORCE only existed." Yet, though he never succeeded in making the reconciliation, a genuine scientific determinism can be reconciled with a belief in the efficacy of the human will

---

[51] Marcosson, *Adventures in Interviewing* (Dodd, Mead & Company, Inc.), pp. 237, 238; quoted by Walker, *op. cit.,* pp. 217, 252–53, 265.

and of human action (a belief which he himself plainly entertained). If human desires, human purposes, the human will are caused, as beyond doubt they are, they in turn become causes in the chain of events. Every scientist in his laboratory, no matter what he professes to believe outside it, is of necessity a determinist. On the other hand, it never occurs to him to abandon the idea of control. Should he lose faith in the determinism of cause-effect and faith also that human purposes may be achieved, his operations would, on the instant, become impossible.

If these observations are true, it follows that Zola was a shrewder man than his American disciple, and a man with clearer perceptions than his critics often give him credit for. Let us hear what he says on the question of naturalistic determinism, and we shall learn why he could be a determinist and also retain a belief in human betterment by human means. We shall understand, further, why there is implied in the naturalistic novelists, however distantly, and beneath much pessimism and fatalism, a sociological bias. Their knowledge of the methods and results of science (though usually a layman's knowledge and imperfect) had forced upon them the concept of determinism. At the same time they knew as a fact of experience that human purposes, whatever the frustrations of circumstance, may, here and there and sometimes, be achieved, or in other words, that something like what we may for the moment call free will appears to exist. Sometimes they were disturbed at what seemed a paradox; sometimes they ignored it; seldom had they thought out the position clearly.

Zola, with the theories of Claude Bernard steadily before his eye, draws an analogy between the work of the physiologist and that of the novelist. After asserting that the object of the former "est d'étudier les phénomènes pour s'en rendre maître," he continues:

nous voulons, nous aussi, être les maîtres des phénomènes des éléments intellectuels et personnels, pour pouvoir les diriger. Nous sommes, en un mot, des moralistes expérimentateurs, montrant par l'expérience de quelle façon se comporte une passion dans un milieu social. Le jour où nous tiendrons le mécanisme de cette passion, on pourra la traiter et la réduire, ou tout au moins la rendre la plus inoffensive possible. ... C'est ainsi que nous faisons de la sociologie pratique ... Être maître du bien et du mal, régler la vie, régler la société, ... apporter surtout des bases solides à la justice en résolvant par l'expérience les questions de criminalité, n'est-ce pas là être les ouvriers les plus utiles et les plus moraux du travail human?[52]

Without pronouncing on the efficacy of naturalistic fiction to the end proposed, it is enough to show in this Zola's compelling sociological interest. How does he reconcile this interest, this confidence in the results of human action, with his determinism? In repelling the attack of those who decried naturalism on the ground that it was fatalistic, he writes (pp. 27–28):

Que de fois on a voulu nous prouver que, du moment où nous n'acceptons pas le libre arbitre, du moment où l'homme n'était plus pour nous qu'une machine animale agissant sous l'influence de l'hérédité et des milieux, nous tombions à un fatalisme grossier, nous ravalions l'humanité au rang d'un troupeau marchant sous le bâton de la destinée! Il faut préciser: nous ne sommes pas fatalistes, nous sommes déterministes, ce qui n'est point la même chose.

In support of the last statement he then quotes Claude Bernard, who asserts that determinism is simply the name given to the proximate or determining cause of phenomena; that in nature we never act on the essence of things, but merely on the conditions of their occurrence; that in this lies the fundamental difference between a scientific

[52] Émile Zola, *Le Roman Expérimental* (Paris: Eugène Fasquelle, 1909), pp. 23–24.

determinism and fatalism, on which it would be impossible to act at all.

Norris was one of those who had not thought out the position clearly. He was at bottom a moralist (let it be said without disparagement) who came finally to believe that the novel should expose evils in order to rouse the public conscience and prepare the way for their removal. Yet characters who voice his thought call men "motes in the sunshine," "mere nothings." There is much talk of destiny, and again much talk of duty and will. Evil does not exist, is a mere negation; truth and justice prevail with the process of the suns. Yet evil is "an abstract principle," an absolute entity.

Norris was attracted to naturalism because it gave scope to his love of the spectacular, of imaginative daring. He was more enamored of "effects" than of philosophical consistency. Adopting the methods of observation, the type of characters and environment favored by the naturalists, he yet called himself a romanticist because romanticism, in his definition, is that kind of fiction which concerns itself with departures from the normal course of life. Franklin Walker says aptly, "Norris accepted determinism only in so far as it appealed to his dramatic sense."[53] Norris did not even take the trouble to study the theories of naturalism, but deduced its aims and method from Zola's novels. If he ever read *Le Roman Expérimental,* he nowhere makes mention of it.

The many and close resemblances between the work of Zola and that of his American disciple are not alone the result of "influence" as it is commonly understood by critics, but depend ultimately on certain correspondences in

[53] Walker, *Frank Norris: A Biography* (Doubleday, Doran & Company, Inc., 1932), p. 85.

the fundamental emotions and mental characters of the two men. Both have the wide-embracing imaginations of epic poets. Both have a romantic Hugoesque love for big effects, striking contrasts, dramatic (even melodramatic) situations. "Never forget," Zola cautioned himself, "that a drama must take the public by the throat."[54] Nothing could be more romantic than the Provençal boyhood of Zola. He devoured the works of De Musset, Hugo, Lamartine, De Vigny; he was a haunter of graveyards and mountain caves. His first writing was verse, a chivalric romance inspired by the reading of Michelet's *History of the Crusades.* As a youth in Paris, Norris eagerly garnered from the stalls along the quais of the Seine a cuirassier's helmet, a skeleton hand with the manacle still clanking upon it, and a quantity of black-letter books. He, too, wrote his poem of medieval love and adventure. When each of the two writers had emerged from this early phase and adopted the doctrines of naturalism, he came to lay a great emphasis on the animal nature of man, if not to celebrate it. In *Thérèse Raquin,* Zola set himself a problem: "Given a strong man and an unsatisfied woman, to seek in them the beast, to see nothing but the beast . . . ."[55] Norris, with whom Zola's *La Bête Humaine* was a favorite, shows the triumph of the brute in Vandover. Both men have a genius for handling men in large masses; they love crowds. Witness the scene at the racecourse in *Nana,* the battles in *La Débâcle;* the scene at the opera which opens *The Pit,*[56] the rabbit drive, the plowing, and the

---

[54] Matthew Josephson, *Zola and His Time* (New York: The Macaulay Company, 1928), p. 150.

[55] *Ibid.,* p. 117.

[56] With the necessary changes for characters, this opera scene is repeated almost verbatim from chapter fourteen of *Vandover and the Brute,* which Norris was never able to get published. He never wasted literary material.

mass meeting at Bonneville in *The Octopus,* the dance at the house of Henrietta Vance in *Vandover.* Like his master, Norris loves to set his people down at Gargantuan feasts which turn into veritable gastronomic debauches during which the faces of the sweating eaters grow scarlet and their veins become distended with their mighty labors. Such are the dinners in *Nana* and *L'Assomoir,* the wedding supper in *McTeague,* the dinner of the plowhands, and the feasting at the conclusion of the rabbit drive in *The Octopus.* Both men intoxicate themselves with swelling paeans to the fecund earth, employing a bold metaphorical language derived from ideas of sex and procreation. Matthew Josephson well says of *La Terre* that it is "a rude poem to the earth and its eternal act of life."[57] This hymning of earth is not a mere literary device, but a genuine feeling in Zola himself (p. 13):

Ah! good earth, take me [he chants], thou who art our common mother. O unique source of life, eternal and immortal, in which circulates the soul of the world, like a sap arising now in the stones and now in the trees, our great motionless brothers! . . . . Yes, I desire to lose myself in thee; I feel thee down there, under my limbs pressing and arousing me; it is thou alone who shalt be as a pristine force in my works, the end and the means at once of all things! . . . .

Norris speaks thus of the land at the moment when the battery of plows is about to attack it:

One could not take a dozen steps upon the ranches without the brusque sensation that underfoot the land was alive; roused at last from its sleep, palpitating with the desire of reproduction. Deep down there in the recesses of the soil, the great heart throbbed once more, thrilling with passion, vibrating with desire, offering itself to the caress of the plow, insistent, eager, imperious. Dimly one felt the deep-seated trouble of the earth, the uneasy agitation of its members, the hidden tumult of its womb, demanding to be

57 Josephson, *op. cit.,* p. 305.

made fruitful, to reproduce, to disengage the eternal renascent germ of Life that stirred and struggled in its loins.[58]

Both writers are capable of alternating delicate fantasies and elevated sentiment with their horrendous pictures of squalor and corruption; after the grim brutalities of *La Terre*, the purity of maiden love in *Le Rêve*;[59] after the harsh and somber *McTeague* and *Vandover*, the *Youth's Companion* "wholesomeness" of *Blix*. And did not Norris write the tender idyl of lost youth and late-recovered love set in an autumnal garden with its tumbled statue of Cupid?[60] and the delicately and reverently imagined *Miracle Joyeux*, in which a youthful Christ smiles upon the innocence of childhood?

Both Zola and Norris sense the world almost as much through their noses as through their eyes and ears. They are extraordinarily responsive to smells—mainly bad smells their enemies averred, though falsely. An interminable catalogue of odors might be compiled from the work of Norris. He notes the smell of hot steam and smoke in the cab of a locomotive, of damp leather and upholstery in a carriage on a rainy night, the "acrid odor of ink" that rose from the branch post office beneath McTeague's "parlors." And in the great plowing scene of *The Octopus* a whole battery of smells discharge themselves upon the sense with smashing impact (p. 130): "the ammoniacal smell of the horses, the bitter reek of perspiration of beasts and men,

[58] *The Octopus* (Doubleday, Doran & Company, Inc., 1929), p. 127.

[59] The name of Vanamee's love, Angéle, suggests that of the girl of similar purity in *Le Rêve*—Angélique. Franklin Walker (p. 250) assigns the origin of the seed ranch, with its bewildering profusion of blossoms, to a similar place observed by Norris during his stay in San Benito County, California. He may equally owe the idea to the garden of Paradou in Zola's *La Faute de l'Abbé Mouret*, to the description of whose intoxicating luxuriance of color and perfume nearly two hundred pages are devoted.

[60] See "A Statue in an Old Garden," *Collected Writings*, p. 291.

the aroma of warm leather, the scent of dead stubble . . . .
the heavy, enervating odour of the upturned, living earth."

Both men have the temperament of the moralist and
the reformer and color their pessimism with hope. "To
tell the truth and still to hope,"[61] Zola enjoined upon himself. But at first neither was sympathetic with agitators or
radicals; rather the contrary. Lantier, in *L'Assomoir,* who
on occasion inveighs against titles and privileges and cries
for the "glorification of the proletariat," is a charlatan.
Marcus Schouler of *McTeague* (though the role of social
malcontent is brief and incidental with him) is equally
a fraud, an ignorant ranter without even a personal griev-
ance. Norris makes him ridiculous (pp. 13–14): " 'It's the
capitalists that's ruining the cause of labor,' shouted Marcus, banging the table with his fist till the beer glasses
danced; 'white-livered drones, traitors . . . . eatun the bread
of widows and orphuns . . . .' " After *L'Assomoir,* Zola
threw himself upon the works of the socialist writers with
the furious energy which he brought to all he did. He was
not constituted by nature, any more than his disciple Norris, to be a thinker on such subjects; but he at least confronted directly the theories of Marx, Proudhon, and
Lassalle, and was ready to call himself a socialist. It is unlikely that Norris ever read a political or economic treatise
in his life; but it is clear from *The Octopus* and from his
later critical writing that his awakening sympathy for the
underdog was beginning to push him, somewhat uncer-
tainly, in the direction of socialism. Whether he would
ever have arrived there or not cannot well be determined.
But there is no doubt that toward the end of his life he had
begun to take the role of social prophet very seriously. In
his defense of the unsentimental rigors of naturalism he

61 Josephson, *op. cit.,* p. 370.

94

declared that if fiction "wears the camel's-hair and feeds upon the locusts, it is to cry aloud unto the people, 'Prepare ye the way of the Lord; make straight his path.' "[62]

Finally, both Zola and Norris were endowed with that kind of moral courage which dares opprobrium and even personal danger in defense of what it conceives to be justice. In Norris this trait is illustrated by an incident which occurred a few months before his death in 1902. The superintendent of the California state home for the feeble-minded at Glen Ellen, Dr. William Lawlor, was accused by his political enemies of brutality toward the inmates of the institution. He was helpless to present his own case; for the press, controlled by the opposition, would print no word favorable to him. The public, systematically misinformed, clamored against the doctor. Norris was indignant, investigated the charges, satisfied himself they were false, and wrote a fiery denunciation which every newspaper in San Francisco cynically refused to print.[63] At length during a dramatic meeting of the board of directors, marked by hot words, a certain Colonel Harrington (appropriately from Kentucky) drew a pistol upon Dr. Lawlor. But before he could fire Norris seized his arm. Dr. Lawlor was eventually dismissed from his post, though officially exonerated. L'Affaire Dreyfus, at the center of which Zola placed himself, shook France from Paris to the borders during two years. The Lawlor episode agitated San Francisco for a few weeks. But for Norris it was his Dreyfus affair—in miniature.

Such comparisons of literary men are apt, however, to bear unjustly on the disciple. It should not be supposed,

---

[62] Norris, *The Responsibilities of the Novelist*, p. 220.

[63] It was published, however, in the weekly *Argonaut*, San Francisco, August 11, 1902.

whatever he owed to Zola, that Norris cannot stand firmly on his own feet as a writer. The words of a French critic, who is little likely to overestimate the worth of Zola's followers in other lands, are here of special interest. M. Marius Biencourt writes:

Le disciple a contracté envers le maître une dette considérable, mais son œuvre n'en laisse pas moins une forte impression de nouveauté et d'originalité. Il est resté américain dans ses défauts et dans ses qualités. ...

Norris dont la devise était: faire de la vie et non de la littérature, a su créer vivant et faire passer dans son œuvre la vigueur et l'énergie de son tempérament épique.[64]

[64] Marius Biencourt, *Une Influence du Naturalisme Français en Amérique: Frank Norris* (Paris: Marcel Giard, 1933), p. 230.

Chapter III

The Cult of the Strong Man

I want man with his shirt off, stripped to the buff and fighting for his life.—FRANK NORRIS*

The world wants men, great, strong, harsh, brutal men—men with purposes, who let nothing, nothing, nothing stand in their way.—FRANK NORRIS, A Man's Woman, *p. 82*

"Did you ever kill a man, Jerry?" asked Wilbur. "No? Well, ... kill one some day . . . ."—FRANK NORRIS, Moran of the Lady Letty, *p. 260.*

IT WAS BUT logical that naturalism, with its theory of the determining influence of heredity on human life and its reduction of psychology to physiology, should focus its attention on the physical man. That man was seen to be a complex of instincts, desires, hungers, toward the satisfaction of which all his energies were bent. All the elaborate machinery of law and custom developed by civilization is scarcely sufficient to hold in check the self-assertive impulses, the hard-driving force of the ego. Hence the continual aggressions, unscrupulous acts, crimes of all sorts, which trouble society. It was readily imagined that man in his primitive state would admit no restraints to the fulfillment of his desires but superior force, whether of things, of beasts, or of other men. As for civilized man,

---

* Quoted in *Frank Norris: A Biography* by Franklin Walker (Doubleday, Doran & Company, Inc., 1932), pp. 230–31. Reprinted by permission.

what Chateaubriand said of the hidden wound in every heart might better be said of the feral, deep-lying, unconscious impulses. "Le cœur le plus serein en apparence," he wrote, "ressemble au puits naturel de la savane Alachua: la surface en paraît calme et pure; mais quand vous regardez au fond du bassin, vous apercevez un large crocodile."[1] Concentration on the animal in man and on instinct tended to diminish the importance of reason and of ethics in human life and to magnify brute strength and energy. In every age of the world, perhaps, a conflict has existed in philosophy and in literature between reason and instinct. The modern phase of that conflict began to show itself during the Renaissance. In his essay, "Of Pedantry," Montaigne, who admired the muscular nation of Sparta, exalted the military virtues and exhorted his readers to beware of the enervating effects of intellectualism. The example of martial states like Sparta teaches us "que l'estude des sciences amollit et effemine les courages plus qu'il ne les fermit et aguerrit." He observes approvingly that the youth of Sparta were furnished, not with tutors to teach them arts and sciences, but "seulement des maistres de vaillance, prudence et justice," which virtues apparently become incompatible with learning. If a man would be virtuous he must close his books and emulate the hardy ignorance of Sparta. Arts and sciences corrupt morals; it is Rousseau's thesis, and we know that Rousseau was a close reader of Montaigne. Montaigne was a reasonable man and a studious man, none more so; but in thus disparaging intellectual culture as the necessary antithesis of "virtue," he prepared the scene for the worship of the "natural man," and the romantic exaltation of instinct, impulse, emotion, above reason.

[1] *Atala* ("Les Funérailles").

The ages of discovery had acquainted Europe with the lives and customs of primitive peoples in remote parts of the earth hitherto unknown, and had provided the eighteenth century *philosophes* and men of letters with exactly the figure they needed in their assault on traditional institutions—the figure of the noble savage, unspoiled by the corruptions of civilization, living close to nature, and surely, safely guided by his instincts. All of cultivated Europe, bored and weary with formalism and rigid social conventions, embarked with a gleam of enthusiasm in its eye on the "return to nature." A long line of romantic writers, descending from Rousseau, raised instinct and natural feeling above reason, above learning, above culture. It is to be observed, however, that thus far there is no cult of force, no emphasis on violent passions and predatory impulses. In the savage paradise pictured by Montaigne in his essay "Des Cannibales," there is no suggestion of a struggle for existence, at least within the tribe or nation. All is forbearance, generosity, mutual aid.

The first half of the nineteenth century brought strong reinforcements to the popular interest in the primitive, set going by the travelers of the Renaissance. The work of the geologists, notably Sir Charles Lyell, the first volume of whose *Principles of Geology* appeared in 1829, and such popular works as Hugh Miller's *Old Red Sandstone* (1841) and Robert Chambers' *Vestiges of the Natural History of Creation* (1844)[2] pushed the human horizon back in time to a distance incredibly remote. The very terms that came into existence for the designation of the geologic ages— Eocene, Miocene, Pliocene—with their beautiful sonorous

[2] Harriet Martineau testified that "the general middle-class public purchased five copies of an expensive work on geology to one of the most popular novels of the time" (quoted by D. C. Somervell, *English Thought in the Nineteenth Century* [London: Methuen, 1929], p. 124).

vowels, were an invitation to the imaginations of ro-
mancers. As the century advanced, the new sciences of
anthropology and paleontology made their contributions
to the fast-accumulating data from which the life of prehistoric man might be reconstructed. With the coming of
Darwinian evolution and the popularization of the concepts of the struggle for existence and the survival of the
fittest, the stage was set for the prosperous appearance in
literature of paleolithic man—the cave dweller, the contemporary of the saber-toothed tiger, the megathere, and
the mastodon.

But an important difference exists between the attitude
of both writer and reader toward the old savage and the
new. The noble savage of the early romantics was admired
because he was—or was thought to be—noble. The new
primitive was admired because he was brawny, because he
took what he wanted by virtue of his brawn, because he
split the skull of his enemy with a stone axe, and because
he dragged his mate to his cave (so it was thought) by the
hair of her head, screaming yet palpitating with desire.

One of the earliest of the dawn-age romances appeared
in French, the work of the brothers Rosny — *Vamireh:
roman des temps primitifs* (1892). It begins, "C'était il y
a vingt mille ans ... Sur les plaines de l'Europe le Mam-
mouth allait s'éteindre ..." Stanley Waterloo published
(ostensibly for younger readers) *The Story of Ab* (1897),
which he later accused Jack London of plagiarizing in
Before Adam (1907). Wells exploited prehistoric times in
Tales of Space and Time (1899). A school of "red-
blooded" literature thus sprang up in which the leading
theme was the celebration of brute strength,[3] in which the

---

[3] Not all fiction of this kind, of course, exalts force or implies that the
law of the jungle is the inescapable law of modern society. Stanley Waterloo,

measure of morality was the measure of the broadest chest, and in which life was reduced to the elemental hungers for food and for sex. Whether scene and characters belonged to prehistory or to the familiar world of today, the purpose was the same. Civilization is but an ill-fitting coat in which men have never been comfortable. In any situation involving self-preservation or the fundamental animal desires they will throw it off with a snarl and stand revealed as the most cunning and most ruthless of the brutes. Writers looked upon their jungle ethic and saw that it was good; and the reading public agreed.

The glorification of force and the elevation of the idea of the struggle for existence and survival of the fittest coincided neatly with the wishes and the practice of nineteenth-century industrialism and with the end-of-the-century imperialism. No doctrine could have been more welcome, and for millions of men, from butcher's boy and petty shopkeeper to steel magnate and beer baron, it was all-sufficient as social philosophy and rule of conduct. Anything "to be a 'success,'" reflected Norris' Charlie Geary, who has cheated his one-time friend Vandover unmercifully; "to 'get there,' . . . . trampling down or smashing through everything that stood in the way, blind, deaf, fists and teeth shut tight. . . . . Every man for himself—that was his maxim. It might be damned selfish, but it was human nature: the weakest to the wall, the strongest to the front."[4]

It was entirely appropriate that the poet of imperialism should be the founder of the "red-blooded" school. Kip-

for instance, instead of emphasizing brutality, is interested rather in showing the faint beginnings of the more humane feelings; and the Rosnys' *Vamireh* makes much of the first stirrings of the creative, artistic impulse.

[4] *Vandover and the Brute* (copyright 1914, 1928, by Doubleday, Doran & Company), p. 328.

ling, in the preliminary verses or "General Summary" to his *Departmental Ditties and Other Verses* (1886), found a certain satisfaction in the belief that we are not much changed from the ape-like men who once roamed prehistoric India; then, he observed, the stronger ran down his fellow as the stronger run men down today.

His first volumes of short stories (which followed each other in rapid succession in 1888 and 1890), filled with soldiers and men who do the rough work of the world in the outposts of civilization, abound in situations calculated to evoke violent and primitive emotions. In *The Jungle Book* (1894) and *The Second Jungle Book*—always more read by adults than by the young for whom they were nominally written—the boy Mowgli is reared by the wolf pack and learns from the bear the law of the jungle, somewhat sentimentalized it is true, and diluted by the introduction of ideas belonging to human social ethics.

Frank Norris is by every right the founder of the red-blooded school in America. A virile fiction fitted the mood of the moment, for with the Spanish war we had taken our place among the imperialistic powers and were undergoing a phase of noisy belligerence. "We find that we want the Philippines," wrote the *Chicago Times-Herald*. "We also want Porto Rico . . . . We want Hawaii now . . . . We may want the Carolines, the Ladrones, the Pelew, and the Marianna groups. If we do we will take them."[5] A popular leader like Theodore Roosevelt was preaching what he called "the strenuous life" and the need of "the big stick." "Thank God," he exclaimed, "for the iron in the blood of our fathers . . . .," and he proceeded to heap scorn on the "timid man, the lazy man, ... the

[5] Quoted by Walter Millis, *The Martial Spirit* (Boston: Houghton Mifflin Company, 1931), p. 317.

over-civilized man, who has lost the great fighting, masterful virtues . . . . whose soul is incapable of feeling the
mighty lift that thrills 'stern men with empires in their
brains . . . .' "[6]

Norris' immediate successor was Jack London, who
owed much to him. After London's early successes the
literary degeneration of the genre was rapid, terminating
in such popular thrillers as *Tarzan of the Apes* (1912).[7]
The stream of stone-age or red-blooded fiction lost itself
in the sandy wastes of the pulp magazines.

Here a distinction must be noted: that though the naturalistic novel may be red-blooded in so far as it gives
prominence to brutality and violent action, the red-blooded
novel is not naturalistic. Terrible things happen to the
people of the former, as Norris remarked; no matter how
strong, they are crushed by yet more powerful forces of
environment, or betrayed by heredity. The strong man of
the latter causes terrible things to happen to others who
may stand in the way of his quest for power and domination. Norris' elementalism derives from both sources—
from Zola and the naturalists on the one hand, and from
Kipling (and to some extent from Stevenson) on the other.

Norris himself has given us no prehistoric characters
or Pleistocene settings. His primitivism reveals itself in
the creation of brutish types like McTeague, or men of
ruthless driving will like Ward Bennett the Arctic explorer; in a general overshadowing preoccupation with
ideas derived from the theory of evolution; in a conscious-

[6] Address delivered to the Hamilton Club, Chicago, April 10, 1899;
printed in *The Strenuous Life* (New York: The Century Co., 1901), see
pp. 5, 7.

[7] Kipling, in his autobiography, recognizes that the *Jungle Books* spawned
this brood. He wrote, with something of asperity of the "jazzing up" of the
motif of the *Jungle Books* by the author of *Tarzan of the Apes* (*Something
of Myself* [New York, Doubleday, Doran & Company, 1937], pp. 235–36).

ness of geologic time and the early state of mankind; in an emphasis on desires and instincts described as "primordial" or "primeval" (two favorite words), on what he calls "life in the raw."

He is fond of subjecting his characters to extreme privation and peril in order that the powerful and cruel instinct of self-preservation may assert itself and the animal appear naked in all his ferocity. A favorite theme is that of atavism—the notion that in every man lies the potentiality of resuming the character of his Neanderthal ancestor, and that to do so he needs only the stimulus of some crisis of danger or conflict. If the man in question is a person of education and culture and wears a dress suit, so much the better, since the contrast is more dramatic.

Thus it was with the polished Bab Azzoun, son of an Arab sheik, who had been educated in France and had become a French citizen. He had graduated with honors from the École Polytechnique and had written several books "couronné par l'Académie"; he had held important diplomatic posts. As a government official he is now with a party of war correspondents accompanying a French military expedition in North Africa. As their scow toils up a shrunken desert river they discourse idly, and Bab Azzoun expounds his theory of the growth of patriotism from loyalty to the family to devotion to the national state. The last stage will not be reached, he says, till "we can look down upon the world as our country, humanity as our countrymen, and he shall be the best patriot who is the least patriotic." He regrets that the powerful French government should be engaged in "terrorising into submission a horde of half-starved fanatics," yawns, and asks for the seltzer water. Suddenly the expedition is attacked by a party of fierce tribesmen. A French cuirassier, "gulping up blood," stumbles out of the battle and falls face downward into the ooze of the river's edge. A troop of wild horsemen dash across the stream just ahead of the scow, shrilling their war cry.

In an instant of time all the long years of culture and education were stripped away as a garment . . . . in a long, shrill cry, he answered his countrymen in their own language:

"*Allah-il-Allah, Mohammed ressoul Allah.*"

He passed me at a bound, leaped from the scow upon the back of a riderless horse, and, mingling with the Kabyles, rode out of sight.

And that was the last I ever saw of Bab Azzoun.[8]

Or perhaps the reversion to type occurs in some innocuous and obscure citizen of laughably prosy occupation. Such a man is Paul Schuster of the short story "A Reversion to Type" (in *The Third Circle*). For ten years he has been floor-walker in a department store that sells "ribbons and lace and corsets and other things." He lives with a maiden aunt and a parrot on a dull street, wears on duty a black cutaway and a white tie and is utterly, painfully respectable. But in him "as in you and me, were generations—countless generations—of forefathers." One evening in his forty-first year Schuster pauses on the sidewalk after locking the door of the store, and with a month's pay in his pocket resolves to get drunk. He does. During the night he gulps copious draughts of fiery whiskey on the Barbary Coast, pours champagne in the piano at the Cliff House, and knocks down a waiter with a catsup bottle and stamps on his belly. When he is sober again he "rides the rods" to a little mining town in the Sierra. He reconnoiters the ground for a few days, and then one dark night in a

---

[8] "Son of a Sheik," in *The Third Circle*, pp. 142–43. Quoted by permission of the publisher, Dodd, Mead & Company, Inc.

narrow defile of the mountains he waylays the superintendent of a neighboring mine who he believes carries the week's gold, and blasts away his face with a charge of buckshot from both barrels of a sawed-off shotgun. It appears that Schuster's grandfather, quite unknown to him, had served a term in San Quentin for highway robbery. And his grandfather two hundred times removed, we may infer, had no doubt dashed out the brains of someone else's grandfather (equally remote) with a knotted club.

To have provided Bab Azzoun and Schuster with extraordinary strength or prognathous jaws would have been injurious to the best literary effect; but McTeague and Ward Bennett are particularly distinguished by the possession of both. Norris has but one word—"salient"—to describe the jutting jaws of his more elemental heroes. Like Buteau in *La Terre,* with his "machoires puissantes de carnassier," McTeague has "the jaw salient, like that of the carnivora." His strength is so great that in contempt of such frivolous implements as forceps he often pulls the teeth of his patients with thumb and forefinger. In his fight with Marcus Schouler at the picnic (a fight growing out of a friendly wrestling match) he snaps the bone in the arm of his antagonist as if it were a dry twig. When, in anger, he lays hold upon a door closed against him, the wood tears like rotten canvas and knob and lock together come away in his hand. Nothing will better illustrate the primevalism which Norris loves to exploit or the gusto with which he dwells on the animal origins of humankind than the language he employs to describe an incident of the fight just mentioned. Schouler has bitten through the lobe of McTeague's ear, drenching the dentist's shirt with blood:

The brute that in McTeague lay so close to the surface leaped instantly to life . . . . He sprang to his feet with a shrill and meaningless clamor, totally unlike the ordinary bass of his speaking tones. It was the hideous yelling of a hurt beast, the squealing of a wounded elephant. He framed no words; in the rush of high-pitched sound that issued from his wide-open mouth there was nothing articulate. It was something no longer human; it was rather an echo from the jungle.[9]

Ward Bennett of *A Man's Woman* is an intensely ugly man, with a narrow forehead—"the forehead of men of single ideas"—and little twinkling eyes. "His lower jaw was huge almost to deformity, like that of the bulldog, the chin salient, the mouth close-gripped, with great lips, indomitable, brutal." There is a suggestion of the same ferocity in him which marks one of the dogs he has brought down from the Arctic. "Your dog has killed our Dan," protests Lloyd Searight, "and, what is much worse, started to eat him." Bennett replies, "it's my fault for setting her a bad example. I ate her trace-mate, and was rather close to eating Kamiska herself at one time."

Perhaps the most striking exhibition of his physical strength, the swiftness of his decision, and his determination occurs in the scene (at the close of chapter iv) where he rescues Lloyd from the cart which is about to be dashed in the canal by her terrified horse. Bennett, who has been hunting for specimens of rock and who still carries his geologist's hammer in his hand, seizes the bit and hauls till the animal's mouth is bloody; but the beast lifts him

---

[9] Frank Norris, *McTeague* (copyright 1899, 1927, by Doubleday, Doran & Company, Inc.), p. 234. Norris borrowed McTeague's great strength and stature, his blond hair, his customary docility, his occasional blind rages, his elephant trumpetings, his concertina, melancholy tunes, canary and all, from Goddedaal, Swedish mate of the brig *Flying Scud* in Stevenson's *The Wrecker* (1892). He owed much to this work, which he admired as greatly as did Landry Court in *The Pit*, who declared that it "Just about took the top of my head off."

clear of the ground and in another instant will be off. Then Lloyd "saw the short-handled geologist's hammer . . . . heave high in the air. Down it came, swift, resistless, terrible—one blow." The horse sinks to the earth like a felled tree and expires with a long shudder. Lloyd is shaken, distressed, even a bit angry at the loss of her fine animal. "I'm sorry I had to do that, ... but there was no help for it—nothing else to do," Bennett apologized briefly. It is such men who are worthy of a "man's woman" like Lloyd Searight.[10]

In a world such as that conceived by Norris, where primordial impulses so largely determine men's actions, frequent revelations of greed or predacity or the sheer lust to kill are to be expected—instances, especially, of the ruthlessness engendered by what is called the first law of nature, self-preservation. The shipwrecked passengers of the "Mazatlan," crowded into their overloaded small boat, who clamor against the wretched Jew trying to board them, are a case in point. As the boat tipped under his desperate clutch, "There was a great cry. 'Push him off! We're swamping! Push him off!' . . . . It was the animal in them all that had come to the surface in an instant, the primal instinct of the brute striving for its life . . . ."

Lauth (of the short story of the same name, written when Norris was twenty-two and still bemused by the Middle Ages) is a student in fifteenth-century Paris. During a street battle between town and gown he posts himself with his arbalest on the roof of a house. The thought

[10] It is a curious quirk of mind which led Norris to give masculine names to so many of his female characters. Thus besides Lloyd Searight we have Turner Ravis (*Vandover and the Brute*), Sidney Dyke (*The Octopus*), Page Dearborn (*The Pit*), Jack Doychert ("His Single Blessedness" in *Collected Writings*), Travis Bessemer (*Blix*), and Travis Hallett ("Travis Hallett's Halfback" in *Collected Writings*). Although his own daughter was christened Jeannette, he never called her by any name but Billy.

of taking human life is intensely repugnant to him, but in the excitement of the struggle he looses a bolt into the surging mass below. It strikes a man dead.

> In an instant a mighty flame of blood lust thrilled up through all Lauth's body and mind . . . . His eyes glittered, he moistened his lips with the tip of his tongue . . . . as his next bolt spun through the brain of a furrier's apprentice in a yellow gaberdine, [he] grew white and stood silent, quivering for very joy.[11]

A certain relish for the depiction of scenes of violent death marked Norris from the beginning. In the story "The Jongleur of Taillebois" (also from his Medieval period and a year earlier than "Lauth"), we learn how Amelot slew his enemy Yéres in the solitudes of the New Forest. Having mortally wounded him with a sword cut in the neck, Amelot stands back and watches his death agonies with curious interest. These are described in minute detail—his writhings and threshings, the blind butting of his head against the exposed roots of the trees. "He streaked his clothes and face with his own blood, the dead leaves stuck to his wet cheeks, and the underlying dust was churned into ruddy mud by the quick, incessant opening and closing of his fingers." At length when Yéres has grown quiet, Amelot, to make sure of him, sets the point of his poniard carefully over the heart of his foe and bears down on the haft; "the skin dinted beneath the point, then suddenly parted, the blade sunk in up to the hilt . . . ."[12] The entire episode is so sharply visualized and its brutality recited with such an air of cool detachment that it was not a little shocking to some readers.

Norris' treatment of nature is in keeping with the "elementalism" of his characters. The immensities of sky and

---

[11] *Collected Writings,* pp. 119, 120.
[12] *Ibid.,* pp. 3, 4.

sea, mountain and desert are never for him merely picturesque or wild in the peculiar, often sentimental, manner of the familiar romantic writers. They suggest to his imagination the vast reaches of geologic time, the younger ages of the earth; for he had a perspective lent by nineteenth-century science which was inaccessible to the literary discoverers of nature. In his hands nature is no longer merely primitive; it is "primordial," "primeval." (The difference in connotation is perhaps a nice one, yet significant.) It is a fit stage for paleolithic man, or for his modern descendant, who is less removed in spirit than he thinks from his skin-clad forebear of the heavy brow-ridges. McTeague, after the murder of Trina, instinctively seeks the wilderness of the Sierra. The scene that breaks on his gaze is tremendous, even terrifying:

At turns of the road, on the higher points, cañons disclosed themselves far away, gigantic grooves in the landscape, deep blue in the distance, opening one into another, ocean-deep, silent, huge, and suggestive of colossal primeval forces held in reserve. . . . . Here and there the mountains lifted themselves out of the narrow river beds in groups like giant lions rearing their heads after drinking. . . . . In Placer County, California, [nature] is a vast, unconquered brute of the Pliocene epoch, savage, sullen, and magnificently indifferent to man.[13]

The same "primordial desolation" confronted Ward Bennett in the far North.

The French naturalists, particularly Zola, were distinguished by the frankness with which they pictured sexual behavior. Norris was clearly eager to explore, yet fearful of this subject, at once so inescapably fascinating and so curiously forbidding. It is the duty of the serious novelist, he believed, to probe "the mystery of sex . . . .

[13] *McTeague*, pp. 379–80.

and the black, unsearched penetralia of the soul of man,"[14] but he cannot put off the feeling that sex, on the whole, is an unfortunate and regrettable arrangement of nature. It is often, in his mind, synonymous with "vice," constantly at war with the upward aspirations of the "better self."

The dawning sexual curiosity, the first vague stirrings of an unknown desire in the boy Vandover are described with great fidelity to common experience. One day in church he receives for the first time into his consciousness what he had no doubt often heard before—the words of the Litany, "all women in the perils of childbirth." On this he speculates long, but without result, "smelling out a mystery beneath the words . . . . with the instinct of a young brute." At length he learns what Norris calls "the brutal truth." "But even then he hated to believe that people were so low, so vile." By chance he stumbles on the article "Obstetrics" in the *Encyclopaedia Britannica* and reads it avidly, poring over the plates and steel engravings that accompany it. What pity that so much sober learning, so much science, should produce an effect so deplorable; for this, we are told, was the last straw: "It was the end of all his childish ideals." Thenceforth Vandover was consumed with the "perverse craving for the knowledge of vice."[15]

Nevertheless sex, as one of the primal human hungers, must have its due in "red-blooded" and in naturalistic fiction; and Norris accordingly contrives to give it a certain prominence throughout his work, though in terms calculated to give the least possible offense to late-Victorian

[14] Norris, *The Responsibilities of the Novelist* (copyright 1901, 1902, 1903, by Doubleday, Doran & Company, Inc.), p. 220.

[15] *Vandover and the Brute*, pp. 10, 11.

sensibilities. Never did he grapple it with the boldness of Zola, whose incessant and heroic ruttings gave pause even to the relatively tolerant French reading public.[16]

The genteelly reared Laura Dearborn, of *The Pit,* is conscious of two natures in herself—the one obedient to the behest of reason, the other impulsive, a little fearsome because incalculable, of unknown potentialities. Vaguely but none the less surely, and without ever formulating her thought in words, she knows this second, emotional nature of hers to rest on desires that belong to her as a woman. It is not Jadwin, the man she marries, who by some subtle telepathy of passion calls urgently to the instinctive Laura, but Corthell the artist, who pays long, assiduous, and skillful court to her. His presence "stirred troublous, unknown deeps in her, certain undefined trends of recklessness; and for so long as he held her within his influence, she could not forget her sex a single instant."[17]

Trina, too, the woman in her for the first time fully aroused when McTeague seized her in his rough embrace, experiences a strange agitation of mingled pleasure and fear. The rich abundance of her blue-black hair, so heavy that the coiled and plaited mass of it tips back her head a little, is a provocation to McTeague; and the heady scent of feminine flesh that diffuses from her person intoxicates him and sets his senses in a whirl. On the occasion when he is a guest at the Sieppes' house, he is given her room. Diffidently he explores the place, touching this object and that—her hairbrush, her clothes, "stroking them softly

---

[16] However cautious his own handling of sex, Norris refused "even to consider apology necessary" for Zola's outspokenness. See H. M. Wright, "In Memoriam—Frank Norris," *University of California Chronicle,* October 1902, p. 243.

[17] Frank Norris, *The Pit* (copyright 1903, 1921, by Doubleday, Doran & Company, Inc.), p. 136.

with his huge leathern palms," a veritable gorilla in a boudoir. "All at once, seized with an unreasoned impulse, McTeague opened his huge arms and gathered the little garments close to him, plunging his face deep amongst them, savoring their delicious odor with long breaths of luxury . . . ."[18]

But it is by suggestion, in the dropped hint, the passing observation, in a physical luxuriousness in certain of his feminine characters that Norris recognizes the all-pervading influence of the sexual instinct, rather than in minute descriptions of scenes of amorous excitement or in any bluntness of language. He notes the "silent ecstasy" of Alberta Bessemer, the twelve- or thirteen-year-old sister of Blix, when she is permitted to wear her first corset: "The clasp of the miniature stays around her small body was like the embrace of a little lover, and awoke in her, ideas that were as vague, as immature and unformed, as the straight little figure itself."[19]

Annixter is unaccountably troubled, waking and sleeping, by Hilma Tree's round white arms, wet, gleaming, and fragrant with milk as she goes about her work in the dairy; by the "full, round curves of her hips and shoulders that suggested the precocious maturity of a healthy, vigorous animal life passed under the hot southern sun of a half-tropical country"; by those "full lips of hers, and her round white chin, modulating downward with a certain delicious roundness to her neck, her throat and the sweet feminine amplitude of her breast."[20]

From his first tentative essays in the short story to his latest novel, Norris thus plucked at the string of his primevalism, running up and down the scale of hunger, sex,

---

[18] *McTeague*, p. 79. [19] *Blix* (Doubleday, Doran & Company, Inc.), p. 5.
[20] *The Octopus* (Doubleday, Doran & Company, Inc.), pp. 82–83.

fear, greed, violence, cruelty. It would be tedious to multiply examples further; but the subject cannot be quitted without more particular notice of *Moran of the Lady Letty* and *A Man's Woman,* the two novels most frankly and obviously representative of the red-blooded school of fiction.

Moran of the Lady Letty chants "the spell of the great, simple, and primitive emotions." Its theme is that civilization, the world of social conventions, vitiates and corrupts and that the only sane life is life in the great out-of-doors where a man now and then can refresh and invigorate his jaded spirit by sinking his knife into the vitals of another—a tonic that Ross Wilbur, the hero of the tale, found remarkably efficacious.

Ross is a member of San Francisco's wealthy "younger set" who fills his days with yachting parties, pink teas, cotillions, and flirtatious badinage with the women of his circle. He has in him the makings of a man, for he is tall, broad-shouldered, and has "plenty of jaw in the lower part of his face"; but at present he is soft, full of squeamishness, and shrinks from direct contact with dirt or vulgarity. He loves, however, to watch the shipping and the life along the water front. One day as he is whiling away an hour or two in this fashion, he manages to get himself Shanghaied aboard a dirty, smelly little schooner anchored in the Bay.

When the fumes of drugged whiskey have cleared out of his head, Ross voices his indignation to the skipper of the craft, a hard-bitten old rascal, who responds with a brand of reasoning, very persuasive, to which the young clubman is unaccustomed—a smashing blow in the mouth, which stretches him full length on the deck. After he has been soundly kicked in the stomach and flung down the fo'c'sle hatch, Ross shows already a marked improvement in manliness and resolves to make the best of his new situation.

During the days that follow, while the schooner—the "Bertha Milner"—holds her course southward into the Pacific, Wilbur's whole outlook on life undergoes a revolution. The existence he has hitherto led appears now vain and empty. Aboard the schooner everything is novel, everything full of interest, from the details of navigation, which Captain Kitchell undertakes to teach him, to the turtle hunt in which he engages with the captain and some members of the crew. He is exhilarated by the blue immensity of sea, the procession of colors in the sky at sunset and dawn. He rejoices in a budding sense of self-reliance.

At length the schooner falls in with the derelict bark "Lady Letty," abandoned by her crew, her decks half blown out by an explosion of gas from her cargo of coal, her Norwegian master dead in his cabin—a grotesque figure with his false teeth half-expelled from his mouth by his last gasp. Behind the wheel lies the captain's daughter Moran, stupefied by the coal gas.

Captain Kitchell is thrown into a frenzy of greed at the prospect of a rich salvage; his jaw "grows salient," and he is ready to do murder on Moran at the least suspicion that she may stand in the way of his claim to the prize. When she has been removed to the schooner and the body of the dead captain has been thrown to the swarming sharks, Kitchell remains behind on the wreck, drunk, singing wildly, and laying about him with an axe. He is now conveniently disposed of by a sudden squall which capsizes and sinks the "Lady Letty." Wilbur and Moran are alone on the Pacific with the Chinese crew of the "Bertha Milner."

It is easy to chaff Norris on his extravagant robustness, but Moran is, nevertheless, a memorable creation, an abrupt departure from the prevalent type of Victorian heroine distinguished by a score of timidities and dishonesties that passed for refinement. Moran is tall, big-boned, muscular, yet not unfeminine—"a thing untouched and unsullied by civilization." Her pale blue eyes are set in a face reddened by sun and wind; her rye-colored hair falls to her waist in two braids as thick as a man's arm. She is often moody, surly, and at times is capable of furious rages. She can be barbarously cruel, as when she binds a file between the jaws of the captive beachcomber Hoang to make him talk and, with horrid sound, rasps his teeth down to the gums. She knows no finesse of language. The men are few whom she cannot out-swear, out-drink, and out-fight, but her "purity was the purity of primeval glaciers." At first Wilbur knows no other tactic with her than his customary politeness and deference to women. These she repels, with deep suspicion, as preludes to treachery. In the end he wins, first her respect, and then her love, in the only way perhaps in which they could be won—by beating her in a bare-fisted fight with no quarter asked or given on either side.

Her life, passed almost entirely at sea, has taught her faith in but one law, the law of the strongest. In Magdalena Bay, on the coast of Lower California, where Moran, a competent navigator, has brought the "Bertha Milner" to anchor, she and Wilbur recover a fortune in ambergris from the carcass of a dead whale but are despoiled of their booty by a crew of piratical Chinese beachcombers; she proposes to regain it by force. When Wilbur questions their right, since the whale, after all, had been the discovery of the beachcombers, she turns on him wrathfully:

We're dumped down here on this God-forsaken sand, and there's no law and no policemen. The strongest of us are going to live and the weakest are going to die. I'm going to live and I'm going to have my loot too, and I'm not going to split fine hairs with these robbers . . . . I'm going to have it all, and that's the law you're under in this case, my righteous friend![21]

It is in the ensuing battle with the beachcombers that Wilbur clears the tepid humors of civilization finally from his blood and effects his complete regeneration as a man— this by the simple act of killing a Chinaman. When he saw his foe writhing at his feet, "the primitive man, the half-brute of the stone age, leaped to life in Wilbur's breast . . . . The knowledge that he could kill filled him with a sense of power that was veritably royal."

When the two adventurers return at length to San Francisco, Wilbur (as well as Norris his creator) is confronted with a very pretty problem. What can he do with his uncouth Viking's daughter? Can he introduce her among the silk-gowned twitterers and tuxedoed young gentlemen of his own circle? Can he endure their snobbery, their lifted eyebrows, their smiles of amused contempt? There is one meeting between Moran and some of his well-groomed friends, including the dainty Josie Herrick, who obviously designs to marry him. Wilbur makes the introductions: " 'I'm sure,' [Josie] said feebly . . . . 'I—I'm sure I'm very pleased to meet Miss Sternersen'."

Can Moran survive out of her proper element? "Mate, how soon can we be out to sea again?" she asks Wilbur when the roofs of San Francisco heave in sight. "I hate this place."

On the other hand, can Wilbur abandon the habits and associations of a lifetime for a life of wandering adventure with Moran—filibustering in Cuba, knocking about the

[21] *Moran of the Lady Letty*, p. 191.

Pacific—as he plans to do? It is intimated that he deceives himself when he thinks he has cut all ties with settled existence.

Norris evades every difficulty by recourse to an easy artifice: Moran is stabbed to death aboard the anchored schooner (where she has remained alone) by Hoang, the leader of the beachcombers. She makes no resistance, for she is like a keen blade from which the temper has been drawn: "she had learned . . . . to know what it meant to be dependent; to rely for protection upon some one who was stronger than she."

Hoang looses the anchor chains and steals ashore with the ambergris. The schooner slips its cables and drives out through the Golden Gate into the open Pacific, its only passenger the dead girl stretched upon the deck, her yellow braids across her breast, while from the shore Wilbur babbles a lyric farewell.

Although Norris yielded to convention in converting Moran at the last into a clinging vine, she belongs with Blix and Lloyd Searight (who are Moran without her savagery and reared in the usual well-to-do, middle-class surroundings instead of on the deck of a ship) as a herald of the "new woman" in fiction, a type since become familiar enough—self-reliant, capable, "practical and sensible" (as Norris asserts of Blix), athletic, drivers of spirited horses like Lloyd, "chums," "pals," the companions of men rather than objects of protection.

Blix wants to study medicine. When Condy voices his consternation, she replies, "isn't studying medicine . . . . better than piano-playing, or French courses, or literary classes and Browning circles? Oh, I've no patience with that kind of girl!" She refuses to "come out," rejects invitations to the social functions that have previously filled so much of her life, and declares, "I'll ride a wheel, take long walks, study something. But as for leading the life of a society girl—no! . . . . I'm done with conventionality for good."[22] Condy applauds her purpose. The two go long rambles on the seacoast, fish, or explore the picturesque corners of San Francisco. These women are one more phase of the revolt from the drawing room in the literature of the 'nineties. Even their physical features are a defiance of tradition. What novelist would dare to give his heroine little twinkling eyes, as Norris gives Blix?

Ward Bennett, of *A Man's Woman,* leader of the Freja Arctic Exploring Expedition, is another of Norris' strong men, who demonstrates his fitness to survive in the struggle for existence. He is hard, selfish, arrogant. "What he wanted he took with an iron hand, without ruth and without scruple." "He had neither patience nor toleration for natural human weakness." When his ship is caught in the ice and crushed, he faces the appalling wilderness of frozen sea which the party must cross, clenches his fist, and grits through his teeth, "I'll break you, by God!"

Day after day, week after week, the twelve men pursue their journey with heart-breaking toil. When a man falls from exhaustion and begs to be abandoned, Bennett kicks him to his feet and drives him forward. But these methods cannot be employed with McPherson, whose foot is ulcered, the flesh eaten away to the bone.

For the fraction of a minute Bennett debated the question, then he turned to the command.

"Forward, men!" . . . .

"Wait—wait," exclaimed the cripple, "I—I can get along—I—" He rose to his knees, made a great effort to regain his footing, and once more came crashing down upon the ice.

"Forward!"

[22] *Blix,* pp. 199, 36, 37.

"But—but—but—*Oh, you're not going to leave me, sir?*"
"Forward!"

There begins a chorus of protests from the others. Several
volunteer to remain with the doomed man.

> Bennett caught the dog-whip from Muck Tu's hand. His voice
> rang like the alarm of a trumpet.
> "Forward!"
> Once more Bennett's discipline prevailed. His iron hand shut
> down upon his men, more than ever resistless. Obediently they
> turned their faces to the southward.[23]

At length the party, now reduced to six, are huddled
in their tent of rotten canvas—foul with the smell of "drugs
and of mouldy gunpowder, ... dirty rags, ... un-
washed bodies . . . . scorching sealskin" — waiting for
death, their arms and legs grotesquely swollen, a curious
effect of starvation. At this juncture the last of the dogs,
which had strayed, returns to camp. Here is food. Bennett
reflects that he is still the strongest of them all. He will
kill the dog, take the meat, and make his way alone to the
nearest settlement: "Was it not right that the mightiest
should live? Was it not the great law of nature?" But in
this instance the great law of nature is obliged to yield to
Bennett's sense of duty to his men. Shortly after, the sur-
vivors of the expedition are picked up by a whaling vessel.

These events occupy but the first two chapters. The
rest of the novel concerns the love of Bennett and Lloyd
Searight. "What a pair they were," thinks Bennett's friend
Ferris, "strong, masterful both, insolent in the consciousness of their power!" A love affair such as theirs resolves
itself inevitably into a struggle for mastery between two
dominating personalities. Each in turn experiences the
humiliation of weakness and the agony of moral self-con-

---

[23] *A Man's Woman*, pp. 32–33.

demnation. Each in turn is restored to his strength. In the end the advantage lies, perhaps, with Lloyd, whose courage is put to the greater test, and who is the agent by whom Bennett recovers his sense of duty to his career as an explorer.[24]

Lloyd is rich in her own right but has rejected the idle social life of women of her class, founded a nursing agency, and chosen nursing as a career—not out of any great love of humanity but because she wanted "with all her soul . . . . to count in the general economy of things." Toward her profession she has the feeling of a well-disciplined and stern soldier toward his duty. Like Bennett when he abandons the crippled McPherson on the ice, she is not moved by compassion when important issues are at stake. In the scene—one of the most vivid and memorable in the novel[25] —of the operation on the little girl Hattie, who must have the end of her thigh bone sawed off ("exsected" is the word used by Norris, who here makes a good display of what he had learned from a visit to the operating room), Lloyd administers the ether with calm efficiency, undisturbed by the piteous cries of the patient.

Shortly after the return of the expedition from the Arctic, Ferris (who has already suffered the amputation of both hands, and whose constitution has been seriously weakened by his terrible experience) falls ill of typhoid fever. It is Lloyd who is summoned to attend him. When

[24] The story "Toppan" (in *The Third Circle*) offers the exact converse of this situation. Toppan is another of Norris' indomitable out-of-doors men who has explored the interior of Tibet, eaten camel's meat when there was nothing better, and rubbed tobacco juice in his eyes to keep awake during a snowstorm on Mount Everest. But he has the misfortune to love a girl who is not a "man's woman," who tames him and converts him into a clerk in an insurance office.

[25] In response to the protests of readers who found it too "strong," Norris rewrote this scene, effectively spoiling it. The publishers of the re-issue of 1928 have inexcusably failed to restore the passage.

Bennett learns this his mind is instantly filled with one idea, one fear, to the exclusion of all else: if Lloyd stays on the case she will contract the disease and she will die. In ignorance as yet of the identity of her patient, he posts to the house where Ferris lies ill, plants his broad back against the door of the sickroom, and forbids her to enter. The moral crisis for Bennett occurs when he learns it is Ferris who lies at the point of death. In his own mind he is convinced that he must choose between the life of the woman he loves and that of his dearest friend. Briefly he makes his decision. "No!" she may not enter. Lloyd is first incredulous, then indignant, then suppliant, then tragic—all in vain. She is broken. Bennett drives her to the station and wires for another nurse. In the interval Ferris dies.

The scene is much too long—twenty-four pages from the moment Bennett enters the house till Lloyd leaves it; yet the time is supposed to be but fifteen minutes while the doctor is gone for a short walk and a breath of air. The effort to drag out suspense is too apparent.

Lloyd believes her professional integrity to be irretrievably lost. Her act, though compelled, seems to her like desertion under fire. She feels an agony of humiliation and crushed pride, and for Bennett no longer anything but hate. But a yet greater ordeal than she has just suffered faces her on her return to the agency. What can she tell her companions? Who will believe her if she tells the truth? They do not know Bennett. If she keeps silence perhaps the facts will never become known. It will be thought that the death of her patient (of which she now first learns) occurred before her departure. But to keep silence is cowardly. We have now another long-drawn-out moral crisis, culminating in Lloyd's confession to the nurses assembled at dinner. Omitting all mention of Bennett, she presents her own conduct in the most damaging light. The truth, however, is soon known, and her professional honor receives no hurt.

Bennett, bowed low under the realization of what he has done, in his turn contracts the fever. By chance it is Lloyd once more who is called in. Distasteful as is the task, she accepts it as an opportunity to redeem herself in her own eyes. Bennett, emerging from delirium to find her in his room, orders her away and, on her refusal, tries feebly to rise and put her out by force. But it is she who is now strong and he who is weak. On his recovery the two strong wills are ready to cry quits; he and Lloyd are reconciled and in due course married. To establish beyond cavil her granite-willed character, she has only to prod awake his now slumbering ambition to plant the American flag at the pole, and to propel him forth to face once more the struggle for existence in the Arctic cold. On his earlier adventure, "in that half-night of the polar circle, lost and forgotten on a primordial shore, back into the stone age once more, men and animals [had] fought one another for the privilege of eating a dead dog." She knows that in all probability the same savage necessity will confront him again. But she cannot falter, for she is "a man's woman."

Franklin Walker feels in *A Man's Woman* the fevered atmosphere of the sickroom; "the clinical thermometer," he writes, "does not go down throughout the entire book." What he takes to be the unhealthy glow of the novel he attributes to Norris' own recent illness, consequent on his sojourn in Cuba as correspondent during the Spanish-American War.[26] The explanation is not implausible, and

[26] Walker, *Frank Norris*, p. 215.

it is true that the moral dilemmas of Bennett and Lloyd are described with an air of emotional strain. But this may be no more than the result of Norris' effort to spur on his (and, as he perhaps feared, the reader's) flagging interest in the tale, for he was not happy in the writing of *A Man's Woman*. His imagination was already astir with plans for *The Octopus,* and he was anxious to be done with the current task.

When Professor Walker ascribes the brutalities with which "the action is incrusted" to Norris' late experience with famine and slaughter in Cuba, he is not convincing; for we have seen enough to know that Norris showed a marked predilection for brutalities long before he viewed the shrapnel-torn Spanish soldiers in the rifle pits at El Caney or smelled there the "strange, acrid, salty smell of blood."[27]

Norris himself has named the fault of *A Man's Woman,* and the critic can do little more than assent. He wrote to Marcosson: "It's a kind of theatrical sort with a lot of niggling analysis to try to justify the violent action of the first few chapters."[28] Then follows the avowal of his purpose to return to what he calls "straight naturalism." He was done with the red-blooded novel as such. In future his paeans to force would be addressed not to brawny men or to stone-age women in modern garb like Moran, but to an impersonal principle of the cosmos which "inevitably, resistlessly" works for good.

In *The Octopus* Norris failed to reconcile his determinism with his social ethics. In *A Man's Woman* he failed to reconcile his survival-of-the-fittest ethics with traditional

---

[27] See "With Lawton at El Caney," *Collected Writings,* p. 259.

[28] Marcosson, *Adventures in Interviewing,* p. 237. Used by permission of the publishers, Dodd, Mead & Company, Inc.

morals. When Lloyd is torn between the impulse to protect herself by silence and the idea that she ought to confess what she believes to be her fault, the "two conceptions of Duty and Will began suddenly to grow." After her confession, "Dimly Lloyd commenced to understand that the mastery of self, the steady, firm control of natural, intuitive impulses, selfish because natural, was a progression."[29]

Moreover, the feminism implied in Lloyd's independence, her self-reliance, her career as nurse, is confused and beclouded by conventional notions of the relative roles of women and men. "Ah! . . . . she was stronger than other women," Lloyd exulted; "she was carrying out a splendid work." It is then an effect of anticlimax to find her tamely accepting the belief that "woman's place is in the home." During Bennett's convalescence she receives a letter from Dr. Street (the surgeon who had operated on Hattie), asking her to take a very important surgical case. Bennett will not selfishly stand in the way of her lifework; but she tears the letter in two, drops the pieces on the floor, and says with finality (p. 235): "That, for my lifework." Later, when she is trying to screw her courage up to the point of sending Bennett into the Arctic again, she reflects, in terms worthy of *McGuffey's Reader* (p. 244): "To be the inspiration of great deeds, high hopes, and firm resolves, and then, while the fight was dared, to wait in calmness for its isssue—that was her duty; that, the woman's part in the world's great work."

Norris came to think it not admirable that "the strong grind the faces of the weak." He was increasingly concerned with social justice, as *The Octopus* and his critical essays reveal. He knew from experience that war (the

[29] *A Man's Woman*, pp. 179, 212.

practical application of "virile" philosophies) is neither romantic nor heroic, nor the proper business of civilized men. The "whole business," he wrote on his return from Cuba, "seems nothing but a hideous blur of mud and blood."[30]

Whence, then, in his work, all this noise of the impact of fists on flesh, these berserk rages, this chorus of primordial bellowings, this splitting of skulls, these exultant chants to the "primal emotions," this harking back to the Stone Age, these strident dithyrambs to the struggle for existence and the survival of the fittest?

Norris might have replied for himself as he replied for the young writer, Overbeck, of the story, "Dying Fires," that "a certain sane and healthy animalism . . . . hurt nobody," and that, in time, like Overbeck, he would outgrow it. Overbeck, it will be remembered, was reproved by the Greenwich Village dilettanti for his *"faroucherie."* But it was not his fault if "the teamsters, biscuit-shooters and 'breed' girls of the foothills were coarse in fibre," or their passions violent. "He had dealt . . . . honestly; he did not dab at the edge of the business; he had sent his fist straight through it." Gradually, however, under the emasculating influence of these pallid little people, Overbeck came to believe "that he must strive for the spiritual, and 'let the ape and tiger die.'" But with the ape and tiger died also all the force and originality of his work. Norris was convinced that it is the "elemental forces" that must provide the novel with "vigorous action." Nothing else would satisfy his dramatic sense: "Vitality is the thing, after all."[31]

His primitivism may be regarded also—along with his

[30] Walker, *op. cit.,* p. 201.
[31] *The Responsibilities of the Novelist,* pp. 27, 142.

anti-intellectualism, his anti-aestheticism, his insistence that life is better than literature, his unconventional heroines— as a part of his revolt against the genteel reticences that so enfeebled American literature. To read the magazine fiction of the 'seventies and 'eighties seemed to him "like entering a darkened room." He was tired of over-refined people "with their everlasting consciences, their heated and artificial activities";[32] of literature whose standards were set by the "'young girl' and the family center table."[33]

But insensibly and perhaps inevitably he slipped over into the frank apotheosis of force, which, however it may be explained, remains a contradiction and a confusion in his work, as it was in the work of his successor Jack London, who called himself a socialist and gave us pictures of ferocious egoists like Larsen, the "Sea Wolf."

That confusion Norris shared with the whole generation following Darwin. Biological evolution scattered the ideas of writers, theologians, philosophers, like a flock of sparrows before the hawk. Moralists sat down, strewed ashes on their heads, and wailed, illogically, that if man had come down from the trilobites or other lowly creatures of the Silurian rocks, if the struggle for existence prevailed in the world of living things, then human ethics was abrogated. It was beyond the comprehension of the confused ones that men might be good at any other behest than God's. Others welcomed the idea of the survival of the fittest as a convenient shield for their predatory acts in the field of industry and finance. Political economy and social theory became dark and bitter.[34]

[32] "The 'Nature' Revival in Literature," *ibid.*, p. 141.

[33] Walker, *op. cit.*, p. 146.

[34] Hans Kohn relates the cult of force and the will to power in politics and economics to nineteenth-century science and to nineteenth-century philoso-

One of the few men of that time who kept their heads was Thomas Henry Huxley. He saw plainly that ethics lost none of its validity if the supernatural sanction was removed; that ethical conceptions are as much a product of evolutionary development as an opposable thumb, and quite as indispensable. He distinguishes two processes in opposition to each other—in nature the "cosmic process" ruled by the struggle for existence and survival of the fittest; in human society the "ethical process," which "repudiates the gladiatorial theory of existence."[35]

> [The ethical process] involves a course of conduct which, in all respects, is opposed to that which leads to success in the cosmic struggle for existence. In place of ruthless self-assertion it demands self-restraint; in place of thrusting aside, or treading down, all competitors, it requires that the individual shall not merely respect, but shall help his fellows; its influence is directed, not so much to the survival of the fittest, as to the fitting of as many as possible to survive. . . . .
>
> It is from neglect of these plain considerations that the fanatical individualism of our time attempts to apply the analogy of cosmic nature to society.[36]

Thus, rightly understood, evolutionary theory yields no support for the worship of force in human affairs. Few, however, understood it rightly. Today, more than a generation after Huxley wrote, social philosophers still find it necessary to point out the fallacy of trying to found

----

phy as shaped by that science. See his *Force or Reason* (Harvard University Press, Cambridge, 1937).

[35] *Evolution and Ethics and Other Essays* (New York: D. Appleton and Company, 1898). It may be asked: If it is the cosmic process that has given rise equally to the state of nature and to human society (and hence to the ethical process), how can the effect be in opposition to the cause? Huxley meets the objection with a simple illustration (p. 13 n.): "When a man lays hold of the two ends of a piece of string and pulls them, with intent to break it, the right arm is certainly exerted in antagonism to the left arm; yet both arms derive their energy from the same original source."

[36] *Ibid.*, pp. 81–82.

a rule of conduct (individual or social) on the fact of man's animal beginnings. "The notion is widespread, indeed," writes Carl J. Warden, "that man is merely an ape-like creature with a thin veneer of culture . . . . the implication that culture is secondary and superficial is contrary to the common facts of everyday life. In a sense, it is true that man created culture but it is just as true that culture created man."[37] The cult of the strong man was erected on such shards and scraps of the doctrine of evolution as gained popular currency. To the men of the 'nineties (such of them as were not too far sunk in the weary languors of the decadents), it came no doubt with the effect of an intoxicating breeze from a Pliocene landscape. In imagination they stripped off their shirts, seized their flint axes, and plunged with prodigious zest into the jungle. If Norris strove in those trampled and gore-drenched thickets as mightily as any, he emerged at length in chastened mood, as will appear in the next chapter, where an attempt will be made to trace in some detail the course of his thinking on social questions.

[37] Carl J. Warden, *The Emergence of Human Culture* (New York, 1936), p. 3. Quoted by permission of The Macmillan Company, publishers.

Chapter IV

Social Ideas of a Novelist: the Mellowing of the Strong Man

. . . . the true patriotism is the brotherhood of man . . . . the whole world is our nation and simple humanity our countrymen.—FRANK NORRIS*

THE EARLIEST evidence that Norris was aware of a social order is, at the same time, evidence of his belief that that order functions on principles something less than Christian—that exploitation of the weak by the strong and the cunning has ever been the law of its existence. In his first published volume, the medieval verse romance, *Yvernelle* (1891), he wrote:

> The feudal baron yet remains today,
>   But, changed into the modern moneyed lord,
> Still o'er the people holds more cruel sway,
>   But 'tis with hoarded gold and not with sword.
>
> Still do his vassals feel his iron heel.
>   His power awes—his government alarms;
> Still rings the world with sounds of clashing steel:
>   'Tis of machinery and not of arms.[1]

These are hardly the sentiments that he could have heard around the hearthstone of his father, who was him-

---

* *The Responsibilities of the Novelist* (Doubleday, Doran & Company, Inc.), p. 81.

[1] *Works* (New York, 1928), VI, 251. Quoted by permission of J. B. Lippincott Company.

self something of a moneyed lord on a modest scale. His mother, busy with her Browning society, was preoccupied with the soul-yearnings of Abt Vogler and Paracelsus rather than with the less ideal concerns of contemporary American politics and industry. Whence Norris derived his early notion of modern society as ruled by lords of finance and the machine must remain a speculation. The muckraking era was far in the future. Attacking the methods of big business lacked the respectability it has since achieved.[2] American fiction since the Civil War had piped an occasional note of social criticism,[3] but that note was drowned in the general roar of applause and self-gratulation raised by a nation rapidly growing in population and wealth and moving confidently into its place as a world power.

But, whatever Norris' inspiration, the incipient social moralist glimpsed in the lines of *Yvernelle* was soon obscured by the college man. Norris became conscious of his position as a gentleman, a sportsman, and a member of the upper classes. The world looked very well to him just as it was. He joined a "good" fraternity, wore his well-cut clothes with an air, and cultivated the role of a regular fellow. "There are three things," he announced, "every man, by virtue of his sex, must know all about, and

[2] See Gustavus Myers' account of his difficulties in obtaining a publisher for his critical *History of the Great American Fortunes* as late as 1909; what was wanted was eulogy, not criticism, no matter how well supported by documentary evidence. One eminent publisher wrote: "The most interesting point about it, commercially, would be its bearing on the idea of American achievement and the suggestion to the ambitious man of today as to how great fortunes have been made—and I know this is by no means the interesting part to you" (Preface to the 1936 edition, New York, The Modern Library).

[3] See Edward E. Cassady, "Muckraking in the Gilded Age," *American Literature*, May 1941. Professor Cassady believes, like Professor W. F. Taylor, that too much has been made of the literary indifference of the Gilded Age to contemporary evils. See W. F. Taylor, "That Gilded Age!" in *Sewanee Review*, January 1937.

must never under any circumstances be afraid of; these are firearms, women, and horses." He affected the aristocratic disdain of one of his feudal barons for what he called the *canaille,* and wished that all radicals might be "drowned on one raft." The whole record of his life during these college years leaves the impression of a certain hard, brassy contempt and arrogance lurking beneath his amiability and his good manners.

It was during his first year at the University of California that the work of Kipling burst on him with the brilliance of a revelation. It became clear to him that civilization was the peculiar property of that branch of the Teutonic race known as Anglo-Saxon. History is only the story of how the Anglo-Saxons carried civilization—on the sword's point—westward around the world against the opposition of "lesser breeds without the law." He wrote in defense of hazing in the universities: "One good fight will do more for a boy than a year of schooling. . . . . it wakes in him that fine, reckless arrogance, that splendid, brutal, bullying spirit that is the Anglo-Saxon's birthright . . . ."[4] Football became for him the type of the Anglo-Saxon virtues in action, and he wrote a story ("Travis Hallett's Halfback," in *Collected Writings*) to show critics of the sport "that the same qualities that make a good football man would make a good soldier; and a good soldier, sir, is a man good enough to be any girl's husband."

During his sojourn in South Africa, after college, in 1895–96, he was vastly excited by the imminence of the British seizure of the Transvaal. In Johannesburg at the time of the Jameson raid he was the admiring guest of John Hays Hammond, American mining engineer and

<hr />

[4] Walker, *Frank Norris: A Biography* (copyright 1932, Doubleday, Doran & Company, Inc.), pp. 46, 88, 66.

able abettor of the international banditries of Cecil Rhodes, the "big fish," as Norris called him, who would swallow up the little stupid ox-like Boers and thus demonstrate once more the supremacy of the Anglo-Saxon. An agricultural economy wherein each man "grow[s] only just so much produce as suffices for [his] own wants," and is content with "his four or five farm buildings of mud and corrugated iron, his Transvaal tobacco . . . . his rifle . . . . and his bullock wagon,"[5] appeared to him ridiculous and destined to give place to the more energetic Anglo-Saxon profit economy.

But if the Anglo-Saxon is superior in conquest he is also superior in the humane virtues. He may be filled with a fine brutal arrogance, but he does not know how to be wantonly cruel. That is left for people of inferior, Mediterranean stock, as appears from a scene in Book II of *The Octopus* (chapter vi)—the scene of the rabbit drive. The entire countryside makes a holiday of it. Men, women, and children take part. On foot, on horseback, in buggies and wagons they form themselves into a vast semicircle. As they close in slowly, rabbits, more and more numerous, start up before them till nothing is to be seen ahead but "a wilderness of agitated ears, white tails and twinkling legs." At length the animals are driven into the corral prepared for them, where they form a mass three or four feet deep—thousands, tens of thousands of squirming, leaping, gray-furred bodies. It now becomes necessary to kill them. Men step into the enclosure, armed with clubs: "Blindly, furiously, they struck and struck. The Anglo-Saxon spectators round about drew back in disgust, but the hot, degenerated blood of Portuguese, Mexican, and mixed Spaniard boiled up in excitement at this wholesale slaughter."

[5] *Collected Writings*, p. 231.

It is the Anglo-Saxons, however, who have organized the drive; and to chloroform the unfortunate rabbits would have been a little impracticable.

In an article published in *The World's Work* for February 1902 Norris developed at some length what may be called his theory of history. The race impulse of the Anglo-Saxons has always been toward a western frontier. When that impulse was checked by the shores of the Atlantic, it swept back upon itself in the form of the Crusades. But these were only a temporary diversion; "all through the Middle Ages we were peeking and prying into the western horizon, trying to reach it, to run it down, and the queer tales about Vineland and that storm-driven Viking's ship would not down." With the discovery of the New World the movement surged forward again, apparently to be stopped once more after three centuries, this time by the Pacific. But not so. Dewey at Manila showed the westward march still under way, and it was not till United States Marines landed in China during the Boxer affair in 1900 that the circle was complete and the frontier gone at last.

Is this all? Will the restless energy of the Anglo-Saxons (for Anglo-Saxons we may read Americans) subside after so many centuries? According to Norris, by no means. As once before when momentarily halted it will roll back upon itself in the other direction. Let the Old World and the East now look to themselves: "we are now come into a changed time and the great word of our century is no longer War, but Trade." The new leaders are not Richard Cœur de Lions and Count Baldwins but men like Andrew Carnegie, who "would have been first on the ground before Jerusalem, would have built the most ingenious siege-engine and have hurled the first cask of Greek-fire over the walls"; or men like the new Baldwin, whose weapons are locomotives instead of mangonels. The conditions may have changed, but the old spirit of conquest marks the new enterprise. "Competition and conquest are words easily interchangeable . . . ." The commercial invasion of England has already begun. The scouts of American trade have even crossed Europe and pressed deep into Asia.

> Is it too huge a conception [Norris asks hopefully], too inordinate an idea to say that the American conquest of England is but . . . . an affair of outposts preparatory to the real maneuver that shall embrace Europe, Asia, the whole of the Old World? Why not?[6]

It is a breath-taking prospect, but why not, indeed? Many were asking the same question.

Beneath his simplifications and the picturesque exaggerations of his rhetoric Norris shows nevertheless a genuine perception. He sensed correctly the direction in which American industrial capitalism was moving: toward the competitive struggle for world markets. And he saw that the new turn was owing (in part, at least) to the disappearance of our western frontier, which had absorbed all energies since the Civil War.

In *The Octopus* he had painted a large and vigorous picture of industrial exploitation, of the corruption of politics and journalism by financial interest, and of the ruin that overtakes the defeated in the economic struggle. The article in *The World's Work* (published two years later, and while he was still engaged in the writing of *The Pit*), taken by itself and regarded as his maturest view, would hardly indicate that he looked upon the ways of a middle-class industrial society with any other feeling than that of

---

[6] "The Frontier Gone at Last," in *The Responsibilities of the Novelist* (copyright 1901, 1902, 1903, Doubleday, Doran & Company, Inc.), pp. 71, 74, 77.

satisfaction. This suggests at once the contradictions that we have found to mark other aspects of his work. It is less accurate to attribute to him the development of social ideas than to say that certain more or less critical attitudes grew up in him side by side with his attitude of acceptance and without ever replacing the latter.

The social implications of *McTeague* are negligible. It is a study of lower middle-class lives by an observer who stands outside. He is a very sharp observer, it is true, and his artist's imagination enables him to realize wretchedness with a painful accuracy. But the sufferings of Trina are due mainly to her own avarice, and the degradation of McTeague to mischance and his own stupidity, for none of which society can well be held responsible. If any attitude is revealed, it is unsympathetic toward social criticism, as may be seen in the slight instance of Marcus Schouler's absurd railings against capitalists.

Again, in *Vandover and the Brute* Vandover's descent through the various stages of poverty to the lowest depths of misery and even hunger is pictured with extraordinary realism. Vandover, however, is the victim of a strange disease, of the weakness of his own character, and of his passion for gambling, although Charlie Geary (who swindles him in conformity with his dog-eat-dog philosophy) contributes to his misfortunes.

Ross Wilbur of *Moran* and Condy Rivers and Travis Bessemer of *Blix* are of the same well-to-do middle-class world to which Vandover belonged. Wilbur has the contemptuous feeling for the unemployed common among the well-dressed; along the waterfront he remarks "caulkers and ship chandlers' men looking—not too earnestly—for jobs." His adventures at sea teach him to scorn lives of well-ordered ease, but this is because they are out of touch with the "great, simple, and primitive emotions," not because his yachting friends are idle at others' expense. Travis (or Blix, as she is called) feels vaguely that her life has been useless, thinks she will "study something," and renounces teas and functions, but not as a result of reading *Progress and Poverty* or *Looking Backward*. In these novels Norris is not interested in the economic relations of class with class.

The point at which he first came into conflict with a business civilization, permeated through all ranks by utilitarian ideals, was the point where it touches the arts. The fact that he began as a painter is important in several ways. The significant thing here is that it provides a clue to the understanding of how he became a sociological novelist. The fiction writer (particularly if he be a purveyor of popular entertainment) may escape collision with middle-class prejudices toward the artist, the poet to a less extent, the painter almost never. His wares are less in demand; his activity seems especially remote from practical life; and tradition has pictured him, even more than the poet, as a queer fish. From critical reflections on the status of the artist (whether painter, poet, or novelist) in a commercial-industrial society, it is no difficult transition to a broader criticism which will embrace the economic and political life of such a society as well. Many have come to radical social doctrines by the same route, as Ruskin, Morris, and Oscar Wilde bear witness. Today young men have traveled from the left bank of the Seine to the left in politics.

Norris' early ambition to be a painter ran squarely into the opposition of his father, who damned art in his own peculiar terms as "thimble-head bobism," and sent his son off to the Boys' High School in San Francisco to train for business. Norris came to see that his own experience was not unique. Years later he wrote:

From the very first the average intelligent American boy is trained . . . . with a view to entering a business life. If the specialization of his faculties along artistic lines ever occurs at all it begins only when the boy is past the formative period. . . . . The boy who is to become a business man finds, the moment he goes to school, a whole vast machinery of training made ready for his use, ... not only . . . . education . . . . but the whole scheme of modern civilization works in his behalf. No one ever heard of obstacles thrown in the way of the boy who announces for himself a money-making career; while for the artist . . . . education, environment, the trend of civilization are not merely indifferent, but openly hostile and inimical. One hears only of those men who surmount —and at what cost to their artistic powers—those obstacles. How many thousands are there who succumb unrecorded![7]

He saw also the inescapable paradox and tragedy of the life devoted exclusively to money-making in the expectation of a future enjoyment of the less material sweets of existence. Vandover's father, during a lifetime in business, has made money; at the age of sixty he comes out to San Francisco to retire and spend his last years in the quiet enjoyment of those things which he has never had time for. Travel, music, books, pictures, a hobby—all are within his reach. But he cannot grasp them. He "discovered that he had lost the capacity for enjoying anything but the business itself . . . . he found himself . . . . forced again into the sordid round of business as the only escape from the mortal *ennui* . . . . that preyed upon him during every leisure hour of the day."[8]

The training Norris received at the Julien Academy in

---

[7] "Novelists to Order—While You Wait," in *The Responsibilities of the Novelist,* p. 130.

[8] *Vandover and the Brute* (Doubleday, Doran & Company, Inc., 1928), p. 6.

Paris, where his tutors were such men as Fleury, Lefebvre, and Bouguereau, made him on his return home peculiarly sensitive to evidences of the prevailing American taste in arts and decoration. He makes the familiar jibe of the sophisticated at the ignorant who always say so confidently, "I don't know anything about art, but I know what I like." In two scenes, one almost the exact copy of the other, he puts this cliché into the mouth of Trina in *McTeague* and of Bessie Laguna (a vulgar little chit of the shopgirl type) in *Vandover*. Trina and the dentist view the pictures at the Mechanics' Fair:

> She knew that she liked the "Ideal Heads," lovely girls with flow-ing straw-colored hair and immense, upturned eyes. These always had for title, "Reverie," or "An Idyl," or "Dreams of Love."
> "I think those are lovely, don't you, Mac?"[9]

Trina and Bessie are poor folk without education, and perhaps no more is to be expected from them. But at the other end of the economic scale stands Jadwin, qualified by his wealth to mingle with the "best people" of Chicago. So far, however, as his understanding of art and literature is concerned, he stands shoulder to shoulder with the two girls at the Mechanics' Fair, admiring "a bunch of yellow poppies painted on velvet and framed in gilt." What then of Laura Dearborn? She has a genteel New England back-ground and a genteel education. But Corthell finds her taste callow and unformed. She ignores an American prod-uct because it is American (especially if it is Western American), and pays deference to European fashions, to whatever is considered "the thing." Very tactfully Corthell undertakes her enlightenment. As they stand before the paintings in Jadwin's private gallery, he points out the

[9] *McTeague* (Doubleday, Doran & Company, Inc., 1899, 1927), p. 198.

obviousness of Bouguereau's "Bathing Nymphs." " 'But,'
she faltered, 'I thought that Bouguereau was considered the
greatest—one of the greatest—his wonderful flesh tints,
the drawing, and colouring—' " Corthell then turns to another canvas, a small landscape, to reveal its superior qualities. " 'Oh, that one,' said Laura. 'We bought that here in
America . . . . I never noticed it much, I'm afraid'." In
music her favorites are Verdi and Gounod. Corthell plays
for her at the great organ the "Appassionata" sonata, ex-
pounding skillfully its theme and mood as he proceeds.
It is a revelation to Laura, for we are told she has an "intuitive quickness" of understanding. But she is appalled,
a little snobbishly, at her own shortcomings; "she was
ashamed and confused at her ignorance of those things
which Corthell tactfully assumed that she knew as a matter of course. . . . . Ah, but she would make amends now.
No more Verdi and Bouguereau. She would get rid of the
'Bathing Nymphs.' Never, never again would she play the
'Anvil Chorus.' "[10] Thus from top to bottom Norris finds
crudities and deficiencies in middle-class society on the side
of the arts.

He has left us a number of portraits of the American
business man, the capitalist, some merely sketched in a few
lines, others solidly painted in at full length like that of
Jadwin. Most are unflattering, but his critical awareness of
the cultural poverty of the type never succeeded in detach-
ing itself from a certain admiration for this masterful and
energetic breed. They are of the same stuff as the old con-
querors, such as Richard the Lion Heart. If that doughty
monarch were alive today he would be a " 'leading representative of the Amalgamated Steel Companies,' and doubt

[10] Frank Norris, *The Pit* (Doubleday, Doran & Company, Inc., 1903,
1921), pp. 247–48, 250–51.

140

not . . . . that he would . . . . underbid his Manchester rivals in the matter of bridge-girders."[11] Craig V. Campbell, of the Hercules Wrought Steel Company, who is active in financing Bennett's second expedition to the Arctic, is filled with a rather blatant patriotism, feels "a little proud that God allowed him to be born in the United States," and believes it the duty of America to beat Britain to the Pole, in an American-built ship every bolt of which should be "forged in American foundries" (presumably those of the Hercules Wrought Steel Company). In the interview which takes place between him and Bennett and Lloyd (present also is Tremlidge, a wealthy newspaper owner) Campbell, without any very obvious occasion for doing so, launches into a kind of lengthy apology for his career as an industrialist and man of wealth. He begins with a thrust at the author of *Progress and Poverty,* admitting facetiously that he and Tremlidge "have more money than Henry George believes to be right." He then enlarges upon the benefactions which men of his kind are accustomed to make, and upon their patronage of arts and learning, and concludes:

but, for the lives of us, we can feel only a mild interest in the pictures and statues, and museums and colleges, though we go on . . . . because we think that somehow it is right for us to do it. I'm afraid we are men more of action than of art, literature, and the like.[12]

But it is plain from the context that though Norris may laugh at the Philistine he admires the magnate.

From the beginning, then, in his character as artist, he viewed middle-class industrial society with a critical eye. But up to the time when he had completed his fifth novel

[11] *The Responsibilities of the Novelist,* p. 74.
[12] *A Man's Woman,* p. 271.

141

(*A Man's Woman*) he had no quarrel with the economic structure of that society, no concern with the problems of political corruption, of rich and poor; no concern with inequalities and injustices. His disdain for the *canaille* and his contempt for radicals show that he identified his social and economic interests with those of the class into which he was born.

In the years from 1892 to 1899 the public mind was agitated by the following movements or events which could not have failed to obtrude themselves on the notice of the most indifferent; and Norris was not, either in theory or in practice, an aloof littérateur: the Homestead strike, the Populist assault on the money power, the Pullman strike, the rise of William Jennings Bryan, and the free-silver crusade. Here was drama enough to satisfy the most avid. Yet not a whisper of these occurrences is heard in the five novels, twenty-odd short stories, and numerous articles which he wrote during this period. Of the concurrent imperialism and truculent braggadocio indulged in by some of the best minds there was on the other hand sufficient, as we have seen. Few could have predicted in 1899, on the basis of the work he had already published, the turn that Norris would take in his next novel, *The Octopus*. Few would have recognized in the accusing tones of such a passage as the following the accents of the debonair youth of a few years earlier, exultantly proclaiming the struggle for existence and nature red in tooth and claw:

You, the aristocrats, who demand the fine linen and the purple in your fiction; you, the sensitive, the delicate, who will associate with your Romance only so long as she wears a silken gown. You will not follow her to the slums . . . . If haply she should call to you from the squalour of a dive . . . . crying: "Look! listen! This, too, is life. These, too, are my children! Look at them, know them and,

knowing, help!" Should she call thus you would stop your ears
. . . .[13]

What effected the transition? We lack exact information. Was Norris' turn to the sociological novel the cumulative effect of influences long at work beneath the surface, influences of which he himself was scarcely cognizant? Or can it be attributed to some more definite circumstance? His new-found sympathy for the underdog in the economic struggle may have been simply the outgrowth of the researches he was obliged to make in preparation for the writing of his novel. The subject he had chosen of necessity led him to examine, perhaps for the first time, the economic machinery of society. His experience may well have been like Presley's. Presley, serious and intense by nature, wants nothing but to write his romantic poem of the West. But gradually he finds his sympathies enlisted on the side of the ranchers till "at times his hatred of the railroad shook him like a crisp and withered reed." He puts away his epic as of little importance, his Milton, Tennyson, Browning, Homer. He "addressed himself to Mill, Malthus, Young, Poushkin, Henry George, Schopenhauer. He attacked the subject of Social Inequality with unbounded enthusiasm."[14] If Norris, however, ever read these or similar writers, no hint of his doing so exists, though this is no conclusive argument against his having dipped, at least, into sociological and economic literature.

Certain events in his private life may have contributed to give him a new insight into what it means to maintain

[13] *The Responsibilities of the Novelist* (Doubleday, Doran & Company, Inc., 1901, 1902, 1903), pp. 218–19.

[14] Frank Norris, *The Octopus* (Doubleday, Doran & Company, Inc., 1901, 1929), p. 307.

life on a decently human level in a competitive world. The divorce of his parents in 1894 and the subsequent re-marriage of his father destroyed his expectations of inheriting a fortune of nearly a million dollars. Thenceforth he was dependent on his own resources, for he made no claims on his father nor did his father acknowledge any further obligations to him, leaving his fortune on his death in 1900 to his second wife. Norris' salary during two years (1898–99) with *McClure's* was fifty dollars a month. At the time of his marriage in 1900 his income (salary and royalties) was a hundred and twenty-five dollars a month. Till the success of *The Octopus* his royalties were negligible.

One item, however, among the probable influences that made *The Octopus* a contribution to the literature of social justice, seems certain: Norris was much impressed by Edwin Markham's *The Man with the Hoe.* The astounding success of Markham's poem (first published in the *San Francisco Examiner,* January 15, 1899) is one of the noteworthy incidents in the literary history of the 'nineties. Without disparagement to *The Man with the Hoe,* it is hardly conceivable that it would meet with similar acclaim today. It arrived at the precise moment fitted to receive it. It seemed to crystallize the long-gathering exasperation and sense of wrong of a whole people beginning to feel that something had gone awry with the fine promise of its democracy; beginning to feel the weight and pressure of the industrial-financial order that had been gathering its powers during the preceding four decades; beginning to understand, as Norris put it, that "an evil tree was growing in the midst of the garden." Presley's poem, "The Toilers," in its inspiration by a celebrated French painting, in its first appearance in a daily newspaper, and in the storm of praise, ridicule, and abuse which it raised, offers an exact parallel to the history of *The Man with the Hoe.*

In *The Octopus* the issue is squarely joined: it is organized wealth against the people. It is Presley who is charged with the responsibility of bearing Norris' "message." Presley views the whole drama of the struggle with the octopus, from the first sly stirring of the monster's tentacles to the final relentless contortion with which it destroys its last victim. He is present at every crisis, witnesses all the agonies, suffers them all vicariously, burns with indignation, and emerges at last, solitary, ineffectual, a dreamer, consoling himself with the thought that the wheat is on its way to feed the starving scarecrows of India and that good can never die—though he has seen it rather roughly handled. But if he is the vehicle of the author's emotions and ideas, Norris maintains toward him at the same time a certain detachment, freely revealing his weaknesses, his confusion of thought, his moral bewilderment. Always Norris strives to keep to what he calls "the larger view," to embrace within his scheme of great impersonal forces both oppressors and oppressed.

In the alignment, however, of his opposing powers, he shows a faulty analysis. The People (always spelled with a capital letter) are represented by the ranchers of the San Joaquin. Who are these men? They are themselves capitalists, and on no small scale. Like feudal lords they command vast areas of ten thousand acres and more. They have great sums invested in equipment and machinery—whole batteries of plows, seed drills, harvesters. They are employers of labor with scores, hundreds of men in their pay. Magnus Derrick has numerous tenants whom he turns off at his convenience. Annixter is a harsh and arbitrary master, as seen in his treatment of Delaney. He feels the agricultural employer's antipathy to the city laborer, the union man. Pausing to inspect the progress of the work on his magnificent new barn, he asks a foreman when the structure will be completed; "a precious long time you've been at it," he declares. The foreman pleads interruption on account of rain. "Oh, rot the rain!" exclaims Annixter impatiently. "*I* work in the rain. You and your unions make me sick" (p. 172).

A chance remark reveals to Presley in a flash the spirit of the gambler and individualist in Magnus Derrick. The ranchers are expecting a decision from the state railroad commission reducing freight rates (an expectation in which they are of course disappointed, since the railroad by its control of state politics virtually owns the commission). "And suppose," says Lyman Derrick, "the next commission is a railroad board, and reverses all our figures?" His father replies: "By then it will be too late. We will, all of us, have made our fortunes by then." It is the spirit of the seeker after sudden wealth, the spirit which has governed the whole economic development of the nation, which has ridden roughshod over all sense of social obligation either to the present or the future:

For all his public spirit, for all his championship of justice and truth, his respect for law, Magnus remained the gambler, willing to play for colossal stakes, to hazard a fortune on the chance of winning a million. It was the true California spirit that found expression through him, the spirit of the West . . . . It was in this frame of mind that Magnus and the multitude of other ranchers of whom he was a type, farmed their ranches. They had no love for their land. . . . . They worked their ranches as a quarter of a century before they had worked their mines. To husband the resources of their marvellous San Joaquin, they considered niggardly, ... To get all there was out of the land, to squeeze it dry . . . . seemed their policy. When, at last, the land [was] worn out, ... they would invest their money in something else; by then, they would all have made fortunes. They did not care. "After us the deluge."[15]

The real struggle is between two types of economy: the one the agricultural, old and ready to pass from the scene; the other, the industrial, new and destined to dominate the future. In the press of the conflict some of the little people are crushed, people like Dyke (one-time locomotive engineer on the railroad, who tries farming on his own account) and his mother and child, or like Hooven (Magnus' German tenant) and his wife and daughters. With the great wheat growers it is not a question of making a living; it is a question of running a large-scale business for profit. In other circumstances Magnus might have been Shelgrim, head of a vast railroad system, in which position he might have found himself applying the principle announced by S. Behrman to Dyke: Dyke has just learned that he has been ruined by a rise in freight charges. Promised a rate of two cents on his hops, he is confronted without warning by one of five cents; but he has already contracted to sell his crop at a certain price. Bitterly he demands to know, "What's your rule? What are you guided by?" S. Behrman, suddenly red with anger, "emphasized each word of his reply with a tap of one forefinger on the counter before him: 'All—the—traffic—will—bear' " (pp. 349-50).

The novel raises a question respecting the means to be employed in the war against social injustice. Is it legitimate to use the weapons of the enemy, to fight fire with fire? Is fraud justifiable? Is violence allowable? In the opinion of Granville Hicks, Norris leaves unsolved the

[15] *The Octopus* (Doubleday, Doran & Company), pp. 298-99.

problems of the use of fraud and of the use of violence. Let us examine the facts.

In the early stage of their contest with the railroad Osterman frankly proposes that the ranchers (or a secret committee of them composed of the leading figures, Annixter, the Derricks, Broderson) by means of bribery seat their own men on the commission. The corporation has checkmated them at every turn. To Osterman's mind all legitimate means have been exhausted. He realizes that the ranchers, if they adopt his scheme, run the risk of seeing their commissioners bought over by the railroad at a higher price or of seeing the hoped-for rate reductions nullified by the subservient courts. But there is no other recourse; they, too, must bribe. Magnus at first repels the idea with stern indignation. But he is placed in a painful dilemma. If the plan succeeds without him, will he refuse to participate in the benefits? Gradually, reluctantly, against every instinct and the fearful pleadings of his wife, he yields; he listens to the specious words of Annixter (p. 184): "But, Governor, standards have changed since your time; everybody plays the game now as we are playing it—the most honourable men. You can't play it any other way, and, pshaw! if the right wins out in the end, that's the main thing." In the dramatic scene which concludes the chapter on the barn dance (and at the same time the first book of the novel) Magnus accepts the leadership of the defensive league spontaneously formed by the ranchers under spur of the news, at that moment received, of the railroad's latest, most dangerous move. In doing so he also tacitly commits himself to the fraudulent tactics of the secret committee. It is a grievous mistake, a fatal error by which the cause of the ranchers suffers in the end; and for Magnus himself it is the source of his personal

148

tragedy, a greater calamity than his material ruin, greater than the death of his son Harran.

Osterman's plan succeeds up to a point. The wheat-growers elect their men to the commission. By a crushing irony, as it proves, one of these men is Lyman Derrick, elder of Magnus' two sons, a lawyer with political ambitions, suave, deceitful, thoroughly corrupt, a born intriguer. "He belonged to the new school, wherein objects were attained not by orations before senates and assemblies, but by sessions of committees, caucuses, compromises and expedients" (p. 75). The railroad buys him with ease, and the ranchers are once more betrayed, their own dishonesty rebounding upon them. The corporation has been perfectly informed throughout of every move of its opponents. After the killing of Osterman, Annixter, and the others in the battle with the deputies, a great crowd of excited farmers and townsmen gathers in the Bonneville opera house. S. Behrman and the other local henchmen of the railroad deem this the strategic moment; and, as Magnus begins to address the meeting, by a preconcerted arrangement they cause to be thrown among the audience copies of the corporation-subsidized newspaper containing a full account of Derrick's part in the fraudulent election. Magnus stands before his friends and all those who have trusted him a disgraced and broken man. Thus the ranchers are outwitted at every turn, public sympathy is alienated from them, their league breaks up, and their cause is hopelessly lost.

Norris, writes Granville Hicks, "wavers between the view that his [Magnus'] surrender is ignoble and the view that it is inevitable."[16] This appears to be true, for Magnus

---

[16] Granville Hicks, *The Great Tradition* (New York, 1933), p. 173. Quoted by permission of The Macmillan Company, publishers.

is said to be "hopelessly caught in the mesh . . . . caught in the current of events, and hurried along he knew not where," and again it is said that he refuses to heed the voice of his better nature. Presley, however, does not blame Magnus, but regards the moral catastrophe that overtakes him as one more crime to be charged against the railroad.[17] Mr. Hicks complains that Magnus' ethical dilemma is unsolved. But a dilemma is by definition a situation in which either course of action presented will lead to a bad result. It is difficult to see what else Norris could have done. Who can deny that in the world of actuality wrong often seems, as it seemed to Magnus (pp. 291–92), "indissolubly knitted into the texture of Right," no matter how neatly these qualities are isolated in the categories of the moralist. Norris' only error was in blaming Magnus; if he must blame anybody he would have done better to blame Shelgrim, who was faced with no such moral dilemma.

As regards the use of violence, none of the characters is put in quite the hard position of Magnus with respect to the use of fraud. The act of the ranchers in defending themselves against the deputies will hardly be condemned. With Presley it is a little different. Filled with grief and rage by the killing of his friends, to which he has been a witness, he spends the whole of the following night pacing his room, or filling the pages of his journal with passionate rushing words: "Oh, come now and try your theories upon us . . . . Oh, talk to *us* now of the 'rights of Capital,' . . . ." And he throws himself across his bed "vowing with inarticulate cries that neither S. Behrman nor Shelgrim should ever live to consummate their triumph" (pp. 538, 540). On the succeeding day, at the indigna-

17 *The Octopus,* pp. 291–92, 187–88, 569, 650.

tion meeting in the Bonneville opera house, carried out of himself, he leaps on the stage and pours out a flood of incendiary eloquence, filled with references to the untimely fate of rulers and painting a lurid picture of revolt (p. 552):

> Liberty is *not* a crowned goddess, beautiful, in spotless garments, ... Liberty is the Man In the Street, a terrible figure, ... fouled with the mud and ordure of the gutter, bloody, rampant, brutal, yelling curses, in one hand a smoking rifle, in the other, a blazing torch.

There is tremendous applause, but the audience finds the speech too literary, and postpones the revolution to some indefinite date in the future.

Presley, however, is ready for some desperate act. On the previous afternoon, rushing out of the room where Harran Derrick had just died from a bullet through the lungs, he had encountered Caraher, the anarchist saloon-keeper, in the crowd gathered round the scene of the battle with the deputies. Grasping the publican by the hand he had said (p. 535): "I've been wrong all the time. The League is wrong. All the world is wrong. You are the only one of us all who is right. I'm with you from now on. *By God, I too, I'm a Red!*"

Caraher's wife has been accidentally killed by Pinkertons in an encounter between these mercenaries and striking employees of the railroad. As a result he is filled with hatred for the corporation and frankly advocates violence in dealing with it. "Ah, yes," he tells Dyke when the latter has been beggared by the road, "it's all very well for your middle class to preach moderation. . . . . That talk is just what the Trust wants to hear. It ain't frightened of that. There's one thing only it does listen to, one thing it is frightened of—the people with dynamite in their hands,—six inches of plugged gaspipe. *That* talks" (p. 357).

Inflamed by Caraher's words and maddened by the wrongs he has seen committed, Presley, on leaving the opera house, takes a bomb of the saloonkeeper's manufacture and hurls it through S. Behrman's dining-room window, just as that worthy is sitting down to his evening meal. But S. Behrman appears to be beyond the reach of human vengeance, for he emerges from the wreck of the room unscathed. He is reserved for poetic justice in more ingenious and picturesque form. But when Presley's blood has cooled he is filled with horror and remorse for what he has done, and trembles to think by what a narrow margin he has escaped the commission of murder. Later he reflects (p. 620) that Caraher is "a bad man, a plague spot in the world of the ranchers, poisoning the farmers' bodies with alcohol and their minds with discontent."

By thus repudiating violence, as he repudiates the dishonest means to which the ranchers resort, Norris provides, in fact, an answer to the question of their use. But from his assumed position of detachment it was not his business to "solve" the problem—either to sanction or to repudiate. The only way in which he could have avoided involvement was to stand unmoved on the neutral ground of his naturalism; but this, from time to time, he abandons in order to take part in the contest. In Presley's interview with Shelgrim we shall see if the author is consistent in his partisanship.

Shelgrim is president of the Pacific & Southwestern, a sinister figure who is seen only on this one occasion, but whose influence is felt in the remotest corners of his vast empire. When he pulls the strings his puppets—S. Behrman, Genslinger the editor of the Bonneville *Mercury*,

Ruggles the land agent of the road in the San Joaquin, the railroad commission, judges on the bench—all move to do his will. Presley is prepared to find a monster. He finds a man of about seventy, of massive frame and equally massive composure, and a little shabby as to dress. While the poet waits to receive the attention of the great man, he overhears a conversation between him and his assistant manager concerning an employee of the road, a book-keeper, a man competent at his task when sober, but given to periods of drunkenness. The assistant manager reminds his chief that the man in question has been repeatedly given another chance; but his latest offense is more outrageous than ever, and the assistant urges his dismissal. After a long silence during which he appears to be lost in the contemplation of matters remote from the present business, Shelgrim speaks (p. 573):

"Tentell has a family, wife and three children. . . . . How much do we pay him?"

"One hundred and thirty."

"Let's double that, or say two hundred and fifty. Let's see how that will do."

"Why—of course—if you say so, but really, Mr. Shelgrim—"

"Well, we'll try that, anyhow."

He then turns to his visitor (whose name he recognizes at once as that of the author of "The Toilers") and delivers him a lecture, first on artistic expression and then on economics. He has read Presley's poem and he has seen the famous French painting which inspired it; "of the two, I like the picture better," he says. "You might just as well have kept quiet. There's only one best way to say anything. And what has made the picture of 'The Toilers' great is that the artist said in it the *best* that could be said on the subject." Presley is astounded. All his preconceived ideas begin to scatter. Instead of "a terrible man

153

of blood and iron" he finds "a sentimentalist and an art critic." "He began to see that here was the man not only great, but large; many-sided, of vast sympathies, ..." When Shelgrim learns that Presley is recently from the Derrick ranch, Los Muertos, in Tulare County, he looks him fixedly in the eye and says: "I suppose you believe I am a grand old rascal." The poet stammers, and the industrial Titan proceeds to enlighten him on the economics of railroading and wheat-growing (p. 576):

. . . . *"Railroads build themselves.* Where there is a demand sooner or later there will be a supply. Mr. Derrick, does he grow his wheat? The Wheat grows itself. What does he count for? Does he supply the force? What do I count for? Do I build the Railroad? . . . . The Wheat is one force, the Railroad, another, and there is the law that governs them—supply and demand . . . . Blame conditions, not men."

"But—but," faltered Presley, "you are the head, you control the road."

"You are a very young man. Control the road! Can I stop it? I can go into bankruptcy if you like. But otherwise if I run my road, as a business proposition, I can do nothing . . . . Can your Mr. Derrick stop the Wheat growing? He can burn his crop, or he can give it away, or sell it for a cent a bushel . . . . but otherwise his Wheat must grow. Can anyone stop the Wheat? Well, then no more can I stop the Road."

Presley allows himself to be completely fogged by these resounding sophistries, which in his ear "rang with the clear reverberation of truth" but which ought not to have deceived a schoolboy. He permits himself to be confused by the generosity of Shelgrim toward the drunken book-keeper, thus tumbling into the "good man" fallacy which Macaulay so brilliantly exploded in connection with the domestic virtues of Charles I.

But Shelgrim's generosity is merely capricious. It falls where the occasion for it comes immediately under his eye. Dyke has been a faithful servant of the road; he has even refused to strike against it, continuing to run his train at some danger to his life. But he is only one of thousands whom Shelgrim has never seen, and when it is deemed expedient to cut wages he suffers along with all other employees; when he protests he is let go without any show of reluctance.

Shelgrim cannot hide so easily behind his impersonal forces. When he bids Presley "blame conditions, not men," he offers us an opponent very slippery in the grasp. Conditions, like principles, like ideals, manifest themselves only through men. Too easily, "bad" conditions become an abstraction like sin. One is tempted to believe here that Ambrose Bierce was right when he wrote:

Sin is not at all dangerous to society; what does all the mischief is the sinner. . . . . I would no more attack [crime] than I would attack an isosceles triangle . . . . My chosen enemy must be something that has a skin for my switch . . . . I have no quarrel with abstractions; so far as I know they are all good citizens.[18]

The naturalists laid out a very severe course when by committing themselves to determinism and consequent moral aloofness they attempted to deny themselves the luxury of blaming wrongdoers. Not to blame is too much for human nature; not to believe that effects must follow their causes is too much for human reason. We must continue to face the hard saying of Scripture: "It must needs be that offences come, but woe unto him by whom the offence cometh." It need not surprise that Norris should blame some of his characters, but only that he should be so maladroit as to blame the wrong ones.

If we are to accept Shelgrim's interpretation of events,

[18] *The Shadow on the Dial and Other Essays* (San Francisco: A. M. Robertson, 1909), pp. 123–24.

the only alternative to bribery, corruption, extortion, and wrecked lives is the bankruptcy of the railroad, a patent absurdity. There is no question of bankruptcy. Harran Derrick knows better. He knows that the road was constructed for fifty-four thousand dollars a mile, but that freight rates and dividends to stockholders are based on a cost of eighty-seven thousand, and on a gross overvaluation of the whole vast property—a trick as common among corporations as brass knuckles among ruffians. He knows that the fine-sounding phrase "a fair return on our investment," which rolls so righteously off the tongue of S. Behrman, conceals all the devious and intricate deceptions of corporation finance.

Norris wants us to believe that the cause of the ranchers is just, wants us to sympathize with them. He puts himself, however, in the position of holding them to account for their lapses from virtue in their struggle with the railroad (though they have been hounded and harried beyond endurance) but at the same time of allowing Shelgrim to take refuge behind the laws of supply and demand, behind "conditions," impersonal forces. When Presley descended to the street after his interview with the great industrialist, his whole scheme of values in disarray, Norris walked arm in arm with him and shared his bewilderment. It is to be suspected that he described his own state when he wrote that Presley, after devouring works on sociology and economics, "emerged from the affair, his mind a confused jumble of conflicting notions, ... raging against injustice and oppression, and with not one sane suggestion as to remedy or redress."

But if, like his ineffectual reformer, he is a bit dazzled by the philosophic splendor of the law of supply and demand, he feels nevertheless a genuine and poignant concern for the poor and outcast. The sore contradiction of poverty in the midst of wealth weighs on his mind, and when he speaks of it he cannot suppress a note of scorn and reproof for the complacently well-fed, the secure, and the smug. So intent is he on driving home this contrast between want and luxury that he prolongs his narrative beyond the dramatic close of the main action in order to record the fate of Mrs. Hooven. After the death of Hooven with the others in the fight at the irrigation ditch, his wife goes to San Francisco in search of work. Her small funds are soon gone and she and the child Hilda are put out of their lodgings into the street. She has not a penny in the world, nor a friend except Presley, who knows not where to seek her. She feels all a countrywoman's bewilderment and terror in the midst of the strangeness and indifference of a great city, where the faces in endless procession reflect, as it seems to her, "every emotion but pity." As she stands helpless on the sidewalk a policeman, for this crime against public order, commands her to move on and threatens her with arrest. Now begins the aimless, hopeless march that leads to her miserable death.

Ah, that *via dolorosa* of the destitute, that *chemin de la croix* of the homeless. Ah, the mile after mile of granite pavement that *must* be, *must* be traversed. Walk they must. Move, they must; onward, forward, whither they cannot tell; why, they do not know. Walk, walk, walk with bleeding feet and smarting joints; walk with aching back and trembling knees; walk, though the senses grow giddy with fatigue, though the eyes droop with sleep, though every nerve, demanding rest, sets in motion its tiny alarm of pain. Death is at the end of that devious, winding maze of paths, crossed and recrossed and crossed again. There is but one goal to the *via dolorosa* . . . .[19]

[19] *The Octopus* (Doubleday, Doran & Company, Inc., 1901, 1929), pp. 594–95.

Meantime Presley, through his aunt, Mrs. Cedarquist, wife of the manufacturer, has been asked to dine at the home of Gerard, one of the vice-presidents of the Pacific & Southwestern, in ignorance, be it said, of the identity of his host till he has reached the door. Again Norris' millionaires are of the first generation, a little raw as yet, still marked by the crudities of the newly rich, essentially vulgar. The women, who sprinkle their conversation with French, coo over Presley. "I have read your poem, of course, ... What a sermon you read us, you dreadful young man," his hostess chides gayly. "I felt that I ought at once to 'sell all that I have and give to the poor,'" she assures him, though she has been successful in resisting this impulse. The magnificent drawing room is minutely described, with its Renaissance cabinets of ebony inlaid with ivory and silver and its brass andirons six feet high for the huge fireplace. Then Presley sits down to a dinner that is a gastronomic masterpiece—course after course: "raw Blue Point oysters, served upon little pyramids of shaved ice," ortolan patties, "*grenadins* of bass and small salmon, the latter stuffed, and cooked in white wine and mushroom liquor," "Londonderry pheasants, escallops of duck, and *rissolettes à la pompadour*," stuffed artichokes. The asparagus, the guests are informed, comes from a particular ranch in the southern part of the state; it is ordered by wire and put on a special train which makes a special stop to take it aboard. "Extravagant, isn't it," the hostess deprecates, "but I simply cannot eat asparagus that has been cut more than a day." Several of the wines are from Gerard's private vineyards in southern France. As Presley sips his Xeres 1815 and looks about at his sumptuous surroundings and the exquisite women seated at the board, he reflects: "It was Wealth, in all its outward and visible forms, the signs of an opulence so great that it need never be husbanded. . . . . For this, then, the farmers paid." He is not entirely satisfied with Shelgrim's explanation, and a sequence of cause and effect seems plain to him which Shelgrim would refuse to accept: "The Railroad might indeed be a force only, which no man could control and for which no man was responsible, but his friends had been killed . . . . because the farmers of the valley were poor, these men were rich." Then a strange fancy enters his mind, a grotesque transformation of the present banquet (p. 608):

It was a half-ludicrous, half-horrible "dog-eat-dog," an unspeakable cannibalism. Harran, Annixter, and Hooven were being devoured there under his eyes. These dainty women, ... with their small fingers and slender necks, suddenly were transfigured in his tortured mind into harpies tearing human flesh.

From time to time Norris interrupts the progress of the feast to follow the ever feebler footsteps of Mrs. Hooven. Four nights she and the child have spent on park benches, shivering with cold, wetted with fog, and surrounded by drunken derelicts. Every day she has begged in the streets, collecting a few dimes and nickels to buy bread and milk for little Hilda. It was by accident that she fell into this last humiliation. A passer-by whom she stopped to ask a direction had misunderstood her and put a quarter in her hand. For three days she herself has eaten nothing but a few apples and a crust of bread rescued from the street. By the night of Mrs. Gerard's dinner she is far gone, wracked by pains and cramps in the stomach, faint and dizzy, hardly able to bear the weight of the sleeping child in her arms. At about the moment when the diners are engaged on their stuffed salmon cooked in white wine and mushroom liquor, or perhaps their Londonderry pheasants, Mrs. Hooven finds on the sidewalk the peeling of a banana:

"Hilda," she cried, "wake oop, leedle girl. See, loog den, dere's somedings to eat. Look den, hey? Dat's goot, ain't it? Zum bunaner."

But it could not be eaten. Decayed, dirty, all but rotting, the stomach turned from the refuse, nauseated.

The dessert, "a wonderful preparation of alternate layers of biscuit glacés, ice cream, and candied chestnuts," arrived at the instant when Mrs. Hooven lay down to die in a vacant lot atop a wind-swept, fog-drenched hill in a thinly peopled part of the city. A pleasant coma stole over her, and gradually she ceased to respond to the frightened pleadings of the child. She was dead. "The gaunt, lean body, with its bony face and sunken eye-sockets, lay back, prone upon the ground, the feet upturned and showing the ragged, worn soles of the shoes, the forehead and gray hair beaded with fog . . . ."

The extended account of Mrs. Hooven's wretched end, contrasted with riches which insult by their very existence, has been called melodramatic. Forming, as it does, a postscript to the principal narrative, it may be regarded as a structural defect. Criticism, however, is forever disconcerted by the fact that a good novel has never been seriously injured by structural defects, any more than a bad one is saved by structural perfection. Critics have raised superior eyebrows at the pathos of the episode. Its pathos is nevertheless sounder than that of a score of scenes in Dickens, or even in some of his less tearful contemporaries. The details are harder, sharper; the tone (except for the *via dolorosa* passage) less emotional.

In *The Octopus* everything is seen from the point of view of the farmers, in their fight against the power of money. In *The Pit* the position is reversed and we are made familiarly at home in the opposing camp, where everything is seen from the point of view of those who wield the power of money. All the characters are either members or satellites of the new aristocracy of wealth created by the rapid industrial and agricultural development of mid-continent America in the years after the Civil War and centered in Chicago, the economic capital of the region. But the "People" of the former novel have here dropped out as one of the antagonists in the drama. The contenders are now financial giants battling for control of the wheat market, the bulls and bears, rending each other with horn and claw. These men neither grow wheat, nor transport wheat, nor mill wheat, nor make bread from wheat, nor do any useful thing with wheat. Now and then they fling a handful to the pigeons which flutter outside the windows of the Board of Trade Building, and this is the only wheat they ever see. Their sole concern is with the buying and selling of wheat which, as wheat, they have no use for and do not want—wheat that is often not yet in existence. The commodity in which they traffic is reduced to an almost intangible state, being represented by nothing more than a series of bookkeeper's entries. At this game, without a shadow of creative activity, without the least contribution to the utility of the wheat as human food, the more fortunate and the shrewder of them may grow rich—those who best master the complicated factors involved: a famine or a drought in some distant quarter of the earth, seasonable rains in some other part, new lands coming under cultivation, the amount of the last year's crop in storage, the state of the market in Liverpool—a score of circumstances that may affect demand or supply. The boldest of them all attempt to corner the market, to gain possession of all the wheat available in order to sell it on their own terms to a world that must have bread.

Of these traders and speculators, gamblers in the food of a nation, the chief is Jadwin. Unlike Shelgrim he is no austere and inscrutable figure, no shadowy presence everywhere felt as the moving power behind events but seldom seen. He is exhibited in a human and sympathetic light with all his foibles and weaknesses; we hear his familiar speech, we see him in his shirtsleeves. Having come out to Chicago in the early days of its remarkable rise, and having entered by mere chance the trade in real estate (another form of nonproductive wealth-getting), he has allowed the natural growth of the city to make him rich. Now and then he makes a little venture in the wheat market, but when the tale begins he has not yet felt the intense fascination of the game.

Jadwin is a generous man. He supports an aunt and a houseful of nephews and nieces; he founds a ward in the Children's Hospital. By an adroit maneuver he restores a fortune to old Hargus, whose business partner, years before, had betrayed and ruined him and whose wits have been enfeebled by his misfortune. With a nice appreciation of poetic justice Jadwin drives the faithless partner, Scannel, into a position where he has no choice but to buy wheat from Jadwin's firm, and Jadwin can dictate the price. Choking with rage, Scannel is forced to disgorge, and Jadwin turns over the money, in his presence, to old Hargus, an outright gift of some five hundred thousand dollars. It is as Mrs. Cressler tells Laura: Jadwin is the "kindliest, biggest-hearted fellow—" Moreover there is a strain of piety in him, of a very practical sort. He has been much influenced by the evangelist Dwight L. Moody.

"The last time I saw Moody," he tells the embarrassed Laura (who is an Episcopalian and likes her religion to be touched with dignity and refinement), "I said, 'Moody, my motto is "not slothful in business, fervent in spirit, praising the Lord" ' . . . . and he said, 'J., good for you; you keep to that. There's no better motto in the world for the American man of business.' "[20] He has applied business principles to the organization of a mission Sunday school on Chicago's West Side, where he himself teaches a class. Having taken charge of a half-dozen thriftless and unflourishing groups always competing with each other, he has, as he puts it (p. 123), "amalgamated them all—a regular trust, just as if they were iron foundries—" Sometimes his generosity pays dividends, as in the instance of the poor boy whom he found in his Bible class and put to work in his office (p. 124): "He does his work so well that I've been able to discharge two other fellows who sat around and watched the clock . . . . so much for taking a good aim when you cast your bread upon the waters." For though he handles millions and can give a fortune to old Hargus (p. 208), "he would put himself to downright inconvenience to save the useless expenditure of a dime—and boast of it."

Shelgrim had evolved a working philosophy to account for the great economic operations in which he was engaged and to justify the part he himself played. Jadwin has no such philosophy. Nor has he learned to think in broad terms, to see the complex relations of wheat trading to the economic life of the nation, to trace the distant results of this gambling (dignified by the name of buying and selling) in the lives of farmers in Nebraska, of factory

[20] *The Pit* (Doubleday, Doran & Company, Inc., 1903, 1921), p. 124.

laborers in Cleveland, of flour-mill workers in Minneapolis, of deckhands on Great Lakes steamers, of millions of people who live as best they can, not because they own but because they labor, and who are of no concern to the voracious parasites in the wheat pit. He does not understand that the social consequences of the exciting and dangerous game into which he presently plunges are, in the main, bad. Norris knows that they are, and as the narrative advances he gives Jadwin an opportunity to acquire the same knowledge. There is no clear evidence, however, that he does. It is true that now and then in critical moments of the struggle he catches a glimpse of the wider significance of what he is about, but he averts his eyes and drives relentlessly ahead. At the end, after the collapse of his corner in wheat, which for a brief time had made him an all-powerful figure, it is not apparent that he has any other feeling than that of having suffered a great and spectacular personal disaster.

The theme that the operations of the pit are socially harmful is introduced casually and without emphasis in the first chapter, when Charles Cressler says of speculation: "it's wrong; the world's food should not be at the mercy of the Chicago wheat pit." Cressler belongs to an older generation. At one time he had made an immense fortune in the pit, only to see the bulk of it swept away by the failure of a corner in wheat which he had held a few days too long. His opinions on speculation are regarded as merely eccentric by Jadwin and his other friends. But when the theme recurs in the fourth chapter it is fully developed in a long speech by Cressler, who addresses his words to Laura while Jadwin listens with an occasional good-natured protest. After asserting that wheat trading is nothing more nor less than gambling (a word which startles Laura, who associates gambling with "depravity of the baser sort"), Cressler continues:

Those fellows in the Pit . . . . don't care in the least about the grain. But there are thousands upon thousands of farmers out here in Iowa and Kansas or Dakota who do, and hundreds of thousands of poor devils in Europe who care even more than the farmer. . . . . It's life or death for either of them. And right between these two comes the Chicago speculator, who raises or lowers the price out of all reason, for the benefit of his pocket. . . . . these gamblers . . . . make the price. They say just how much the peasant shall pay for his loaf of bread. If he can't pay the price he simply starves. And as for the farmer, why it's ludicrous. If I build a house and offer it for sale, I put my own price on it, and if the price offered don't suit me I don't sell. But if I go out here in Iowa and raise a crop of wheat, I've got to sell it, whether I want to or not, at the figure named by some fellows in Chicago. And to make themselves rich, they may make me sell it at a price that bankrupts me.[21]

Such, in Cressler's view, are the general economic results of market speculation. But, he points out, there are yet others—the moral and psychological effects on those who participate in it. It generates in men the lust for easy money, destroys "the taste, the very capacity for legitimate business." Young clerks at seventy-five dollars a month discover that they can make in a few hours (if they are lucky) five hundred or a thousand dollars "without so much as raising a finger"—sums that would take them ten years to save in the normal course. They are fortunate if they do not become such flotsam as Jadwin has

[21] *The Pit*, pp. 129–30. Note Shelgrim's fallacy in trying to draw a parallel between wheat-growing and railroading. Derrick, he tells Presley, like himself, must make a profit if he wishes to remain in business. He, Shelgrim, prefers to remain in business and sets his rates accordingly. But it is not within Derrick's option whether or not he will make a profit, since he cannot set the price of his wheat.

The consequences of speculation for the farmer and laborer are seen even more concretely than in Cressler's speech in the short story "A Deal in Wheat" (in the volume of the same name), apparently a by-product thrown off by Norris during the writing of *The Pit*.

observed in the customers' room at the Board of Trade Building, shabbily dressed men to be found every day slouched in the same chairs, "always with the same fetid, unlighted cigars, always with the same frayed newspapers two days old . . . . their decaying senses hypnotised and soothed by the sound of the distant rumble of the Pit . . . ."[22] To Cressler's exposition Laura listens attentively, made very thoughtful; "for the first time in her life she looked into the workings of political economy."

Though Jadwin has no fault to find with the ethics of wheat trading, he is at first cautious. When his broker friend Gretry invites him to take part in a bigger deal than he has previously ventured, he replies: *"I don't want to make any more money, Sam. I've got my little pile, and before I get too old I want to have some fun out of it."* But he yields to the urging of the other and comes out of the affair fifty thousand dollars richer. On being told by Cressler that the "bull" trader to whom he had been opposed in the maneuver has been obliged to take a job as a bookkeeper, he merely pulls his mustache and remarks dryly (p. 111) that he didn't suppose the fellow would "be getting measured for a private yacht." Gradually he is drawn into the activities of the Pit, which Norris likes to describe (p. 79) with a Zolaesque largeness and ruggedness of imagery reminiscent of *Le Ventre de Paris:*

within the Board of Trade Building . . . . a great whirlpool, a pit of roaring waters spun and thundered, sucking in the life tides of the city . . . . as into the mouth of some tremendous cloaca, the maw of some colossal sewer; then vomiting them forth again, spewing them up and out, only to catch them in the return eddy and suck them in afresh.

During three years Jadwin makes ever bolder and bolder sallies into the market, always successful, always

[22] *The Pit* (Doubleday, Doran & Company, Inc., 1903, 1921), p. 83.

(as a bear trader) forcing the price of wheat lower and lower, in this aided, of course, by abundant crops in all parts of the earth. Himself now taking up the burden of the theme earlier carried by Cressler, Norris reminds us that, though bread is cheap in other regions, in the United States, "New mortgages were added to farms already heavily 'papered,'" and that throughout the Middle Western farming communities people have ceased to buy plows and binders and buggies and parlor organs.

Then one day, with his acute sensitivity to the slightest movements in the undercurrents of the market, Jadwin feels intuitively that the trend of the past few years has reached its lowest point. Abruptly he reverses his tactics, becomes a "bull" trader, and begins to force up the price of wheat, buying steadily all that is offered. With all his faculties he becomes ever more deeply engrossed in the tremendous and hazardous game he is playing. Laura, wounded in her possessiveness and self-love by his absorption in a business which she cannot understand and of which he tells her nothing, cries bitterly (p. 235), "When it's a question of wheat I count for nothing." When she reminds him that they have already more money than they know how to use, "Oh, it's not the money," he replies (p. 231). "It's the fun of the thing; the excitement—" His resolution of a few years earlier to have some "fun out of his pile" has vanished, for though he is only half as old as was Vandover's father, he finds himself in the same predicament (p. 232): he can find no pleasure in anything but business, "the game"; "what am I to do?" he asks helplessly of his wife. "What are we fellows, who have made our money, to do? I've got to be busy. I can't sit down and twiddle my thumbs."

At length there comes the moment when, with exultation mixed with awe, Jadwin sees clearly that he can corner the market. He gives his days and his nights to the strategy of the campaign, neglects food and sleep, and drives mind and body to the limit of endurance. Within a few weeks he is absolute master of the pit. The sense of his power makes him drunk. As he views his beaten adversaries (pp. 350, 351), "a vast contempt for human nature grew within him. . . . . The more the fellows cringed to him, the tighter he wrenched the screw." Sometimes, capriciously, it pleases him to let them escape without loss; "but in the end the business hardened his heart to any distress his mercilessness might entail. He took his profits as a Bourbon took his taxes, as if by right of birth." A story which reaches his ears about a poor youth in Italy who can no longer buy the loaf, "small as the fist, and costly," troubles him a little and lingers at the back of his mind. But he exclaims angrily (p. 335), "It's a lie! . . . . Of course it's a lie," and puts up the price of wheat to a dollar and twenty cents. In his own city, too, the poor suffer by his act; "from all the poorer districts . . . . came complaints, protests, and vague grumblings of discontent."

From this point forward the humanitarian theme is obscured and lost in the rapidly accelerating rush of the narrative toward the crisis of Jadwin's personal fate, which Norris handles with great dramatic skill. (He is indeed remarkably successful throughout in imparting narrative interest to the operations of commerce, which in less expert hands would have proved but recalcitrant material.) But in view of the vigorous and sustained note of protest against economic injustice which distinguished *The Octopus* it is curious that with equal opportunity he omitted to give it the same prominence in *The Pit,* where it is never anything but a minor note.

It may be claimed for *The Octopus,* more truly than Thackeray claimed for *Vanity Fair,* that it is a novel without a hero. But Jadwin is unquestionably the hero of *The Pit.* However Norris deplored the economic consequences of speculation, he could not withhold his admiration from Jadwin for his boldness, his energy, his resource, and the magnificent scope of his designs. Author and character have a good deal in common; both admire action and men of action; both are essentially "practical." In her efforts to impart literary culture to Jadwin, Laura read him some of the novels of Howells: "He never could rid himself of a surreptitious admiration for Bartley Hubbard. He, too, was 'smart' and 'alive.' He had the 'get there' to him." Pinkerton in Stevenson's *The Wrecker* is a caricature of the American businessman, his head seething with ingenious money-making schemes many of which seem to his friend Loudon Dodd to be distinctly shady. For Jadwin, Pinkerton "long remained . . . . an ideal," because he also was "smart" and "alive." Howells' Silas Lapham "he loved as a brother" (p. 216). In the last year of his life Norris wrote: "The United States in this year of grace nineteen hundred and two does not want and does not need Scholars, but Men—Men made in the mould of the Leonard Woods and the Theodore Roosevelts . . . ."[23]

One last time, however, Norris reminds us of the evil which Jadwin has wrought:

The great failure had precipitated smaller failures, and the aggregate of smaller failures had pulled down one business house after another. For weeks afterward, the successive crashes were like the shock and reverberation of undermined buildings toppling to their ruin. An important bank had suspended payment, and hundreds of depositors had found their little fortunes swept away.

[23] *The Responsibilities of the Novelist,* p. 265.

But as Jadwin sets his face toward the farther West and prepares to rebuild his fortunes, is there a suggestion that his experience has given him an insight into social ethics, a hint that he feels any great responsibility for the train of disasters he has set in motion? None. Jadwin is not a reflective man; he applies himself to the railroad timetable. Nor would Laura "admit her husband was in any way to blame. He had suffered, too." His own words recur to her: "I simply stood between two sets of circumstances. The wheat cornered me, not I the wheat." As they depart from their great empty, echoing mansion on North Avenue to drive for the last time through the streets, past the Board of Trade Building, looming "black, monolithic" against the sky, "under the night and the drifting veil of rain," troubled thoughts flit through her mind:

> For a moment, vague, dark perplexities assailed her, questionings as to the elemental forces, the forces of demand and supply that ruled the world. This huge resistless Nourisher of the Nations—why was it that it could not reach the People, could not fulfil its destiny, unmarred by all this suffering, unattended by all this misery?
> She did not know.

Is it, then, this abstraction, this "law" of demand and supply alone that pinches men's bellies, that flings men in the dust?

Norris was not an economic or political thinker. But as he looked about him at the social order with its irrational inequalities, he felt that something was wrong, and generous sympathies came to life in him.[24] For the arro-

---

[24] It is difficult to reconcile the opinion of Professor Walker—that Norris "was comparatively untouched by suffering and misery"—with many passages in *The Octopus* or with many of the utterances in the critical essays. "By nature," states Professor Walker, "he was almost as detached from his subjects as was Flaubert" (*Frank Norris: A Biography*, p. 257). Artistic detachment, however, does not preclude sympathy.

gant egoism and worship of force in his earlier work he substituted a humanitarianism none the less genuine for the retention of a few inconsistencies.[25] It is not unlikely that in describing the transformation which took place in Annixter's character after his marriage to Hilma he describes in some sort the shift that occurred in his own point of view, to whatever cause it may be ascribed. Annixter had at one time prided himself on being a hard man, and a sharp man in his dealings. "I'm a 'driver,' I know it, and a 'bully,' too," he told Hilma in the early stage of his courtship, and boasted, "There's nobody can get ahead of me." If people hated and feared him he only exulted, for it showed his power over them. But after his marriage he is found performing various acts of unaccustomed kindness, as when he gives a home to the mother and small daughter of Dyke after the latter's sentence to life imprisonment for robbing a train of the Pacific & Southwestern. On one occasion Presley, arriving at the ranch house, finds his friend in his room shaving, his face covered with lather, and his sky-blue suspenders dangling against his legs. In these informal circumstances, Presley having commended him for giving asylum to Mrs. Dyke, Annixter expounds, in his homely, slangy speech, his new philosophy of conduct:

I began to see that a fellow can't live *for* himself any more than he can live *by* himself. He's got to think of others. If he's got brains, he's got to think for the poor ducks that haven't 'em, and not give

[25] Symptomatic of the change is the loss of his enthusiasm for British imperialism in South Africa. Hamlin Garland reports a conversation which occurred in New York, January 20, 1900, at the home of Juliet Wilbor Tompkins: Norris "questioned the justice of England's rule, and this stirred Seton-Thompson's British blood. Filled with English imperialism, he defended the war in Africa with fiery eloquence. His black eyes glowed with a menacing light, but Norris held his own with entire good humor. He knew what he was talking about" (*Companions on the Trail* [New York, 1931], p. 11). Quoted by permission of The Macmillan Company, publishers.

'em a boot in the backsides because they happen to be stupid; and if he's got money, he's got to help those that are busted, and if he's got a house, he's got to think of those that ain't got anywhere to go.[26]

Annixter here does no more than proclaim the duty of charity, in particular, charity to the "busted" on the part of the prosperous. It is far from his thought to suppose the need of any general readjustment in the social scheme. But with one stroke he cuts through a fallacy implicit in a great deal of social theorizing, namely, that the possession of superior intelligence confers the imprescriptible right to exploit, cheat, sweat, humiliate, and brutalize those who have (or are conveniently supposed to have) less intelligence. Apologists for systems of privilege have always made much of the incontrovertible fact that men are not created equal with respect to their brains and abilities, with the inference (spoken or unspoken) that this fact gives moral sanction to every species of trickery and injustice.

In contrast to Annixter, Corthell views the problem in somewhat wider perspective. He is not satisfied that individual or private charity is enough; there are, as well, obligations to society at large. "A little good contributed by everybody to the race is of more, infinitely more, importance than a great deal of good contributed by one individual to another." He acknowledges that "One must do one's own hoeing first. That's the foundation of things." But, he asks, "Isn't that certain contribution . . . . which we make to the general welfare, over and above our own individual work, isn't that the essential?"[27]

[26] *The Octopus* (Doubleday, Doran & Company, Inc., 1901, 1929), pp. 231, 467-68.

[27] *The Pit* (Doubleday, Doran & Company, Inc., 1903, 1921), pp. 246, 245.

By such tentative essays, using now one character and now another for his spokesman, asking a question here, suggesting an answer there, Norris groped his way from the notion of the primordial struggle for existence to the concept of a common social enterprise in which individual self-assertion must yield to the general good. In the concluding paragraphs of one of the last things he wrote—the article in which he viewed with such satisfaction the prospect of an American commercial conquest of the Old World—he envisioned a very lofty goal for human progress. Is "it not possible," he asks, "that we can find in this great destiny of ours something a little better than mere battle and conquest, something a little more generous than mere trading and underbidding?" At present, he realizes, "we cannot get beyond the self-laudatory mood," but he bids us "take the larger view." He then traces the historical enlargement of group loyalties—first loyalty to the family, then to the clan, the city, the province, and at last the nation: "but if all signs are true, ... and the tree grow as we see the twig is bent, the progress will not stop here."

Will it not go on, this epic of civilization, ... until at last . . . . we who now arrogantly boast ourselves as Americans, supreme in conquest, whether of battle-ship or of bridge-building, may realize that the true patriotism is the brotherhood of man and know that the whole world is our nation and simple humanity our countrymen?[28]

Thus Norris came seriously to pronounce the words which a few years before he had put into the mouth of the Europeanized Arab, Bab Azzoun, only for the purpose of showing their futility.

[28] Frank Norris, *The Responsibilities of the Novelist* (copyright 1901, 1902, 1903, by Doubleday, Doran & Company, Inc.), pp. 78 ff.

Tell your yarn and let your style go to the devil.
—FRANK NORRIS, *letter to Isaac Marcosson in Marcosson,* Adventures in Interviewing, *p. 235**

FEW WRITERS exemplify better than Frank Norris the famous saying of Buffon that the style is the man. His style is what we would expect from his character as a man, his interests as a writer, the subjects of his fictions, his deep distrust of aestheticism, his belief that literature must be understandable to the "Plain People," his cry, "We don't want literature, we want life." The qualities of that style are energy, animation, impetuosity of movement, spaciousness, directness, and an almost unfailing concreteness and sensory vividness. In a much-quoted passage Conrad once wrote: "My task . . . . is, by the power of the written word to make you hear, to make you feel—it is, before all, to make you *see*."[1] Far apart as are the two men in nearly every particular, Norris yet shares with the more deliberate artist the power to make us hear, to make us feel, and to make us see, though Conrad's "unremitting never-discouraged care for the shape and ring of sentences" was ever outside his intention. Such care Norris would have considered a danger to his robustness, his virility. He was

---

* Used by permission of the publishers, Dodd, Mead & Company, Inc.

[1] From the original preface to *The Nigger of the Narcissus,* by Joseph Conrad (copyright 1897, 1914, by Doubleday, Doran & Company, Inc.).

not the conscious craftsman with words, not a manipulator of rhythms and cadences, not a weaver of sentence harmonies. Delicacy or subtlety of thought subtly expressed was not his purpose. He does not wish to charm; he would rather bear us down and trample us under a rush of brawny adjectives and slashing verbs. "I detest . . . . 'elegant English,'" he wrote; "tommyrot. Who cares for fine style!"[2] Much as he admired Stevenson it is impossible to imagine him concerning himself, like the latter, with assonance and alliteration, with tracing the melodies to be won by a skillful repetition and variation of liquids and labials, or with the dexterous involution and resolution of sentences.

The faults of his style are but the excess of its virtues. He saw everything a little larger than life size, and dramatized everything; hence in communicating what he has seen he frequently raises his voice above the normal pitch. Sometimes he shouts; sometimes he becomes strident; often he gives the sense of an undue heightening of effect. Wishing to inform us that the wheat crop in Nebraska was unpromising, he writes: "The wheat had been battered by incessant gales, had been nipped and harried by frost; everywhere the young half-grown grain seemed to be perishing." This appears to be adequate; but, as if not satisfied that he has created a full sense of something tremendous and appalling, he adds, "It was a massacre, a veritable slaughter." He had already applied the same words to the killing of the sheep by the locomotive in *The Octopus;* but he must have a massacre. The bent of mind which led him to view events, even the most commonplace, in terms of some dynamic, or splendid, or spectacu-

[2] Marcosson, *Adventures in Interviewing*, p. 235. Used by permission of the publishers, Dodd, Mead & Company, Inc.

lar action may be seen in his description of the way spring came to Chicago:

the minute sparkling of green flashed from tree top to tree top, like the first kindling of dry twigs. . . . .

At length came . . . . full-bodied, vigorous winds straight from out the south.

Instantly the living embers in tree top and grass plat were fanned to flame. . . . . Branch after branch caught and crackled; even the dryest, the deadest, were enfolded in the resistless swirl of green. . . . . From end to end . . . . of the city, fed by the rains, urged by the south winds, spread billowing and surging the superb conflagration of the coming summer.[3]

He is at his best in animated scenes filled with the restless movement of people and the myriad sounds that arise from crowds. Several of these have been more than once referred to—the opera scene in *Vandover and the Brute* and in *The Pit,* the plowing, the supper of the plowhands, the barn dance, the rabbit drive in *The Octopus.* Of a like concreteness and producing the same illusion as of things actually seen and heard and smelt are the descriptions in *Vandover* of the reception at Henrietta Vance's, of the crowd at the Mechanics' Fair, of the barroom of the Imperial (a favorite resort of Vandover and his friends and of the "fast" women of the city), where we watch the ceaseless coming and going through the flapping swing doors, hear the "rattle of chairs and glassware," the "cluck" of the cash register as it rings its bell, fill our nostrils with the smell of sweetened whiskey, tobacco, musk, and cooking food, and watch men bending over plates of stewed tripe from the free lunch counter; or the pictures in *The Pit* of the railroad yards—a swift impression of furious motion and terrifying clamor; of South Water Street—

[3] Frank Norris, *The Pit* (copyright 1903, 1921, by Doubleday, Doran & Company, Inc.), pp. 193, 147–49.

the quarter of wholesale produce with its endless files of dray horses "suggestive of an actual barrack of cavalry," with its wilderness of crates, baskets, boxes, and sacks, stored with "the fatness of a hundred thousand furrows."

Scores of such passages tempt to more-extended quotation; but one must suffice, a scene from *Blix* of the San Francisco waterfront, which well exhibits certain of Norris' qualities:

Ships innumerable nuzzled at the endless line of docks, mast overspiring mast, and bowsprit overlapping bowsprit, till the eye was bewildered, as if by the confusion of branches in a leafless forest. In the distance the mass of rigging resolved itself into a solid gray blur against the sky. The great hulks, green and black and slate gray, laid themselves along the docks, straining leisurely at their mammoth chains, their flanks opened, their cargoes, as it were their entrails, spewed out in a wild disarray of crate and bale and box. Sailors and stevedores swarmed them like vermin. Trucks rolled along the wharfs like peals of ordnance, the horse-hoofs beating the boards like heavy drum-taps. Chains clanked, a ship's dog barked incessantly from a companionway, ropes creaked in complaining pulleys, blocks rattled, hoisting-engines coughed and strangled, while all the air was redolent of oakum, of pitch, of paint, of spices, of ripe fruit, of clean cool lumber, of coffee, of tar, of bilge, and the brisk, nimble odor of the sea.[4]

Here are the profusion and the magnitude that Norris loved; here is bustling activity with just a suggestion in the military similes, faintly menacing, of the shock of powerful forces, able to crush and destroy; here are color and sound and a multitude of arresting smells.

Without in the least impairing his capacity for minute observation, he was enamored of vastness, of all things large, powerful, and excessive; enormous, tremendous, colossal, gigantic, titanic, immense, mammoth, inordinate—

[4] *Blix* (Doubleday, Doran & Company, Inc., 1899, 1928), pp. 48–49.

these words form the backbone of his vocabulary. Crowds, great cities, even inanimate nature in its larger features—mountains, forests, deserts, seas—these have for him an independent life of their own; they breathe, and the sound of that breathing, composed of innumerable smaller sounds, manifests itself to the ear attuned to catch it in the form of a ceaseless, profound, all-pervading monotone. This almost mystical sense of an exhaustless life reaching down into the very roots of being stirs and excites him; it is almost an obsession. He has three words with which to name this sound that "always disengages itself from vast bodies"—murmur, diapason, bourdon. Verrill, of the story "The Guest of Honour" (in *The Third Circle*), raises a window on the top floor of a tall building and looks out over the city at night:

At once a subdued murmur, prolonged, monotonous, ... rose to meet him. It was the mingling of all the night noises into one great note that came simultaneously from all quarters of the horizon, infinitely vast, infinitely deep,—a steady diapason strain like the undermost bourdon of a great organ as the wind begins to thrill the pipes.

It was the stir of life, the breathing of the Colossus, the push of the nethermost basic force, old as the world, wide as the world, the murmur of the primeval energy, coeval with the centuries, blood-brother to that spirit which in the brooding darkness before creation, moved upon the face of the waters.[5]

In all the novels we hear the same profound note. In *McTeague* it is the "vast and prolonged murmur" of Polk Street, or "the noises that the mountains made in their living . . . . like the breathing of an infinitely great monster, alive, palpitating"; in *A Man's Woman* the "prolonged, indefinite murmur" of the great crowd come to witness

[5] *The Third Circle*, pp. 282–83. Used by permission of the publishers, Dodd, Mead & Company, Inc.

the departure of Bennett's ship; in *The Octopus* the "vague murmur . . . . like the sound of very distant surf" produced by a vast flock of sheep. He is responsive to all deep, heavy, swelling sounds; to all prolonged, pervasive sounds, which he describes by his three favored words—the sound of breakers, of a locomotive speeding over a trestle, the rumbling voice of Dyke in his anger, the baying of bloodhounds, the "vast monotonous murmur" of the rain.

The style he employs for his realistic or naturalistic scenes and episodes is objective, confining itself to what the senses can perceive, the diction plain, harsh where needful. This objective style may be seen in such passages as those which describe McTeague's dental parlors, Polk Street, the picnic in Schutzen Park, the vicinity of the B Street station, the variety show at the Orpheum; or Vandover drunk in the back room of a Barbary Coast saloon, sprawled over a table, face down in his own vomit, with "a great swarm of flies buzzing about his head"; or Charlie Geary's block of cheap houses. But the manner here is not Norris' only manner, for his work is veined and seamed with idyllic, "poetic," "idealistic" passages, where the intention is to be eloquent, tender, to convey lofty sentiment. Unfortunately these are apt to be invaded by rhetoric and sentimentality, by triteness of both thought and expression. When he lets himself go we get something like the following, which pictures Hilma during the time of her approaching motherhood:

She moved surrounded by an invisible atmosphere of Love. Love was in her wide-opened brown eyes, Love—the dim reflection of that descending crown poised over her head—radiated in a faint lustre from her dark, thick hair. Around her beautiful neck, ... Love lay encircled like a necklace—Love that was beyond words, sweet, breathed from her parted lips. From her white, large arms downward to her pink finger-tips—Love, an invisible electric fluid, disengaged itself, subtle, alluring. In the velvety huskiness of her voice, Love vibrated like a note of unknown music.[6]

But his lyrical, empurpled prose may be seen to better advantage in those parts of *The Octopus* that deal with the Vanamee–Angéle Varian story.

In *A Man's Woman* occurs a passage untouched by the rhapsodic intensity seldom absent when Vanamee is the subject, and showing Norris' style in a phase of unwonted calm and repose:

A vast, pervading warmth lay close over all the world. The trees, the orchards, the rose-bushes in the garden about the house, all the teeming life of trees and plants hung motionless and poised in the still, tideless ocean of the air. It was very quiet; all distant noises, the crowing of cocks, the persistent calling of robins and jays, the sound of wheels upon the road, the rumble of the trains passing the station down in the town, seemed muffled and subdued. The long, calm summer days succeeded one another in an unbroken, glimmering procession. From dawn to twilight one heard the faint, innumerable murmurs of the summer, the dull bourdon of bees in the rose and lilac bushes, the prolonged, strident buzzing of blue-bottle-flies, the harsh, dry scrape of grasshoppers, the stridulating of an occasional cricket.[7]

Taken together these specimens exhibit the full range of Norris' prose—his realistic, objective style; his dramatizing style; his rhapsodic, romantic style; and his quiet style.

Norris held that the great principle in writing, as in other arts, is simplicity. He illustrates by relating how he once went to buy a silver soup ladle. He was shown a large assortment, "ladles with gilded bowls, with embossed handles, with chased arabesques," but none of these were to his taste. Then the salesman displayed a ladle "as plain and as unadorned as the unclouded sky—and about as beautiful." But, strangely, this one cost more than any

[6] *The Octopus* (Doubleday, Doran & Company, 1901, 1929), p. 497.
[7] *A Man's Woman*, pp. 263–64.

of the others. "You see," explained the salesman, "in this highly ornamental ware the flaws of the material don't show, and you can cover up a blow-hole or the like by wreaths and beading. But this plain ware has got to be the very best." Here, he asserts, is the standard of comparison for all things, "whether commercial or artistic." The perfection of bare and simple beauty he finds in the Bible. Suppose, he asks, the story of Christ's birth were to be told today for the first time. "How the adjectives would marshal upon the page . . . ." But the New Testament account is given without one unessential word, "with the terseness of a military report, and yet—there is the epic, the world epic, beautiful, majestic, incomparably dignified."[8]

Ornamental diction, a copious flow of words, metaphorical language, "violent colour" may be pardoned, he believes, in slack parts of the narrative, though they are too frequently devices to conceal defects of structure. But in the crisis "We want no adjectives to blur our substantives. The substantives may now speak for themselves." If they do, the writer has no need of comment.

He is often successful in achieving the ideal of simplicity here set forth. The account of the murder of Trina is admirably plain and objective, as is that of the fight between ranchers and deputies at the irrigation ditch in *The Octopus*. In the latter scene, confining himself to the barest statement, he relates the deaths of the several characters in such unemotional terms as the following (p. 522): "Annixter, instantly killed, fell his length to the ground, and lay without movement, just as he had fallen, one arm across his face." This compares favorably with Thack-

---

[8] "Simplicity in Art," in *The Responsibilities of the Novelist* (Doubleday, Doran & Company, Inc., 1901, 1902, 1903), pp. 242–43.

eray's quiet announcement of the death of George Osborne, if it is not superior: "Darkness came down on the field and city; and Amelia was praying for George, who was lying on his face, dead, with a bullet through his heart."

In general, however, Norris does not practice a rigid economy in the use of words. To strip his idea down to its naked bones seems to him miserly, ungracious, a needless self-denial. His reliance is rather on a prodigal opulence. He prefers to get his effects by piling up words, by exhibiting his thought in a succession of phrases each revealing it in a slightly different aspect and at the same time enlarging it till it stands at its maximum development. The following sentence will illustrate the propensity:

It was the season after the harvest, and the great earth, the mother, after its period of reproduction, its pains of labour, delivered of the fruit of its loins, slept the sleep of exhaustion, the infinite repose of the colossus, benignant, eternal, strong, the nourisher of nations, the feeder of an entire world.[9]

In the other matter, that of withholding comment, he not infrequently ignores his own injunction. If the picture is pathetic, he warns, never say, "It was pitiful to the point of tears"; if beautiful, let the beauty shine by its own light; if terrible, never say, "It is terrible!" Yet he says of the slaughter of the sheep, "The pathos of it was beyond expression," and the cries of the wounded sheep were "heart-rending, pitiful."

In his figures of speech he is often original, apt, and striking. He was constantly on the alert for vivid images, and it was his habit always to record them in his notebook. From these memoranda one example is preserved by his

[9] *The Octopus* (Doubleday, Doran & Company, Inc., 1901, 1929), pp. 46–47.

brother: "The hands of the village clock closed like a pair of shears, and cut the night in twain."[10] It comes with an agreeable novelty to find a woman's teeth called "as white and even as the kernels on an ear of green corn." [11] On a wet day on Polk Street, "The asphalt of the sidewalks shone like the surface of a patent leather boot; every hollow in the street held its little puddle, that winked like an eye each time a drop of rain struck into it."[12] As the wrecked "Mazatlan" heaved its stern out of the water for its final plunge, Vandover noted "the screw writhing its flanges into the air like some enormous starfish already fastened upon the hulk." In the idyllic "A Statue in an Old Garden" we find (p. 293) "a red leaf fell like a blood drop from the heart of the dying summer."[13] In *Moran of the Lady Letty* (pp. 28, 47, 89, 90) we read of the schooner "Bertha Millner" that she "scooped the nor'wester in the hollow palms of her tense canvases," and again, during a season of gentle winds, she "rolled lazily southward with the leisurely nonchalance of a grazing ox." In a rising storm "the sun was wiped from the sky like writing from a slate," and "the sky shut down over the troubled ocean like a pot-lid over a boiling pot." When the cowboy Delaney, drunk and seeking to square accounts with Annixter, rode the mettlesome buckskin into the barn in the midst of a waltz, the dancers were cleared from the floor

[10] Charles G. Norris, *Frank Norris, 1870–1902: An Intimate Sketch*, pp. 7–8. Norris used the figure in "Outside the Zenana," in *Collected Writings*, p. 184, changed to read, "The hands upon the huge clock . . . . closed slowly together like the blades of a great pair of shears, and clipped the night into equal halves . . . ."

[11] *McTeague*, p. 24. Said of Trina; curiously, Norris applies the same words to the teeth of Flossie, a prostitute, in *Vandover and the Brute* (p. 51), surely an instance of his inadvertent repetitions.

[12] *Ibid.*, p. 182.

[13] *Collected Writings*, p. 293.

"like sand blown from off a rock." On "Ladies' Day" at Lyman Derrick's club the women "entered the room—this unfamiliar masculine haunt . . . . with a certain show of hesitancy and little, nervous, oblique glances, moving their heads from side to side like a file of hens venturing into a strange barn." Geology and paleontology sometimes provide him with an image. During the harvest on Los Muertos a threshing machine "moved belly-deep in the standing grain . . . . a dinosaur wallowing through thick, hot grasses";[14] and the yellow wallpaper of Vandover's shabby room was "stamped with a huge pattern of flowers that looked like the flora of a carboniferous strata."[15]

It is not often that, like Stephen Crane, he wrests an adjective from its accustomed uses, but when he speaks of a group of picnickers gazing out from a photograph with "monolithic cheerfulness,"[16] he suggests Crane's "great crimson oaths" and "squat, ignorant stables."

His fondness for personification, commonly achieved with a capital letter, is often carried to excess, as Hawthorne carried allegory. Vandover heard the "prolonged and sullen diapason" arising from the sleeping city "like the breathing of some infinitely great monster, alive and palpitating, the sistole and diastole of some gigantic heart. . . . . It was Life . . . ."[17] Always prodigal of monsters and colossi, Norris seldom fails to invest "Life" with awe-inspiring personality. In *The Octopus* the Wheat takes on the character of a living force, and the People has its collective identity, the identity, when aroused, of a brute, "many-tongued, red-eyed." In *A Man's Woman* we are

14 *The Octopus*, pp. 256, 309, 616.
15 *Vandover and the Brute*, p. 318.
16 *A Man's Woman*, p. 65 of the later, revised edition.
17 *Vandover and the Brute*, p. 230.

confronted twenty-three times by a personified "Enemy," which undergoes rapid transformations. It is first the polar ice, then death by cold and starvation, then death by disease, the ever-present adversary of Lloyd's corps of nurses; it now becomes in turn Lloyd's fear that Bennett has perished, the death that threatens the girl Hattie in the operating room, Bennett's self-will, the typhoid fever that attacks first Ferris and then Bennett.

Norris' most characteristic sentence pattern is distinguished by the placing of nouns, adjectives, or phrases in series of two, three, four, or even more members (commonly without the connecting "and"), by the frequent use of two or three appositives in succession, and by the placing of adjectives (frequently three) after the noun, again without the conjunction. This practice is evidently related to his dependence on cumulative effect in building up his thought. Consider the following examples:

Heaps and heaps of blue-black coils and braids, a royal crown of swarthy bands, a veritable sable tiara, heavy, abundant, odorous.[18]

As yet she was almost, as one might say, without sex—savage, unconquered, untamed, glorying in her own independence, her sullen isolation.[19]

But once in a remoter field, solitary, magnificent, enormous, the short hair curling tight upon his forehead, his small red eyes twinkling, his vast neck heavy with muscles, Presley came upon the monarch, the king, the great Durham bull, maintaining his lonely state, unapproachable, austere.

It was one of those legendary passions that sometimes occur, idyllic, untouched by civilization, spontaneous as the growth of trees, natural as dew-fall, strong as the firm-seated mountains.[20]

[18] *McTeague* (Doubleday, Doran & Company, Inc., 1899, 1927), p. 23.
[19] *Moran of the Lady Letty*, p. 104.
[20] *The Octopus*, pp. 375, 36.

He follows, however, a certain traceable course in the use of such sentences as the foregoing (which constantly suggest to the ear a dactylic rhythm). In *McTeague* and *Vandover* they are the exception; in *Blix* and *Moran* they are even less evident; in *A Man's Woman* they begin to be more prominent; in *The Octopus* they suddenly swarm; in *The Pit* they fall off perceptibly. In dialogue, of course, it is another matter. The talk of the characters approximates actual speech, particularly when they use the vernacular—such characters as McTeague, Trina, Schouler, Vandover and his friends, Annixter, Jadwin, Landry Court, Mrs. Cressler, Aunt Wess. But does anyone ever say "hark!" for "listen!" as do Trina in *McTeague* and Crookes the speculator in *The Pit*?[21]

As might be expected from his temperament, Norris' writing shows marks of carelessness and haste. His enthusiasm for his story left him no patience for scrupulous attention to minutiae. Nor was he oversensitive to clichés, which are plentiful in all of the novels. Despite the importance which he attached to technical accuracy, he sometimes blunders in his details, as when he makes Annixter hang up the transmitter of a telephone instead of the receiver, or when he makes Magnus' fields produce forty-three sacks of wheat to the acre—an impossible yield, since a sack contains more than two bushels, and that he means bushels is evident a few sentences later. But mistakes of this sort are of small account.

Of more interest is the recurrence of certain favorite words—words associated with his peculiar sense perceptions, dominant emotions, and leading ideas. He is as far removed as possible from the painful scrupulousness with which Flaubert sought to avoid the repetition of a word

---

[21] *McTeague*, p. 296; *The Pit*, p. 272.

within twenty or thirty pages. Some of these words have already been noticed—"salient," "bourdon," "diapason," "murmur." The innumerable odors with which he flavors his pages are almost invariably accompanied by one of three words: "disengaged," "exhaled," or "redolent."

It is not alone particular words that constantly appear and reappear with stubborn reiteration, but scenes, situations, traits of character, images, descriptive phrases, as well. This is due in part to his method of driving home an impression or idea by repeated hammer blows, by the steady sounding of a motif;[22] in part to the circumstances under which his work was published. But much of it is clearly inadvert and unpremeditated, the result of the fact that many of his observations early crystallized into verbal formulas so commanding as to reassert themselves later through some association, to the exclusion of other possibilities. Concrete details, images, phrases that appear in his first novel are found again in the last, six years later. The cable cars that jolted over Polk Street in *McTeague* "with a strident whirring of jostled glass windows" also jolted over Chicago streets in *The Pit* "with a strident whir of vibrating window glass." The cry of newsboys "chanting the evening papers" reached alike the ears of McTeague, of Vandover, and of Lloyd Searight. Hunger, or the fear of pursuit, "rode and rowelled" McTeague, and infatuation for the Mexican woman Felice "rode and

---

[22] For each person in *The Octopus* "Norris prepared a character sketch which included notes on the physical appearance, the personality, whatever symbolic value there might be, and the labeling phrases which he intended to repeat, like Homeric refrains, whenever the character appeared in the story" (Walker, *Frank Norris: A Biography;* reprinted by permission of Doubleday, Doran & Company, Inc., 1932, p. 259). The notes given by Professor Walker for the character of Annixter show the striking similarity of Norris' method to that of Zola, which may be studied in Matthew Josephson's *Zola,* Appendix, containing extensive selections from the notes and plans for *L'Assommoir.*

rowelled" the mine superintendent Lockwood in the story "The Wife of Chino" (in *A Deal in Wheat*).

Sometimes traits of one character are given to another quite different. McTeague and Schouler and the other unpolished dwellers on Polk Street are accustomed to slap their thighs in token of mirth or pleasure. But Condy Rivers employs the same gesture. The dentist, dull of wit and always slow of comprehension, is forever stammering bewilderedly when addressed, "Huh, what, what?" Condy on occasion also exclaims, "Huh! what? what?" in a manner disconcertingly like that of McTeague.

During more than three years Norris had on his hands the manuscripts of two novels, *McTeague* and *Vandover and the Brute;* from these he drew freely for an uninterrupted stream of sketches and stories contributed to the San Francisco *Wave* and other periodicals, and even for some of his later novels. This fact largely accounts for the air of familiarity which many incidents, scenes, and characters have for the reader of his complete works. Had these two novels been published as soon as written, some of this duplication no doubt would not have occurred. But other instances show that publication did not deter him from making second use of an idea. The opera scene from *Vandover* went first into the *Harvard Advocate* under the title "The End of the Act";[23] rewritten, it was later incorporated into the first chapter of *The Pit*. A deaf and dumb person who can talk only when drunk he thought of sufficient interest to use twice, first in *Vandover* and then in "The Third Circle," in the volume of the same name, where, however, the character is a woman. One of

[23] Reprinted in *The Wave*, November 27, 1897; it is possible, of course, that the piece was first written for the *Advocate* and then used in *Vandover and the Brute*. It was included in *Collected Writings* (1928), where it is stated that it first appeared in the *Harvard Crimson*.

Vandover's frivolous amusements was playing two banjos simultaneously; this feat is transferred to Osterman in *The Octopus*. *Vandover* supplied six other items to Norris' later writing. In the second of the series of sketches, "Man Proposes," in *The Wave*, May 30, 1896 (reprinted in *Collected Writings*), the crude proposal of marriage made by a coalheaver to a washerwoman is lifted, with slight changes, from *McTeague*. "The Plumber's Apprentice" (*The Wave*, May 2, 1896) and "Judy's Service of Gold Plate"[24] (*The Wave*, October 16, 1897)—where is seen again Maria Macapa's fabulous set of gold dishes—are also borrowed from *McTeague*.

On the other hand, in a number of the short stories may be seen ideas, characters, or episodes repeated in the subsequent novels. The restaurant in Chinatown pictured in "The Third Circle," the talk of Hillegas and Miss Ten Eyck, who chance upon the place during a quiet hour, and who regard it as a happy discovery, are obviously models for a similar scene in *Blix*. Manning, of the same story, a former deep-sea diver who has burst his eardrums at his occupation and who can blow tobacco smoke out of either ear, becomes Captain Jack of the lifeboat station in *Blix*. The old shabbily dressed woman in "Little Dramas of the Curbstone," painfully leading, now and then attempting to carry, a small crippled girl, evolves into Mrs. Hooven, tramping the streets of San Francisco with little Hilda. The fifth and last of the "Man Proposes" series supplies a piquantly dramatic situation to *A Man's Woman:* Bennett and Ferris, without either being aware of the other's feeling, are both in love with Lloyd Searight. When death seems but a matter of hours, Bennett reveals his mind and urges his friend to tell him if she has ever

[24] Both reprinted in *Frank Norris of "The Wave"* (1931).

spoken a word that might have given him hope. Ferris, thinking the lie will be only a last kindness, assures him she has. Then the rescue ships steam into the bay.

The seed of the idea for his epic of the wheat was apparently planted in Norris' mind unawares as he watched the shipping along the San Francisco waterfront. As early as *Moran of the Lady Letty* (beginning of 1898) we find Ross Wilbur of that novel lounging on the wharves and watching with keen interest the grain ships "slowly gorging themselves with whole harvests of wheat from the San Joaquin Valley." In *Blix,* Condy Rivers is assigned to write a special article on a certain whaleback steamer; he visits the vessel (p. 50) where it is moored at its pier and finds it "sucking in entire harvests of wheat from the San Joaquin valley—harvests that were to feed strangely clad skeletons on the southern slopes of the Himalaya foothills."

Norris' repetitions, of both matter and manner—the continual recurrence of phrases, fragments of observation, similes, his borrowings from himself, the pressing of situations into renewed service—stamp his work with a certain character. They are partly due, of course, to the necessity he was often under of grinding out copy; but at the same time they define the extent and suggest the limitations of his literary resources. The conviction forms in the mind of the reader that his ideas, large and small (carrying with them his peculiar manner of expression), had described their full orbit, and would continue thenceforth to swing in the same track without much deviation. He would move on to new scenes, it is true—a famine-stricken community of Europe for the third member of the wheat trilogy, *The Wolf,* or the battle of Gettysburg for a new epic, or some region of the South Seas for which he was about to depart at the moment of his death—but would he see them in fresh terms, would he tell what he saw in new language?

At its worst Norris' style may become strident, rhetorical, emotionally overwrought; at its best it moves with majestic rhythms, as often in *The Octopus,* or with a forceful plainness and directness, as mostly in *McTeague.* It shows considerable powers of modulation to suit the matter. He can achieve passages of quiet beauty or remarkable effects of simplicity and economy. His strength lies greatly in his sharp, concrete visualizations of objects, of people, of human behavior—a rich array of sense impressions that linger in the mind longer than wisdom, like those images which every man carries in memory, trivial it may be, detached and irrelevant, sole remaining fragments of forgotten yesterdays. Clear and distinct is the picture of the drab little suburban B Street station, bare of all save "a couple of whittled and carven benches." All around stretch salt marshes, expanses of black mud uncovered by the tide, dump heaps prowled by Chinese ragpickers. Here, amidst the odors of tar, dead seaweed, and bilge, Trina and McTeague exchange passionate kisses, and Trina gains the husband who one day will crush the life from her body with his enormous fists.

We see Vandover's sick mother seated in a wheel chair on the platform of a railway station: "she drew a long sigh, her face became the face of an imbecile, stupid, without expression, her eyes half-closed, her mouth half-open. Her head rolled forward as though she were nodding in her sleep, while a long drip of saliva trailed from her lower lip." So she died.

We see Vandover returning to the big empty house

after his father's funeral and finding on the rack his father's hat, "a stiff brown derby hat, flat on the top . . . . He took the hat in his hands, turning it about tenderly, catching the faint odour of the Old Gentleman's hair oil that hung about it . . . . he put his arms clumsily about the old hat, weeping and whispering to himself."[25]

The rains have come to the valley of the San Joaquin. We hear with Annixter the faint humming of the telegraph wires "under the multitudinous fingering of the myriad of falling drops," see with him the poles "dark and swollen and glistening with wet," see the glass insulators shining dully in the somber light of the day's end.[26]

Norris' style is like the life he describes—vigorous, robust, often tumultuous. It is like a flood, sometimes a turbid flood, bearing the débris of its banks. But like a flood it moves, with a powerful impulse, sweeping along his mannerisms, his clichés, his rhetoric, which may encumber its surface but cannot seriously impede its movement or diminish its strength.

In him is neither any *fin de siècle* lassitude nor any wish to burn with a "hard gem-like flame"; when he burns it is with the red glare and the crackling roar of a forest fire.

His style is no unfit instrument for that symphony to whose profound harmonies his ear was ever attuned—"the symphony of energy, the vast orchestration of force, the paean of an indestructible life, coeval with the centuries, renascent, ordained, eternal."[27]

[25] *Vandover and the Brute*, pp. 4–5, 157 (Doubleday, Doran & Company, Inc., 1928).

[26] *The Octopus*, p. 93.

[27] "The Guest of Honour," in *The Third Circle* (Dodd, Mead & Company, Inc.), p. 298. Used by permission.

Chapter VI

Contemporary Estimates and After-Fame

To say: "This man is great" means: "He is accepted by the right people." . . . . No critic knows, and every critic likes to play safe.—ALBERT LÉON GUÉRARD*

Who shall guard the guardians of literature? . . . . criticism is, in the first instance, merely the expression of opinion about authors, books, and theories of art generally. The opinion is usually expressed dogmatically; that is, it is expressed as if it were a fact, a reality. It is a reality in so far as it has existence in the mind of the critic who utters it; it is a fact of what has been happily called the "existential" sort.—WILLIAM TENNEY BREWSTER†

DURING the forty years that have elapsed since Norris first claimed the attention of the public, a considerable mass of commentary has accumulated around his work. This body of criticism reveals that engaging diversity of opinion which always affords a malicious satisfaction to the man skeptical of absolute values in literature. The student who makes his way patiently through the contemporary reviews, and through all that has since been

---

* *Literature and Society* (Boston: Lothrop, Lee & Shepard Co., 1935), pp. 3, 402.

† Introduction to *Specimens of Modern English Literary Criticism*, pp. ix, xi–xii. Quoted by permission of The Macmillan Company, publishers.

written of Norris, will learn a good many things about him and his work that cannot lie down peaceably together in the same mind.

He will learn that Norris was a great novelist, and that he was not a great novelist; that his best work is *The Pit,* that it is *The Octopus,* that it is *McTeague,* and even that it is *Moran of the Lady Letty;* that *The Pit* was "frankly written down,"[1] calculated to delight "cheap people";[2] that although *The Pit* was less successful than *The Octopus,* the fact is due to the subject and not to the fault of the author.[3] The seeker after critical certitudes will learn further that Trina's miserliness is skillfully introduced and developed,[4] and that Norris failed properly to prepare for it.[5] He may have his choice of the opinions, (1) that the conclusion of *McTeague* is "ludicrously meretricious";[6] (2) that few novels end "as effectively, as inevitably, as much to the purpose";[7] (3) that its ending, though melodramatic, "does nothing that denies the reality of [the] characters."[8]

He will hear that the mysticism of *The Octopus* is "preposterous"[9] and, on the other hand, that it is the

[1] H. L. Mencken, *A Book of Prefaces* (New York: Alfred A. Knopf, 1917), p. 71.

[2] Thomas Beer, *The Mauve Decade* (New York: Alfred A. Knopf, 1926), p. 99.

[3] Milne B. Levick in *Overland Monthly,* June 1905, p. 508; Carl and Mark Van Doren, *American and British Literature Since 1890,* p. 48; Edward Wagenknecht, "Frank Norris in Retrospect," *Virginia Quarterly Review,* April 1930, p. 319.   [4] Levick, *op. cit.,* p. 506.

[5] Granville Hicks, *The Great Tradition,* p. 169.

[6] Geoffrey Hellman, "Trail-Blazer of Realism," in *New York Herald Tribune, Books,* December 4, 1932, p. 25.

[7] John Curtis Underwood, *Literature and Insurgency* (New York: Mitchell Kennerley, 1914), p. 150.

[8] Howells in *North American Review,* December 1902, p. 773.

[9] Mencken, *loc. cit.*

saving feature of the work.[10] He will hear that there is a "lack of vivid character drawing" in this novel: "the characters . . . . love and suffer and die, and their joy and their misery fail to wake a responsive thrill";[11] but against this it is declared that the wrongs and sufferings of Magnus, Dyke, Annixter, and Hilma "touch us as if they were personal friends, and we feel our hearts throb with the grief and indignation that moved Presley."[12] Norris' "interest was not that of the ethical teacher, the reformer who turns on the light";[13] not so: "He never hesitated to assail a social evil, never stopped short of trying to right a wrong."[14] The sumptuous dining of the Gerards and their guests while Mrs. Hooven dies of hunger is a masterly scene, big;[15] nonsense! it is nothing but yellow journalism.[16] Corthell is "well portrayed";[17] mistaken! he is "a feeble caricature."[18] Norris could not handle "drawing-room small talk"; he lacked "a certain light sureness of touch in presenting men and women of the world";[19] on the contrary, "he moves through the lake-side palaces of Chicago with a . . . . *ton* as admirable as [was] ever Mrs. Ward's in any ducal mansion of them all!"[20] And so the catalogue of irreconcilables might be extended to

[10] William B. Cairns, *A History of American Literature*, rev. ed., pp. 486–87.

[11] Frederic Taber Cooper in *The Bookman*, May 1901, pp. 246, 247.

[12] A. L. Muzzey in *The Public*, May 3, 1902, p. 64.

[13] Hamlin Garland in *The Critic*, March 1903, p. 216.

[14] V. F. Calverton, *The Liberation of American Literature* (New York: Charles Scribner's Sons, 1932), p. 354.

[15] *The Literary World*, March 1903, p. 54.

[16] *The Outlook*, April 20, 1901, p. 882.

[17] *Public Opinion*, January 22, 1903, p. 121.

[18] *The Independent*, February 5, 1903, p. 332.

[19] Owen Wister in *The World's Work*, February 1903, p. 3134.

[20] Harriet Waters Preston in *The Atlantic Monthly*, May 1903, p. 692.

include every aspect of Norris' work down to the last detail. It is possible nevertheless to discern amidst this variety certain currents of opinion from the time of the earliest reviews to the present.

From the very beginning Norris threw many of his critics into confusion by publishing first the third of his novels. Reviewers naturally assumed that it was a first book; but at this time (September 1898) two of Norris' three best novels (that is, *McTeague* and *Vandover and the Brute*) were already three years behind him. *McTeague* was published in February 1899. The fact that it was Norris' first novel was soon known, was referred to in print,[21] and was accessible to all who cared to inform themselves on the matter. Yet, for long, critics continued to speak of *Moran of the Lady Letty* as prentice work, and to view *McTeague* as an advance from it. *Moran,* though it was an experiment, an interlude, is in no sense prentice work. But the assumption was general, and has persisted to the present, that up to the date of the publication of *McTeague,* and even beyond, he was "trying to find himself," "feeling his way," "testing his powers," "seeking his direction."

This assumption was fostered by three of the four posthumous collections of Norris' short stories and sketches, namely, *The Third Circle* (1909), *Collected Writings Hitherto Unpublished in Book Form* (1928), and *Frank Norris of "The Wave"* (1931).[22] "Here collected are the longest and most important of his prentice products," wrote Will Irwin in the Introduction to *The Third Circle;* "they are," he continued, "an incomparable study

21 By John D. Barry in *The Literary World,* March 18, 1899, pp. 88–89.

22 The remaining volume, the first to be published, was *A Deal in Wheat and Other Stories of the New and Old West* (1903). Reviewers, apparently, did not take it to be early work, as in truth it is not.

in the way a genius takes to find himself. . . . . Admirable in themselves, ... they are most interesting when compared with the later work which the world knows. . . . ." But of the sixteen pieces in the volume only three antedate *McTeague.* The brief sketch entitled "The Dental Parlors" (contributed to *The Wave,* March 13, 1897, and nowhere reprinted) is not, as Irwin says, "the nucleus for" the description of McTeague's room, but is drawn *from* the already-written novel to help make up Norris' weekly stint for the paper.

It was apparently Gelett Burgess who first set on foot the legend that Norris during his two years on *The Wave* (1896–97) was serving his apprenticeship. "This," he wrote, "was Frank Norris' season of experiment; he was feeling his way toward style, plot, construction and that graphic force which became more and more compelling with every book."[23] Applied to the man who had already written *McTeague* and *Vandover,*[24] these words have little meaning. Charles Norris takes the same view as Burgess of Frank's journalistic years on *The Wave.* "In my opinion," he writes in the Introduction to *Collected Writings,* "with which his contemporaries and many literary critics agree, some of his best work was written at this time." But the critic would be hard pressed to name anything Norris wrote in 1896 or 1897 which deserves a

[23] "One More Tribute to Frank Norris," *Sunset,* January 1903, p. 246.

[24] *Vandover and the Brute,* of course, remained unknown to the public till 1914. The first mention in print of its existence (so far as can be discovered) is by Denison Hailey Clift, who wrote: "There is one unpublished novel that Norris wrote at the time of his literary beginnings. This book is a story of a college generation, and its title is *Vandover and the Brute.* The manuscript is at present in New York. The realism of the work is too intense and too true to life to render its publication possible." ("The Artist in Frank Norris," *Pacific Monthly,* March 1907, pp. 321–22.) How the manuscript could be in New York in 1907 is not clear in the light, itself rather vague, of Charles Norris' Foreword to the novel.

place among his best work, just as he would be sorely puzzled to demonstrate exactly how stories like "The Heroism of Jonesee," "A Case for Lombroso," "His Single Blessedness," and "His Dead Mother's Portrait" "show the development of the writer," as Charles Norris asserts. Three years later in his Foreword to *Frank Norris of "The Wave"* (the last meager gathering from a twice-gleaned field), Charles Norris reaffirms his belief that Frank's two years with *The Wave* were "his most formative" and that he was "finding himself during this time." In reviewing the last-named volume, John Chamberlain, Florence Haxton Britten, and C. Hartley Grattan[25] all make the mistake of supposing that the sketches called "Fantaisie Printanière" and "Judy's Service of Gold Plate" are preliminary studies for *McTeague,* and have thus a special interest, whereas they were merely drawn from the yet unpublished *McTeague* to serve Norris' need for copy. Mr. Grattan, however, does something to restore the perspective on Norris' journalism when he asserts that from the *Collected Writings* of 1928 and the *Wave* volume of 1931 "we learn precious little about why Norris was able to write a small group of first-rate and important novels .... We do not discover here more than the merest faint indications of the way he would write [had already written, Mr. Grattan should have said] when he was at the top of his bent."

This firm determination to see in every potboiler of a writer, in all his run-of-the-mill work, evidences of "development" is but an indication of the extent to which ideas borrowed from biological evolution have penetrated

[25] In *New York Times Book Review* (May 3, 1931), *New York Herald Tribune, Books* (August 23, 1931), and *American Literature* (November 1931), respectively.

literary criticism. Such subtle domination have these ideas acquired that they are applied, with dubious fitness, to the criticism of literature even by those who fancy themselves opposed to the materialism of science. An author is supposed to unfold himself with the sequential precision which evolves a chicken from an egg.

It is a cardinal principle of many reviewers and critics that a novelist's second book is better than his first, his third still better, his fourth better yet, and so on to the end of the calendar, when he achieves his masterpiece. Thus it is asserted of the patently inferior *A Man's Woman* that it "shows a decided advance over 'McTeague' in the development of character." And Owen Wister captioned his review of *The Pit* "the last and best novel of the late Frank Norris."[26] To raise these objections is not to hold that writers do not grow in mastery of their craft; it is not to contend perversely that Norris never learned anything; nor is it to take refuge in some mystagogical theory of genius. It is merely to repeat, what is obvious enough, that the factors involved are too numerous and too complex to be accommodated by an easy scheme of development—that eccentricity is quite as common as regularity in the products of the mind. And it is to advance the belief that Norris' real prentice work must be sought before 1894 when he began to write *McTeague*.[27] That work was

[26] *The Outlook,* March 3, 1900, p. 486; *The World's Work,* February 1903, p. 3133.

[27] The exact date of composition of *McTeague* remains uncertain. In his *Frank Norris* Professor Walker writes: (1) "in his senior year he started *McTeague*" (p. 53), i.e., 1893–94; (2) "probably in his senior year" (p. 82); (3) "It was just the first ideas of a novel which Norris had in mind when he finished his fourth year at Berkeley" (p. 90). In 1914 Charles Norris was of the opinion that *McTeague* "was begun and the bulk of it was written before he left California" (Foreword to *Vandover and the Brute,* p. vi); in 1928 he stated that the novel was begun in Frank's "twenty-first or twenty-second year" (Introduction to *Collected Writings,* p. ix), which would put the inception of *McTeague* as early as the beginning of 1890, an unlikely date.

meager enough, and it throws but a feeble light on what was to follow.[28]

We may now sample the reviews to learn how a realist fared in the days of *Janice Meredith* and *Castle Craney-crow*. Although Bailey Millard once offered the unique opinion that *Moran of the Lady Letty* was "the best thing Norris ever did,"[29] it was not a book to excite wide comment and in truth not a great deal was said of it. Few could have inferred from it that its author had already created two such sturdy pieces of naturalism as *McTeague* and *Vandover*. A writer in *The Independent* (October 20, 1898) found it "amateurish in tone," its romance "dyed with the accepted colors well known to Bret Harte, Stevenson and Joaquin Miller . . . ." Perhaps the greatest success of Norris' first published novel was in attracting the favorable notice of Howells (in *Literature,* December 17, 1898), who praised its "fresh and courageous invention" and thought its contemporaneous action and American scene to its credit.

But the most noteworthy feature of the reception of *Moran* is that its author was nowhere reproached for brutality and coarseness, offenses which formed the burden of complaint against *McTeague* when it reached the reviewers a few months later. Yet Norris' tale of battle,

---

28 The early poems on medieval subjects—*At Damietta, A.D. 1250* (1890), *Brunhilde* (1890), *Poitier* (1891), *Les Enervés de Jumièges* (1890), *Yvernelle* (1891)—and such stories as *Le Jongleur de Taillebois* (1891), *Son of a Sheik* (1891), and *Lauth* (1893) already reveal Norris' love of violence and primitive emotions. The last-named shows the first handling of the idea employed in *Vandover*—the sinking of a man into actual brute semblance. Lauth having died of the wound received in the street battle, one of his ingenious friends, a doctor of medicine, restores him to life by a transfusion of sheep's blood. But the soul has gone, and the body progressively degenerates through various animal forms till it becomes a shapeless mass of protoplasm which yields at length to putrefaction.

29 "A Significant Literary Life," *Out West,* January 1903, p. 53.

murder, and sudden death, as it is described in its first sentence, was plentifully seasoned with brutality. Was it less brutal for Captain Kitchell to fell Wilbur to the deck and kick him in the stomach than for McTeague to amuse himself by biting Trina's fingers? Was it more refined for the worthy captain to spit and suck the nicotine from his moustache than for McTeague to wipe his mouth with his hand after eating? The difference, of course, is that *Moran* was "adventure," "romance," in recognizable form, where violent or brutal acts have their accepted, even indispensable, place and where coarse characters are permitted to be coarse. But to put the coarseness and brutality and vulgarity of common people in common circumstances under the magnifying glass and to observe them with detachment is another matter. This is "realism," and realism was a fighting word in the 'nineties. Above all, perhaps, *Moran* escaped the censure of the genteel critics because its hero was rich, respectable, and a gentleman, whereas McTeague, as reviewers were quick to remark, was an "ill-born lad," and the book dealt with "a class of people that story-tellers generally avoid, or at least seldom select for their chief characters."[30]

The reviews of *McTeague* make melancholy reading today. The violence of the revolt against the genteel tradition, especially among the generation that began to be heard about the time of the World War of 1914–1918, is sometimes decried; but the browser among these old reviews will feel that it was amply justified. The keen-nosed watchdogs of literature sensed immediately that here was something new and disturbing in native writing, and promptly set up their growl. *McTeague* came

[30] *Review of Reviews*, June 1899, p. 749.

just at the moment when the critics were congratulating themselves that the invading foreign heresy of naturalistic realism, after a twenty-year struggle, had been stamped out—"swept out of sight," as one reviewer wrote, "five or six years ago by the sudden on-rush of works of ideality and romance, which arose like a fresh, sweet wind to clear the literary atmosphere."[31] With mingled prudery, priggishness, and Pecksniffery, Norris was admonished and chided and his novel deplored. A veritable chorus arose: "we trust that Mr. Norris's next plot will fall in more pleasant places"; "to be hoped that Mr. Norris will find subjects better worthy of his power"; "to be hoped he may henceforth use [his ability] in the writing of books that will be not less true but a good deal more agreeable." The author was accused of "searching out the degraded side of humanity." It was deemed "a misfortune that he should have devoted so much skill and virility to the description of a life so essentially without spiritual significance, and so repulsive in its habit and quality." His manner was "hard and cold." His book was "a monotony of brutality from beginning to end"; it was "about the most unpleasant American story that anybody has ever ventured to write"; it had "no moral, esthetical or artistic reason for being," and no one would "be the better for reading it."[32]

From the reviewer in *The Outlook* we learn why Kipling could concern himself with the lives of "coarse and even vulgar" men and yet become popular with a tender-minded generation intensely intolerant of ugliness, squalor,

[31] Nancy Huston Banks, "Two Recent Revivals in Realism," *The Bookman*, June 1899, p. 356.

[32] So *Public Opinion* (March 16, 1899), *The Outlook* (March 18, 1899), *The Review of Reviews* (June 1899), Nancy Huston Banks (*Bookman*, June 1899), and *The Independent* (April 6, 1899).

or brutality—in its books. Kipling, the writer explains, "has always exhibited such men at some point as possessing deep human feeling, a sense of duty, courage, fellowship, or humor. In Mr. Norris's story there is not a trace of these higher qualities with the single exception of the two lovers."

Being themselves of a severe intellectual and verbal chastity, the critics were considerably embarrassed in their efforts to warn against Norris' "coarseness." They could deal only in cautious allusion. Thus the writer last quoted: "In two instances at least, ... he descends to descriptions of incidents which have no place in print; to comment upon or even suggest them is vulgar to the last degree." It is likely that the chief cause of these fastidious shrinkings was the incident of little Owgoost's unfortunate urinary incontinence at the theater.[33]

Yet *McTeague* wrung from its adverse critics on all hands admissions, however grudging, of its original force and of its author's high talents. *The Literary World* (April 1, 1899), of Boston, was typical. To avoid compromising itself it was obliged to voice strongly its editorial[34] dissent from the opinion of its New York correspondent, John D. Barry, whose favorable review it had recently printed. It accused Norris of "grossness for the sake of grossness," declared the spirit of his work to be "false to the highest standards," prayed that the book might fall into the hands only of those of "vigorous mind

---

[33] This entirely innocuous passage was removed by the publisher after the first copies had been sent out, and has not subsequently been restored till the appearance, in December 1941, of the limited edition issued by the Colt Press, San Francisco. The curious may also find the omitted passage in Walker's *Frank Norris,* pp. 221–22.

[34] The editors were the Reverend Edward Abbott (brother of Lyman Abbott) and Madeline Vaughan Abbott.

. . . . and strong stomach," and concluded that though he had reason to be proud of his novel "the world will not be proud of it in that distant tomorrow which irrevocably sets the true value on books of today." But with all this it could not deny that he was a powerful writer, that his characters were drawn "with rare skill," and that the deterioration of McTeague's character was pictured with a "relentless truth" which would not afford the reader the "consolation of saying that in real life it could not have happened so." Neither the public, however, nor the official guardians of literature were prepared to accept excellence, no matter how commanding, on the terms offered by such a novel as *McTeague*. For from the preceding survey of the reviews may be inductively drawn the rules governing the writing of fiction, as that art was understood by the defenders of the genteel tradition: (1) fiction must deal with pleasant subjects; (2) the chief characters must be good people, respectable, such as one might safely introduce to his wife and family; (3) the chief figures may be poor if they go to church, are industrious, and are respectful to their betters; (4) since even the most happily circumstanced heroes or heroines are likely to meet bad, coarse, or vulgar people, let the latter be always redeemed by some conspicuous virtue; (5) lest there be any mistake about where the author stands on the subjects of beauty, goodness, and truth (always remembering that there are certain "untellable truths"), let him roll his eyes heavenward from time to time, or wipe away a tear of compassion and thus avoid the imputation of being hard and cold; (6) shun unhappy endings.

Several honorable exceptions, however, may be found to the general thin-lipped disapproval which greeted *McTeague*. Charles F. Lummis in *The Land of Sunshine*

(July 1899) of Los Angeles, of which he was editor, thought it a "hideous story" but was not to be daunted by a hideous story when it was well done. And in *McTeague* he found "a fine and a powerful piece of work, an honor to its smith and a matter of pride to those of us who love literature . . . . and respect honest craft."

One of the earliest and one of the most intelligent of the reviews was that by John D. Barry, whose "New York Letter" to *The Literary World* (March 18, 1899) put the editors of that journal to the necessity of a rebuttal. *McTeague* "seems to me," he began boldly, "worthy to rank among the few great novels produced in this country." He declared himself astonished by the "profound insight into character . . . . shrewd humor . . . . brilliant massing of significant detail, and . . . . dramatic force" of Norris' novel, which he already knew at this early date was composed before *Moran of the Lady Letty*. Aware of the irrelevant objections provoked by the theme of the work, he replied: "for those who do not go to fiction merely to be amused and diverted, and who believe that fiction may profitably be made an expression of life, *McTeague* will be a revelation." An "authoritative reviewer" had recently disparaged the novel by calling it "a study of people who were on the verge of the criminal class." But even supposing the statement were true, why, Barry asked, should it be considered a reproach to the author? "People on the verge of the criminal classes, as well as the criminal classes themselves, offer excellent material for serious study in fiction."

The Old Grannis–Miss Baker love affair has always been a *locus criticus* in all discussion of *McTeague*. A majority of the reviewers, in their dogged search for something sweet in this lump of corruption, seized on it desperately as the only palatable episode in the novel. A minority saw it as an artistic defect. Thus Barry thought it had "a little of the unreality of romance."

He was one of the very first to link the name of Norris with that of Crane, an association that has been maintained in criticism ever since. The handling of the theme of *McTeague* suggested to him Crane's manner, but without a hint of imitation and with none of Crane's "striving for effect." If the novel had a fault it was that occasionally the author explained his characters "in a way that suggests superiority," whereas when he found it necessary to speak at all, he should have used language "wholly in harmony with theirs."

But it was again Howells who proved Norris' most influential champion. He had been sniffing the air and had ventured to predict that a shift in the wind was imminent. A period of expansion in American fiction, he believed, was drawing near, a time when it would lay aside the puerilities of romance and become a closer reflection of American actualities; when it would quit the provincialisms that had long confined it and become continental in scope. And the impulse which would set the new currents in motion would come from the foreign realists whose spokesman Howells had long been. *McTeague* seemed to him "A Case in Point" for all he had been prophesying, and with these words he entitled his review (*Literature,* March 24, 1899) of the novel. *McTeague,* he believed, posed an important question:

Whether we shall abandon the old-fashioned American ideal of a novel as something which may be read by all ages and sexes, for the European notion of it as something fit only for age and experience, and for men rather than women; whether we shall keep to the bonds of the provincial proprieties, or shall include within the imperial territory of our fiction the passions and the motives of the savage world which underlies as well as environs civilization, are points which this book sums up and puts concretely . . . .[34a]

Professing to have seen already in *Moran* signs of the coming change "from the romantic to the realistic temperament," he found that change fully accomplished in *McTeague,* "suddenly, and with the overwhelming effect of a blizzard." After drawing parallels with Zola and offering a close résumé of the narrative, he praised its "vivid insight," its "simple and subtile expression," the skill which could manage a mass of detail without encumbering the action, the creative power which showed no relaxation in the drawing of minor figures: "the subordinate persons are never shammed or faked; in the equality of their treatment their dramatic inferiority is lost." He demurred only, as we have seen, at what he considered the anticlimax of the conclusion and at "those silly elders," Old Grannis and Miss Baker. In one of its larger aspects, however, he found *McTeague* wanting, and here he resorts to the argument and the language of the romantic and "idealistic" school of critics who had been belaboring Norris' novel in the reviews. "Mr. Norris," he wrote, "has . . . . learned his lesson well, but he has not learned it all. His true picture of life is not true, because it leaves beauty out. Life is squalid and cruel and vile and hateful, but it is noble and tender and pure and lovely too." By this assertion it might be thought that he would have welcomed the old lovers, for did not their romance form an oasis of the "noble, tender, pure, and lovely" in the dreary waste of Polk Street? The idyl appeared to him, however, too obvious an effort at contrast, patched on, not organic to the whole.

But does Howells' dictum about life (which was every-

[34a] Quoted by permission of Miss Mildred Howells.

body's dictum and surely nothing profound) carry with it any imperative to the artist? Why must the artist put everything into every picture? May he not, must he not (whether he wills or no) select? And if so, may he not, if he likes, use only the darkest pigments, and for objects only of the harshest outlines? The question answers itself; and as a criticism of *McTeague* Howells' complaint that beauty has been left out falls to the ground. *McTeague* has·a beauty of its own, of another sort than Howells had in mind—the beauty of an imaginative creation executed with a high artistry.

Howells is a little like the veteran propagandist of revolution who, when the revolution comes, finds himself an exile. It is as if when he saw in action the forces he had invoked, he felt himself already assailed by regrets and a sense of loss. For all his tolerance and liberality of mind, the taboos of the genteel tradition "rode and rowelled" him, as Norris might have said, and he could never forget that vast audience of pious matrons and pure maidens to whom for a quarter of a century he had been addressing his own mild fictions. At the close of his review he wrote:

It is a little inhuman, and it is distinctly not for the walls of living-rooms, where the ladies of the family sit and the children go in and out. This may not be a penalty, but it is the inevitable consequence of expansion in fiction.

Blix was greeted with expressions of relief by the reviewers, good fellows only too ready to praise when their sensibilities were not outraged. "Compared to the horrible realism of 'McTeague,'" wrote one who signed himself "M." in *The Pacific Monthly* (December 1899), "this story is almost ideal." But Norris' tendency to break with the conventional heroine of fiction was not allowed to pass unchallenged. The critic just quoted saw in such a tendency a serious threat to the dignity of letters. "No matter," he declared, "how well told and clever a story may be, we never forgive the author who, having the power to do so, fails to make his heroine beautiful." Just as later the dull blue eyes of Lloyd Searight were an offense to reviewers, so in this instance were the little twinkling eyes of Blix:

He makes a noble, sensible, lovable, physically perfect creature, and then deliberately ruins his creation . . . . if the exigencies of the case called for a physical blemish, she might . . . . have been totally blind—no eyes at all are preferable to eyes that suggest rodents. The character of the heroine does not harmonize with her eyes. I refuse, therefore, to consider her seriously. . . . . Let her creator confess that he has no sense of the fitness of things and then stop writing books.

All the critics were struck by the character of Lloyd Searight in *A Man's Woman*. Like the reviewer in *The Critic* (April 1900) they found her "as far from any ideal of a man's woman heretofore presented as the east is from the west," and hence the admiration they accorded her was often reluctant. Several missed in her the brilliance of coloring which they felt to be the imprescriptible right of heroines and commented with astonishment and distaste on her dull blue eyes, the dull glow of her cheek, and the dull red of her hair. The *Overland Monthly* (May 1900) could not understand why a hero should be ugly and was particularly distressed by the cast in Bennett's eye: "Why that cast at all, Mr. Norris? But if we must have it, why not a slight one?"

Those who had been pained by what they thought the brutality of *McTeague* found the same cause for dissatisfaction in *A Man's Woman*. *The Outlook* (March 3, 1900), under the pious editorship of Lyman Abbott, always one of the most vigilant guardians of the literary proprieties, said severely: "The author of 'McTeague' again in his new novel finds it necessary to his ideas of realism to present the most repellent and brutal narratives of human suffering." The writer could describe the operation scene only by the words "sickening and disgusting," and pronounced it without "legitimate place in a work of fiction."

It is clear from the foregoing that most of the critics of *A Man's Woman* concerned themselves with irrelevant objections. Few were able to form anything like a true estimate of its worth in relation to *McTeague*. The most pertinent remarks came from *The Overland Monthly* and *The Literary World* (July 1, 1900), the first pointing out the obviousness of Norris' effort to "create bigness, to make great, overwhelming effects," and the second asserting brusquely that the book could be best described as "piling on the agony."

Had Norris ceased to write after *A Man's Woman* it could not be said that he achieved any but a very modest recognition with the contemporary reading public. It was *The Octopus* that first gained him a hearing with respectable numbers, and *The Pit* which brought him something like fame. Journals like *The Atlantic Monthly, The Dial,* and *The Nation,* which had hitherto ignored him entirely, now came forward with reviews, though the last-named held off till the appearance of *The Pit*.

The Octopus by its sheer massive proportions compelled attention, and the effect was no doubt magnified in the minds of readers by the fact that the book was announced as merely the first of a grand trilogy. Its energy and passion bore down indifference or hostility, even when the presence of the terrible Zola was glimpsed behind the scenes. No such book had ever been written by an American. Where could it be matched for largeness of design, for its almost barbaric richness of color, for its profound sense of the teeming earth and of the play of cosmic forces, for the sweep and intensity of its drama? Californian in its locale it was national in its implications; for it seized on what was characteristic in an epoch of a people's life— the vanishing frontier and the death struggle of an agrarian order in conflict with an emerging industrialism.

No doubt the novel owed something of its immediate success to a certain timeliness of theme. When it appeared, the assault on the money-power was in full swing and had its political expression in Populism and Bryanism. Hence the attitude of critics toward the book was often determined by their political and social sympathies. Some scented propaganda, though none could deny the power of the novel.

Writing in *The Dial* (September 1, 1901), William Morton Payne was offended by what he called Norris' too-evident partisanship. "If only he had given the devil his due, we might be willing to admit the diabolic character of the corporation," said he, failing to perceive that Norris had given the devil rather more than his due— that in the Shelgrim speech he had virtually (and quite unnecessarily) thrown in his hand. But for his part, Payne averred, he was inclined to sympathize with the octopus, which after all acted fully within its rights under the law. The acts of the wheat-growers, on the other hand, "illustrate nearly every form of violence and anarchy."

In his next statement Payne raises one of the knottiest problems in social and political ethics. "If the writer means to preach anything," he asserts, "it is that a certain degree of outrage justifies individuals in taking the law into their own hands, and this is the most dangerous sophistry that now confronts our civilization." Would Payne have undertaken to condemn the American Revolution, for instance, on the same grounds? It is to be feared that the problem will never be settled by a statement of general and inviolable principle, but will ever be dealt with pragmatically, however repugnant this may be to the absolutist in morals.

The Independent (May 16, 1901) did not like the hint of revolutionary excitement to be detected in the novel, nor was it pleased by its determinism:

The final impression on the reader is that the individual human will has no sway or freedom, but is beaten down by inanimate force . . . . It is our favorite contention that the aim of art is to enlarge the human will, not to contract it. In this enlargement lie both the joy and the morality of true literature.

The reviewer is nevertheless constrained to grant that *The Octopus* "contains scenes of real beauty, and elements of power that only need to put off hysterical license to rival anything written in recent years."

Henry Walcott Boynton (*The Atlantic Monthly,* May 1902) experienced ascetic shrinkings from the voluptuousness which he found in Norris' portraits of women. Hilma he thought "subtly colored after the manner of D'Annunzio's creatures," and the emphasis on odors in the description of Angéle Varian he condemned as "the sort of romantic vulgarity of which only the realist of the French school is capable." But with the exception of Presley and Vanamee he found the characters "indigenous" and the source of the novel's power. Indeed it is his evident desire, by bestowing all his praise on the characters, to brush aside the social significance of the book: "what," he asks, "is the value to creative fiction of world-movements and commercial problems compared with such breathing human nature as this?" The attitude here revealed is a cliché of traditional criticism. Must the novel be forever bound by the purely personal relations, above all by the relation of a man and a woman? Is it not a confession of eternal puerility to say that it must? Does human nature reveal itself in no other direction? H. L. Mencken's words are to the point: "the destiny and soul of man are not moulded by petty jousts of sex, as the prophets of romantic love would have us believe . . . ."[35]

That most indefatigable of reformers, Benjamin Orange Flower, editor of *The Arena*, hailed *The Octopus*—with its "noble passion for justice" equal to Zola's—as "a work so distinctly great that it justly entitles the author to rank among the very first American novelists." But not content with his otherwise sensible remarks, he added primly as a commendation of the novel that it was free from Zola's sexualism, "so revolting to the refined and healthy imagination." If not the only one to see, Flower was at least the only reviewer to point out the "palpable sophistry," as he names it, of Shelgrim's speech to Presley. He is probably wrong, however, in thinking that Shelgrim in uttering this speech violated the nature given him by the author and that Presley in allowing himself to be so staggered by it also acted out of character. To avoid frightening off those who profess to believe that a novel ceases to be a work of art at the moment when it looks beyond the loves and fortunes of private men, Flower assured his readers that *The Octopus* "must not be imagined . . . . primarily a social study," and that the author was "at all times the artist." He urged all who could afford but one

[35] "Joseph Conrad," in *A Book of Prefaces* (New York: Alfred A. Knopf, 1917), p. 35.

novel in the spring of 1901 to buy Norris' book; "read it aloud to your family," he bade, "and then lend it to your neighbors."[36]

A corps of reviewers prevailingly romantic in their sympathies and (even more pertinent) incorrigibly sentimental, singled out the romantic parts of *The Octopus* for commendation, as they had fixed on the love idyl in *McTeague*. But Frederic Taber Cooper, one of the most interested observers of Norris' work from the beginning, strongly deplored his romantic divagations. He declared himself (in *The Bookman,* May 1901) exasperated to find a man who could do such work as the realism of the Polk Street scenes in *McTeague* and the Arctic scenes in *A Man's Woman* "deliberately choosing every now and then . . . . to look at life through rose-coloured glasses, instead of adhering fearlessly to the crude colours and the harsh outlines." He was not greatly satisfied with *The Octopus.* More astounding than his curiously wrong notion that it was deficient in the creation of vivid, living characters is his opinion that it ranks below *A Man's Woman* in truth to life. Further, though he had deprecated the melodramatic conclusion of *McTeague,* he was extravagant in his praise of the yet more obviously manipulated scene of S. Behrman's death, which he thought nearly wiped out the faults of the work.

S. Behrman, it may be explained, having escaped Presley's bomb and having gained possession of Magnus' vast acres with their rich harvest, betakes himself to the dock where the steamer "Swanhilda" is filling her hold with the spoil. He boards the vessel and stands near the open hatch to enjoy the sense of his triumph and to watch the

[36] "The Trust in Fiction: A Remarkable Social Novel," *The Arena,* May 1902.

wheat, his wheat, pouring in a mighty cascade from the elevator into the depths of the ship. Suddenly he trips on a coil of rope and falls headlong on to the mounting cone of wheat below. His first sensation is merely one of dismay, but as the realization of his peril dawns upon him he is seized by mortal terror. He rises to his feet and strives to mount the ever shifting pyramid of grain toward the square of light far out of reach above. He shouts, but his voice is lost in the vast rustling whisper of the descending torrent. The pelting kernels sting his face like bullets; chaff and dust blind and choke him; sweat streaked with blood streams down his florid cheeks. Time after time he flings himself at the treacherous sliding mound, only to be buffeted from his feet. At length, exhausted, he can no longer free his arms and legs from the heavy close-pressing grain. There is a last glimpse of clutching fingers above the flood that in the next moment submerges him completely, and extinguishes the life in his fat carcass. As a final irony it is the "Swanhilda" on which Presley, seeking relief for his oppressed spirit, takes passage for India, unaware as he treads the deck that beneath his feet lies the man whom mortal justice could not reach, his mouth stuffed with wheat—the avenging and all-victorious wheat.

Considered by itself, S. Behrman's unpleasant death in the hold of the grain ship is entirely credible. As a piece of writing, the incident is highly effective, done with all of Norris' descriptive and dramatic skill. Considered, however, in relation to the whole, it is open to objection. In the first place, S. Behrman is plainly the victim of a conspiracy on the part of the author. In the second place, if poetic justice were to be meted out at all (and that it should be is not apparent), it should have fallen, not on

S. Behrman, but on Shelgrim. That the ranchers should have concentrated their hatred of the railroad on the oleaginous Behrman was only natural, since he was its visible representative and willing servant; Shelgrim they never saw. But for the author to take his revenge on the agent instead of the principal is illogical.

The attitude of critics toward the Zola influence in Norris' work varied, of course, with the feeling of those critics for Zola himself. For, though it is possible to admire the Frenchman in his own sphere and yet believe his method ill-adapted to the depiction of American life, objections to his influence on American writers meant as a rule that the critic disliked Zola on moral rather than artistic grounds. Thus Higginson and Boynton taxed Norris and Garland with inconsistency in breaking with the literary traditions of the Eastern states, only to look for models still farther east, in France and Russia:

. . . . Mr. Norris's novels could not have been written but by a worshiper of Zola. It cannot be expected that the spirit of the West will find perfect expression under such a method. If America cannot find utterance in terms of England, she certainly cannot in terms of France. There are certain racial prescriptions of taste and style which cannot be safely ignored.[37]

These remarks have a superficial air of truth, but, as with other generalizations, the test comes in their particular application. They fail as a criticism of the work of Norris, whose people feel and think and speak and act like Americans, and like no other. To forbid writers to borrow a foreign method or to look at a foreign model is indeed a large prohibition. The real animus of Higginson

[37] Thomas Wentworth Higginson and Henry Walcott Boynton, *A Reader's History of American Literature* (Boston: Houghton Mifflin Company [1903]), p. 255. This work is apparently the earliest of its kind to take cognizance of Norris. "Apart from the question of method," say the authors, "the substance of Mr. Norris's books is of exceptional power . . . ."

and Boynton comes out in their phrase, "certain racial prescriptions of taste and style which cannot safely be ignored." It is merely the familiar prudery which speaks here.

The Bookman, however, in its "Chronicle and Comment" department (May 1901), thought Norris' mistake in *The Octopus* lay, not in his following Zola, but in taking for his model the later Zola of *Paris* and *Fécondité,* which are smothered by their theses and in which the characters become types. But Norris was fully aware of the weakness of such a work as *Fécondité,* which he cites as an example of what to avoid in writing a purpose novel. It is traces, rather, of several of Zola's best novels—*L'Assomoir, Germinal, La Terre*—which are to be found in *The Octopus.*

Howells struck at once to the essential quality of *The Octopus* when he proclaimed its author "a poet among the California wheat-fields." He believed the influence of Zola on the book not harmful. Norris, he wrote in "The Editor's Easy Chair" of *Harper's* (October 1901), "owes to the great romantic realist nothing but the conception of treating a modern theme epically." Far from thinking the characters not realized as individuals, he pronounced them "not the less personalities because of their typical function." Regretting as always Norris' penchant for romantic digression, he yet found the loosely connected episodes (such presumably as the Vanamee story) good in themselves: "we would prefer to have [them] another time rather than lose [them] altogether." At the end of his review he did not hesitate to assert that *The Octopus,* granted its defects, was still "a great book, simple, sombre, large, and of a final authority as the record of a tragical passage of American, of human events, which, if we did not stand in their every-day presence, we should shudder at as the presage of unexampled tyrannies."

But of all Norris' novels *The Pit* gave most satisfaction to his contemporaries. To both critics and readers it seemed that here he was back on familiar ground after his willful sojourn in regions outlandish and fearful, where monstrous beings performed monstrous acts in the midst of a savage landscape. In such a figure as Jadwin readers had the type hero of their generation. They could at the same time admire his ruthless will to power through riches and lay unction to their souls in witnessing his fall and in reflecting with him that, after all, money isn't everything. The sentiment had about it an engaging air of moral and philosophic truth, though nobody seriously believed in it.

The novel was first published serially in *The Saturday Evening Post*,[38] and did not appear in book form till three months after Norris' death. Hence a number of reviewers took the opportunity to sum up his work and to cast his literary horoscope. Frederic Taber Cooper placed *The Pit* with *McTeague* as most likely to endure. *The Octopus,* he thought, had been a failure and a grave disappointment to those who had most confidence in Norris. But with his last work all was redeemed: "what he failed to do then he has done, and done brilliantly, in . . . . *The Pit.*"[39] Owen Wister (*World's Work,* February 1903), Arthur Goodrich (*Current Literature,* December 1902)—

---

[38] September 27, 1902—January 31, 1903. It is not without significance that *The Pit* could be accepted by the *Post,* then in its third year under the editorship of the late George Horace Lorimer, who gave it the character it has ever since maintained. It was in 1902 also that Lorimer's creation, Old Gorgon Graham, the shrewd Chicago pork packer (of the *Letters from a Self-Made Merchant to His Son*), enjoyed his huge success, both in the pages of the *Post* and in the volume published by Small, Maynard & Co.

[39] *The Bookman,* December 1902, p. 335.

who had known Norris during their days together with the firm of Doubleday, Page—and the reviewer for *Public Opinion* (January 22, 1903) all applied the "last and best book" formula. Some, however, like Albert Bigelow Paine (*Bookman,* February 1903), were ready to concede superior workmanship and style to *The Pit,* but not its superiority to *The Octopus* as an imaginative creation. A few spoke more sharply. *The Independent* (February 5, 1903) averred: "the book is not far from a glorification of the basest passions in the American character."

But that review which perhaps most surely penetrates to the fundamental weaknesses of *The Pit* appeared in *Harper's Weekly* (March 14, 1903). Norris had given too great prominence to the "unimportant society side of the business" and to his vain, half-cultured heroine, when the only proper heroine of the novel should have been the wheat. He had failed sufficiently to clarify his own thought and feeling with respect to Jadwin and Laura.

It is not alone the luxury of our Jadwins which is vulgar; it is the Jadwins themselves who are vulgar . . . . It is for such brute state as theirs that the earth groans with harvests and her children with hunger, and we have not quite an assurance from the novelist that he senses their vulgarity. He leaves us to fear that somehow the woman's beauty and the man's courage have blinded him.

Such "unessential lives" cease to excite either the interest or the pity of the reader. Let the one sink to ruin through her "greedy vanity," and the other through his "ruthless lust of power." It is all one, concludes the reviewer, whether they rejoice or suffer.

The year following Norris' death saw the expected offering of obituary notices, personal reminiscences, friendship's garlands, and summaries of his work—some dozen in all (exclusive of newspaper items), after which he began to fade quietly from public notice, yielding place to new names of the hour. Through most of these articles may be traced one theme, the theme made mandatory when Keats died at the age of twenty-six; it begins something like this: "Cut off in the flower of his youth and at the dawn of his powers, had he lived he would undoubtedly have gone on to greater triumphs, of which the work he left behind was hardly more than the ample promise." But there is not much reason to think that most writers who have died young died too soon. A fantasy of Hawthorne's, tart beneath its humor, comes to mind. In it he imagines interviews in 1845 with Byron, Shelley, and others of the romantic rebels. We see Byron gouty, enormously fat, and wearing a brown wig and spectacles; he has been reconciled to his wife, is intimate with Southey, makes speeches in the House of Lords vigorously denouncing radical notions in politics, has embraced Methodism (with embellishments from the doctrines of Pusey), and is preparing a new edition of his complete works, carefully revised and expurgated for reading in the family circle! Shelley has taken holy orders, and writes poetical tracts establishing the proofs of Christianity on the basis of the Thirty-Nine Articles![40]

Not for more than a decade did the regrets subside respecting what Norris did not live to write. In 1917 Mencken expressed doubt that it would have surpassed what he left behind. *The Pit* he thought a disquieting sign; "the evil lures of popular success lay all about him. It is no wonder that he sometimes seemed to lose his direction."[41] To Thomas Beer, writing in 1926, it seemed that

---

[40] "P's Correspondence," in *Mosses from an Old Manse,* Vol. II.

[41] H. L. Mencken, *A Book of Prefaces* (New York: Alfred A. Knopf, 1917), p. 71.

in the battle waging in Norris between the artist and the moralist, the artist had succumbed and turned into a "bitter pamphleteer, still powerful, still adroit." For Beer *The Octopus* is no more than a "tremendous melodrama with Jehovah thundering at its close."[42]

By allowing Norris greatness in an impossible future, certain critics were able, with every appearance of generosity and acumen, to disparage what he actually did. Thus William Dallam Armes wrote (*Sunset,* December 1902) that the work he left entitles him to honorable mention but to the end he was "somebody's disciple" and his work was crude; if, however, he had lived, concludes Armes with the familiar refrain, "I believe he would have gone far, even into the front ranks."

At his death he left no immediate successors, and the naturalistic realism of which he and Crane had been the advance guard came to a halt. It is true that Norris had seen in Dreiser his legitimate heir, and it was largely through his enthusiasm that *Sister Carrie* first got into print. But the prudery of a publisher's wife impounded the whole edition (except for reviewers' copies) in the storerooms of the firm, and Dreiser remained unknown to the general public for another half-dozen years.[43] The field appeared to be in full possession of costume romance. Maurice Thompson, whose literary aversions were nothing if not extensive, looked about him and exulted that the noisome "Flaubert-Maupassant-Zola-Ibsen-Hardy-Tolstoï tide" had subsided. He wrote:

. . . . I suggest that we hold on as long as possible to the sort of

---

[42] Thomas Beer, *The Mauve Decade* (New York: Alfred A. Knopf, 1926), p. 99.

[43] Norris read the manuscript of *Sister Carrie* for Doubleday, Page & Company. For Dreiser's account of the misadventures of his first novel, see his "Early Adventures of Sister Carrie," *The Colophon,* Part V, 1931.

stories just now so popular. A little history, a little courage, a strong measure of lawful and pure love, a dash of rattling adventure and a happy marriage to come out of it all, may not be a mixture agreeable to the taste of the "higher critics" of fiction; but it is wholesome and conducive to a healthy longevity.[44]

But by the end of 1903 the vogue of the "hysterical historical" novel (as it was called by a critic in the *Review of Reviews*) was on the decline. "The people are tired of 'Odzooks!' and 'S'Blood!' and 'What ho, without there!' " This writer continues:

The result is a large number of novels of modern times, studies of life as the writer has seen it, and therefore with fundamental truth. And the more courageous, more earnest writers, with much creative imagination and with little, are taking the great problems, political, commercial, and social, into the material they are molding.[45]

The influence of such works as *The Octopus* and *The Pit* in turning the novel into this new channel is obvious. Thus Norris may be regarded as a forerunner of the "muckraking" movement which filled the first dozen years of the new century. During this period, naturalism, though it exerted a strong pull on such writers as Herrick and London, was in abeyance. But Carl Van Doren, looking back from 1922, was able to say (in the Preface to his *Contemporary American Novelists*) that the most striking fact of the preceding twenty years had been the tendency toward naturalism.

At rare intervals up to the World War of 1914–1918 articles on Norris appeared in the magazines. Two essays

[44] Maurice Thompson, "Breezy Books for Summer," *The Independent*, June 7, 1900, p. 1387.

[45] *Review of Reviews*, December 1903, p. 753. The writer mentions Richard Whiteing's *The Yellow Van*, Will Payne's *Mr. Salt*, David Graham Phillips' *The Master-Rogue*, Samuel Merwin's *The Whip Hand*, Frederick Upham Adams' *John Burt*, Alfred Henry Lewis' *The Boss*, Frederick Trevor Hill's *The Web*—all faded beyond recovery.

achieved book covers, one by Frederic Taber Cooper, the other by John Curtis Underwood, and by consequence for long constituted almost the whole bibliography of Norris criticism. Cooper, writing in 1911, testified that already the work of Norris had been "thrown into an unjust and misleading remoteness" as if he belonged to a past generation, and as if his influence had suddenly and permanently perished. But the appearance, he thought, was deceptive: "As a matter of fact, Norris's influence has never for an hour been dead. In a quiet, persistent way, it has spread and strengthened, leavening all unsuspectedly the maturer work of many of the writers who have since come into prominence."[46] For the rest, Cooper's essay is compounded mainly of his earlier reviews and offers nothing new except its ten-year perspective. In that perspective, it seemed to him, Norris stood taller than ever, dwarfing all those who had come forward in the interval.

A few years later Underwood wrote: "Norris is still a prophet without honor in some sections, some classes, some literary, scholastic, cultured and educated circles of his own country." But for his part he was convinced that Norris stood in the new century "so far unrivaled, unassailed and unassailable." He saw rightly that *The Octopus* "in its broad results" justifies capitalistic aggression; he also rightly praises its author for his humanitarian "hatred of sham, of pretense, of special privilege of any sort," for his democratic sympathy as great as Mark Twain's, for his love of justice. He then swallows the paradox without apparent discomfort, indeed without even being aware of it.[47]

<hr>

[46] "Frank Norris," in *Some American Story Tellers* (New York: Henry Holt and Company, 1911), p. 295.

[47] "Frank Norris," in *Literature and Insurgency* (New York: Mitchell Kennerley, 1914), pp. 152, 175, 177.

The posthumous collection of short stories, *The Third Circle* (1909), stirred but little interest. None but Jeannette Gilder[48] has ventured to think that Norris had in him the makings of a notable short-story writer. In his short stories he worked on a lower level of thought and emotion than in his novels. He could not compress his large vision of human life in space and time within their limits. Showing largely the impress of Kipling and of Richard Harding Davis—the dress-suit snob of American fiction—they make plentiful use of surprise and contrast; they are by turns clever, smart, ingenious in plot, momentarily exciting, humorous, for Norris, despite the impression he gave many to the contrary, had humor, both in his work and in his private converse—that best of humor which enables a man to smile and to jest at himself.

His bantering spirit is well seen in his letters. On occasion he referred to *The Octopus* as "The Squid," and sometimes signed himself "The Boy Zola." But his humor makes no clamorous demands on laughter, and so has gone unnoted by many. His talent for parody may be seen in a little group of "Perverted Tales," imitations of Kipling, Crane, Harte, Harding Davis, Bierce, and Anthony Hope. With uncanny accuracy he reproduces Crane's peculiar abruptions and startling adjectives, and turns into hearty burlesque what the reader will recognize as Bierce's "One of the Missing," from *In the Midst of Life.*[49]

But few of Norris' short stories have distinction. Two of the more noteworthy are not exercises in realism, but rather sheer fantasy—"The Guest of Honour" (in *The Third Circle*) and "The Puppets and the Puppy" (in *Frank Norris of "The Wave"*). In the first, the guest of

[48] In *Putnam's Magazine*, August 1909, p. 631.
[49] See *Frank Norris of "The Wave,"* pp. 77–100.

honor is death—not a figure of terror but a healer, a physician whose remedy is heroic but sovereign. The second is in the spirit of Voltaire's *Micromégas* or Franklin's *The Ephemera*. It embodies Norris' sense of the ironic relation between humanity's conception of its role in the cosmos and the inscrutable powers that shape its destiny.

Between 1897 and 1902 Norris' view of the position and future of the short story underwent a reversal. At the earlier date he believed the short story offered a more promising field than the novel—at least to the San Francisco writer, to whom his remarks are particularly addressed: "we are not settled enough yet," he wrote, "for the novelist, who demands large, co-ordinated, broad and simple lines upon which to work . . . . But the short stories? There's the chance. Who shall be our Kipling?"[50] By 1902 he had come to think, prophetically enough, that the cheap popular magazine would "in time to come, engender a decay in the quality of the short story." The conscientious writer, he continued,

will turn his attention and time, his best efforts, to the writing of novels, reverting to the short story only when necessary for the sake of boiling the Pot and chasing the Wolf. He will abandon the field to the inferior men, or enter it only to dispose of "copy" which does not represent him at his best.[51]

That this described his attitude toward his own short stories is confirmed by the fact that he made no effort to preserve them in book form.

Since its publication in 1914 *Vandover and the Brute* has enjoyed a steady rise in critical esteem. Many of its

[50] "An Opening for Novelists," San Francisco *Wave*, May 22, 1897; quoted by Charles G. Norris, Introduction to *Collected Writings*, p. xii.

[51] "Salt and Sincerity," in *The Responsibilities of the Novelist* (Doubleday, Doran & Company, Inc., 1901, 1902, 1903), p. 253.

first reviewers, with their fixed ideas of "development," learning that it was an early book and ignoring that it was contemporary in composition with *McTeague,* could see nothing in it but a crude and tentative effort. Charles Norris in his Introduction to the volume asserts that the "dominant idea of the novel possessed its writer to the exclusion of the less important details of the plot"; that the meeting of Haight and the prostitute Flossie in the "Imperial" was obviously meant to be more important; and that Turner Ravis, so carefully introduced, is allowed to fade out of the story. Following this hint several reviewers detected the same faults. One speaks of "several characters . . . . elaborately introduced and then apparently forgotten." Another repeats this charge and discovers "currents that lead us to look for crises never fulfilled . . . ."[52] But it is a necessary consequence of Norris' main conception that the secondary characters should recede as the narrative advances. When Vandover's seduction of Ida Wade becomes a public scandal, his old set promptly ostracizes him, not of course for the act itself but because he has been found out. His former acquaintances fall away naturally as he sinks stage by stage in the social scale, even those like Haight whose friendship is sincere. As for the meeting of Haight and Flossie, it appears to be merely a part of Norris' naturalistic theme—an irony of chance by which the innocent are punished equally with the guilty. By it Haight, the chaste young man, suffers as greatly as Vandover, a thorough debauchee.

Edwin Francis Edgett perceived that these supposed inadvertences were a part of Norris' artistic purpose: "He has

---

[52] *Literary Digest,* June 20, 1914, p. 1494; *Current Opinion,* June 1914, p. 456.

concentrated his attention and the reader's interest upon one man and one man alone, and he has compelled us to follow him to the bitter end." It is therefore proper that the other characters should exist only in their relation to Vandover. Among the reviewers, Edgett was the stoutest champion of *Vandover and the Brute*. He saw that it was not perfect and that revision might have made it "more coherent and more compact" but not, he believed, "more forceful or more truthful." Nor would he concede that it was incomplete. "Apologies for 'Vandover and the Brute' because it is a posthumous novel, a first novel, a youthful novel, an unrevised novel are unnecessary. It is a novel of which any writer might be proud . . . ."[53]

How the notion got abroad that *Vandover* is incomplete is uncertain. Parrington called it "An unfinished work—but a huge and terrible torso."[54] But too much has been made of this alleged incompleteness. We could speak more to the point on the subject if we could compare the manuscript with the published version. We learn that Charles Norris added some five thousand words, at what points it would be useful to know. (He has been skillful in conforming his style to that of the original.) He also omitted an entire chapter—to quiet the fears of the publisher, it is true, but with what effect on the structure we cannot tell. The question always remains: Would Norris have submitted a novel he considered unfinished to Doubleday & McClure Company and would John S. Phillips of that firm, fearing to publish it himself, have sent it to William Heinemann?

[53] "Norris' Posthumous Novel" (signed "E.F.E."), *Boston Evening Transcript,* April 22, 1914, Part Two, p. 8.

[54] V. L. Parrington, *The Beginnings of Critical Realism in America* (New York: Harcourt, Brace and Company, 1930), p. 332.

The first to place *Vandover and the Brute* definitely ahead of *The Pit*—and even of *The Octopus*—was Edith Wyatt. Disapproving of trilogies, she adjudges the earlier work more spontaneous than the epic of the wheat and much superior to *The Pit* in its "evocation of a city atmosphere." She praises its "admirable realization" of the period of the 'nineties—the era of cotillions and leg-of-mutton sleeves. But while this last is just, it hardly supports her opinion that what is essentially an individual study is a "large and radical presentation of a social picture."[55]

C. Hartley Grattan (*The Bookman,* July 1929) puts *Vandover* with *McTeague* and *The Octopus* as one of Norris' three novels which are "undoubtedly of the first rank." Disregarding its lack of revision, he pronounced it "as it stands, an American masterpiece. It is consistent, accurate and powerful realism," and the picture of Vandover's degeneration compares for excellence with that of Hurstwood in *Sister Carrie.* Three years later, in reviewing Professor Walker's biography (*The Nation,* November 30, 1932), he is more reserved about *Vandover* and includes it among Norris' best novels with some show of reluctance. Professor Blankenship accords the book only "flashes" of merit; but those flashes, he asserts, have not been surpassed in American fiction.[56] Mencken grants it high rank in Norris' work, understands that its defects cannot conceal its "general merit," and commends its "occasional touches of delicate and mature artistry," its "boldly and clearly" imagined characters, its scenes of

[55] Edith Wyatt, *Great Companions* (New York: D. Appleton & Co., 1917), pp. 51 ff.

[56] Russell Blankenship, *American Literature as an Expression of the National Mind* (New York: Henry Holt and Company, 1931), p. 529.

"genuine dramatic power," and its "striking and effective" dénouement.[57]

The revival of interest in Norris which began about the time of the World War of 1914–1918 is but a part of the final assault, made all along the line, against the genteel tradition. The sacred figures of the New England enlightenment—as well as their heirs, the Gilders, Stedmans, Stoddards, Aldriches—were all in the camp of the enemy, whether as volunteers or as conscripts. Willy-nilly they had all been pressed into service and put into the uniform of the genteel and academic battalions. Hence the younger novelists, poets, and critics who together made the renaissance of the 'twenties looked about them eagerly for allies. They found them in the men, neglected or half-forgotten, of the 'nineties or earlier—men who at one point or another had challenged the genteel tradition and defied its taboos. Various "rediscoveries" began to be made, and old reputations were reappraised, sometimes with a biting tongue. First biographies of Melville, Crane, and Bierce appeared in 1921, 1923, and 1929, respectively. Early in the period Van Wyck Brooks, in *America's Coming of Age* (1915), had proclaimed the new day. Thomas Beer in the brilliant and scornful *Mauve Decade* (1926) made his attack on the pruderies and hypocrisies of the 'nineties. The *American Mercury* (founded 1924) under the editorship of Mencken carried the campaign forward for ten years with great verve and gusto. The fight was won when the tone changed from indignation to humor. Politicians, financiers, evangelists, writers, soldiers, popular heroes of every kind from the last thirty years of the nineteenth century were resurrected in biogra-

[57] H. L. Mencken, Introduction to *Vandover*, Vol. V of Norris' *Works* (1928).

phies of the "new school," stripped of their haloes without anger, and held up for the tolerant amusement of a generation now happily freed (so it hoped and believed) from the delusions of its fathers.

Recent critics of Norris, whether or not they like present-day literary trends, are agreed on one point: his importance, first, as a pioneer of naturalism, and, second, as an example for those who would deal boldly and honestly with American life. This, in the words of John Chamberlain, is his "extrinsic" value to American literature. "More than anyone else he broke the ground for Dreiser . . . . more than anyone else he brought 'realism' from its theoretical stage . . . . to the stage where it became an active virus."[58] Hartley Grattan places him with Bierce, Crane, and London as one who bore a part in the coming of age of our literature.[59]

V. F. Calverton, fixing his attention on the novels alone, sees Norris as one who "gave early voice to the defeatist mood which has pervaded American literature since his day." He it was who "taught us that tragedy was abroad in the land." In him the romantic exuberance generated by "the early rhythm of the West," the soaring optimism whose great prophets had been Emerson and Whitman, "broke down . . . . into pessimism and despair."[60] This drift toward pessimism was the natural consequence of fundamental changes in American life, of the restriction of economic opportunity, of the steady hardening of a once plastic social order. Although Calverton takes no account of the optimism which Norris

[58] *New York Times Book Review*, May 3, 1931, p. 10.

[59] Hartley Grattan, *Bitter Bierce: A Mystery of American Letters*, p. 273.

[60] V. F. Calverton, *The Liberation of American Literature* (New York: Charles Scribner's Sons, 1932), pp. 350–51.

superimposes on the theme of *The Octopus,* he is nevertheless substantially correct in emphasizing the determinism and pessimism of the novels. For Norris' optimism is cosmic; he has transferred his hope from the individual to the race and entrusted final good to the action of cosmic forces. The individual suffers and is trampled by an iron destiny; the power to prevail over his environment is taken out of his hands. But the race endures and good will ultimately triumph. This is but cold comfort and a poor substitute for the tangible rewards of individual effort, for the intense conviction that (to return once more to Emerson's words) "every young man of good faculty and good habits can by perseverance attain to an adequate estate." Norris' cosmic optimism is in effect a retreat from the faith of the fathers.

Such are the implications of a novel like *The Octopus.* Curiously, however, a different impression may be gained from the critical essays, where, as we have seen, is to be found an explicit statement of the traditional optimism engendered by the expanding frontier, of faith in progress, of faith in the democratic ideal, of faith in the power of literature as an instrument of social betterment. It is thus that Bernard Smith is able to place Norris with Garland as last in the succession of Emerson and Whitman, rather than as first of the prophets of pessimism and disillusionment.[61] That two such diverse interpretations of Norris' significance in American literature are possible— the one finding support in his fiction, the other in his critical utterances—is but a final instance of the mingling in him of contrary elements.

Few have discovered in Norris any talent for criticism.

[61] Bernard Smith, *Forces in American Criticism* (New York: Harcourt, Brace and Company, 1939), pp. 180, 184.

His posthumously collected essays were roughly handled by *The Nation* (November 19, 1903): "Assurance of his splendid possibilities can hardly survive the republication of these casual papers . . . . for they show defects . . . . of knowledge, of judgment, of taste—that militate against achievement of greatness in any direction." But what really troubled the reviewer, as soon appears, was Norris' full-voiced contempt for the rectory–tea-party conception of literature. Later critics like Hartley Grattan and Professor Bixler have dwelt on his intellectual deficiencies. He was "intellectually lost," writes the latter; he "dabbled in learning to the extent of one or two half-baked ideas which he thought the whole of philosophy."[62]

George E. DeMille, however, has pointed out that some of Norris' pronouncements in *The Responsibilities of the Novelist* are by no means contemptible. Two ideas in particular reveal his critical ability: (1) "his discovery of the frontier as a chief 'matter' of American literature"; and (2) his novelist versus story-teller distinction. Of the first, Mr. DeMille writes: "The thing itself was old enough. . . . . But it was Norris who first labeled and ticketed the frontier in American literature, who traced its various developments from Cooper to Garland, and who noted that in his own day the frontier was no more." Though Emerson had long before suggested the literary possibilities of the West, this claim for Norris could be plausibly defended. The second idea, Mr. DeMille believes, is a contribution to the theory of the novel which shows genuine insight, and which "alone marks out Norris as potentially a great critic."[63]

62 Paul H. Bixler, *American Literature*, March 1933, pp. 85, 86.

63 G. E. DeMille, *Literary Criticism in America: A Preliminary Survey* (New York: The Dial Press [Lincoln MacVeagh], 1931), p. 201.

Norris was not a great critic, actual or potential, of the kind who erect imposing systems or provide the intellectual world with a universal passkey to the truth. In this sense a "great critic" is merely a man who is greatly mistaken. But that Norris had thought about literature, and thought to some purpose, cannot be denied. He had "insights," as Bernard Smith says justly, "frequently profound." His rejection of the genteel and his perception that literature overleaps purely aesthetic boundaries are enough to earn him respect. That rejection and that perception were useful for his generation and they will be useful again.

It remains to glance briefly at what some believe to be the "intrinsic" value of Norris' work, as against his "extrinsic" importance, generally agreed upon by the critics.

Professor Pattee greets Norris at the front door of the somewhat austere mansion where literature abides, with some kind words about his vitality, his imaginative power, his truth. But this is only preliminary to showing him around to the tradesmen's entrance at the rear. For, in Professor Pattee's view, "restraint," "reserve," "good taste" are necessary for admission to the drawing room, and in these Norris was woefully deficient; hence what he wrote was not literature at all, but journalism: "In the higher sense of the word they [*The Octopus* and *The Pit*] are not literature; they are remarkably well done newspaper 'stories.'" So the old ladies of Cranford, remembering the great Doctor Johnson, must have spoken about Mr. Dickens. But there is journalism and journalism. If the journalism of one generation survives into the next, it is already literature. In his remarks on *McTeague* and *Vandover* Professor Pattee revives the language of the reviewers of twenty years earlier. With Norris, "To tell the truth was to tell with microscopic detail the repulsive things of physical life." Of all Norris' memorable work in the naturalistic vein he can only say, "True to life it undoubtedly is," and then ask, "but to what end?"[64]

In the opinion of Ludwig Lewisohn, Norris is a man of one book. That book is *McTeague,* and nothing else he wrote belongs any longer to living literature. Of *Vandover and the Brute* he has no word. *McTeague,* however, "has what no other book of the period has, what very few American novels have yet had at all: concentration, density, impassioned exactness, depth of tone, even an approach to severity of contour," and this for a special reason—that it expressed something very personal in Norris and "therefore released an obscure inner appetence and conflict of his own."[65] Not Zola but Octave Mirbeau determined the shape and quality of *McTeague,* Mr. Lewisohn believes. If this be true, it is a genuine discovery of considerable interest, for it has escaped the notice of all other critics; and if, as Mr. Lewisohn thinks probable, Norris "soaked himself" in Mirbeau, it is curious that he very carefully concealed the fact, for among the hundred-odd writers he mentions, the name of that author nowhere occurs. Zola is more apparent to Mr. Lewisohn in *The Octopus* and *The Pit.* Believing as he does that the method of Zola is "very tiresome and pitifully shallow," he is not sorry that Norris has had no greater influence.

Dreiser is one of the few who without saving clauses give *McTeague* its proper rank. Its characters, he asserts,

[64] F. L. Pattee, *A History of American Literature Since 1870* (New York: The Century Co., 1915), pp. 400, 398, 399.

[65] Ludwig Lewisohn, *Expression in America* (New York: Harper & Brothers, 1932), p. 322.

have become as permanent fixtures of his mind as the people of *Wuthering Heights, Vanity Fair, Crime and Punishment,* and *Père Goriot.* It is "as sombre and yet true a presentation of reality as has been conceived by any writer in any land."[66]

Professor Bixler in calling *McTeague* "a minor American masterpiece" does the novel an injustice. A minor American masterpiece is Brockden Brown's *Wieland* or Ed Howe's *Story of a Country Town.* Unless we can find an explanation for *McTeague,* thinks Professor Bixler, we must accept the book as "a kind of miracle, a flash of lightning in the midst of philosophic and artistic blackness." But this makes too much of a mystery where no mystery exists greater—or less—than attaches to the origin of any other novel of high rank. To say further that Norris "held surprisingly few scruples about his vocation" is to run counter to the evidence, both of those who knew him and of his essays on writing. Severe, however, as he is with Norris in general, Professor Bixler makes the handsome acknowledgment that "no more gifted painter of the objective scene ever graced American literature."[67]

How does Norris stand with recent critics in relation to other novelists of the realist group? His revival has never reached the proportions of that which established Crane. The latter had the early advantage of such a belligerent champion as Thomas Beer. His reticence and certain rumors persisting vaguely around his name fitted him to catch the public interest. Carl Van Doren believes Norris wrote nothing to excel *The Red Badge of Cour-*

<hr>

[66] Theodore Dreiser, Introduction (p. x) to 1928 edition of *McTeague* (by Frank Norris, copyright 1899, 1927, by Doubleday, Doran & Company, Inc.).

[67] Paul H. Bixler, *American Literature,* March 1933, pp. 85, 86.

age.[68] Dreiser on the contrary thinks Crane not "the equal in any sense"[69] of Norris. Parrington saw in Crane "the genius of his generation"; in Norris the "most stimulating and militant of our early naturalists."[70] Professor Harlan Hatcher believes correctly that Norris' "understanding of the real forces at work in American life and their appropriateness for the novel was . . . . much more penetrating than Crane's,"[71] though the latter's critical reputation is admittedly the greater.

Mencken has no hesitation in putting Norris above Howells in the creation of living characters,[72] in imaginative power, in intuitive perception of the surge and rhythm of a people's life. "No figure even remotely comparable to . . . . McTeague or Dreiser's Frank Cowperwood is to be encountered in his novels. He is quite unequal to any such evocation of the race-spirit, of the essential conflict of forces among us, of the peculiar drift and color of American life."[73] As between the two naturalists, "Dreiser, in truth," he wrote in 1917, "was a bigger man than Norris from the start . . . ."[74] Some years later he had modi-

[68] *Cambridge History of American Literature,* III, 93.

[69] Introduction to 1928 edition of *McTeague,* p. viii.

[70] *Beginnings of Critical Realism in America* (New York: Harcourt, Brace and Company, 1930), pp. 328, 329.

[71] *Creating the Modern American Novel* (New York: Farrar and Rinehart, 1935), p. 20.

[72] With shrewd insight Professor Firkins accounts Jadwin a creation superior to Silas Lapham for the reason that Howells in dealing with Lapham could not overcome his aristocratic bias. As a result he makes of him a "dancing bear" and puts "the emphasis on the vulgar side, rather than the human or natural side, of acts which are susceptible of either treatment." If Norris had drawn Lapham, "the result would have been less vulgar even if equally accurate, because taste, if a juror at all, would not have been the foreman of the jury" (Oscar W. Firkins, *William Dean Howells: A Study* [Harvard University Press, 1924], p. 160).

[73] *Prejudices: First Series* (New York: Alfred A. Knopf, 1919), p. 54.

[74] H. L. Mencken, *A Book of Prefaces* (New York: Alfred A. Knopf, 1917), p. 70.

fied, even reversed, this judgment: "Dreiser lacks his craftsmanship, his versatility, his elastic intelligence."[75]

The last ten years have seen a dozen new histories or surveys of American literature and of American fiction. In these works Norris receives at least a respectful attention and a due recognition of his importance for recent developments in our fiction. Several of academic authorship, however, show a certain reserve toward an uncompromising realism, and find Norris' redeeming virtues on his romantic or "idealistic" sides. Thus Professor Knight writes: "his brand of realism is never pocked like so much of the French; it is refined with an idealism which was Norris' inescapable inheritance."[76]

Professor Quinn, likewise tender-minded, prefers the clean running and shooting of the last part of *McTeague* to its "squalid love story," which would have been but "a photographic account of an unimportant matter" without the dentist's flight through the mountains. In this episode Norris "added the imaginative touches that lifted the book into significance." Professor Quinn also finds satisfaction in the visionary parts of *The Octopus* and thinks the "final note of optimism . . . . lifts the novel into imaginative surety."[77] In a long list of permanent portraits in the gallery of American fiction, he finds room for Elsie Venner, Mrs. Lecks and Mrs. Aleshine, Peter Stirling, and Ben Hur, with others more distinguished; but not for Maggie, Hurstwood, Frank Cowperwood, Doc Kennicott, George F. Babbitt, Trina, or McTeague.

Writers may be divided into two groups: those marked

---

[75] Introduction to 1928 edition of *Vandover and the Brute*, p. x.

[76] Grant C. Knight, *The Novel in English* (New York: Richard R. Smith, 1931), p. 301. Quoted by permission of Farrar & Rinehart.

[77] Arthur Hobson Quinn, *American Fiction: An Historical and Critical Survey* (New York: D. Appleton-Century Co., 1936), pp. 626, 628.

by an abundance of life and energy, by fertility of imagination, by a free play of emotion, by a large vision of mankind, by ardent enthusiasms. Sharp incongruities are apt to appear in their work. They show but a scant respect for "the rules," and at one point or another they are likely to reveal defects of craftsmanship. Among men of this description one thinks of Mark Twain or of Hugo (as novelist).

In the other group are those of colder blood, of more deliberate processes of thought and feeling, of narrower range in interests and sympathies—men who hover over their art with an austere solicitude. The name of Henry James comes inevitably to mind. The separation between the two kinds of writers cannot be better seen than in the remark of James about Twain: that he could appeal only to infantile minds. Here too may be recalled Norris' attitude toward men like Pater. Hartley Grattan accuses Norris of ignoring Flaubert entirely in preference to Zola because the former held to the ideal of style.[78] Mark Twain despised the confined and level art of Jane Austen.

Norris, who obviously belongs to the first group, has suffered from his imperfections perhaps more than most writers of equal creative power and similar defects. With exceptions noted, critics have preferred to say that had he lived he might well have written the mythical great American novel, and that he was a worthy pioneer of realism, rather than to accept *McTeague, Vandover,* and *The Octopus* in their own right.

Two men as far apart in temper and intellect as Howells and Mencken have best appreciated Norris and have best understood his essential quality. Howells (for

[78] *The Bookman,* July 1929, p. 507. Norris mentions Flaubert but once, in such a way, however, as to imply respect; see *The Responsibilities of the Novelist,* p. 297.

whom his best book was *The Octopus*) saw in him an epic poet with a fine and true feeling for "the stir of dumb cosmic forces." Mencken (for whom his best book is *McTeague*) sees in him the artist of tragedy who got from Zola the "essential secret of the serious novel: that its foreordained . . . . subject is the vain battle of man with his fate . . . ."[79] In most great creative artists, Mencken writes elsewhere, dwells the "conviction that human life is a seeking without a finding, that its purpose is impenetrable, that joy and sorrow are alike meaningless . . . ." This conviction, he believes, Norris shared with such men as Synge, Gorky, Crane, Dunsany, Dreiser, Moore, and Conrad. At their most reflective, no "first-rate race or . . . . enlightened age . . . . ever gave more than a passing bow to optimism."[80] Norris, it is true, gave his passing bow to optimism at the end of *The Octopus*. Under a momentary excitement he heard the pounding of his own blood in his ears and mistook it for the voice of a cosmic hope. But by and large he sensed the "doubtful doom of humankind" when viewed *sub specie aeternitatis*. "He remains," in Mencken's final judgment, "after a quarter century, the most considerable American novelist of the modern period."[81]

McTeague, The Octopus, and *Vandover and the Brute* are substantive works. What American novel except *Moby Dick* is overarched by a wider sky or moves to a more majestic groundswell of emotion than *The Octopus?* What other novel has a truer sense of the relation of man to the earth which bears him and returns him again to

[79] Howells, in "The Editor's Easy Chair," *Harper's Monthly Magazine,* CIII (October 1901), 825; H. L. Mencken, Introduction to *Vandover and the Brute* (Doubleday, Doran & Company, Inc., 1928).

[80] H. L. Mencken, *A Book of Prefaces,* pp. 15, 14.

[81] H. L. Mencken, Introduction to *Vandover and the Brute.*

the dust? *Giants in the Earth* is its equal in this; but that was left for a Norwegian-American to write. Elizabeth Roberts has this sense in her rarely beautiful *Time of Man,* though her novel, conceived on a smaller scale and written in a minor key, forbids comparison in other respects with Norris' epic.

What other American tragedy in prose fiction excels *McTeague? Ethan Frome,* perhaps, but only in economy and concentration, not in strength and poignancy. *An American Tragedy?* Its sprawling length, its prolixities, its *gaucheries* of style rob it of half the power of *McTeague.*

What American novelist has imagined people more real than Annixter, McTeague, Trina, Vandover, Hilma, Dyke, Osterman, Jadwin? Norris' power to make his creatures come alive extends even to the lesser figures which crowd his pages—the silent old man Dabney, for instance, who was killed with the others in the fight at the irrigation ditch and "of whom nothing was known but his name." Norris does not even take the trouble to describe his dress or appearance. Not once does he speak. At supper at the barn dance he "ate and drank quietly, dipping his sandwich in his lemonade." That is all; yet he exists as surely as that briefly seen pilot of Conrad's who was afflicted with a perpetual sniffle and who was forever coming to dry his damp handkerchief before the galley stove.

Which of our writers observes details with a sharper, fresher vision? Which is a greater master than Norris in the art of evoking a scene, with all its accompaniments of smell or sound or movement, as if it were actually present to the senses? Which, in sum, has greater skill to create the illusion of life?

Bibliography

ARMES, WILLIAM DALLAM. "Concerning the Work of the Late Frank Norris," *Sunset,* X (December 1902), 165–67.

BANKS, NANCY HUSTON. "Two Recent Revivals in Realism," *The Bookman,* IX (June 1899), 356–57.

BARRY, JOHN D. Review of *McTeague, Literary World,* XXX (March 18, 1899), 88–89.

BEARD, R. O. "A Certain Dangerous Tendency in Novels," *The Dial,* III (October 1882), 110–12.

BEER, THOMAS. *The Mauve Decade.* New York: Alfred A. Knopf, 1926.

BIENCOURT, MARIUS. *Une Influence du Naturalisme Français en Amérique: Frank Norris.* Paris: Marcel Giard, 1933.

BIERCE, AMBROSE. *The Shadow on the Dial and Other Essays.* San Francisco: A. M. Robertson, 1909.

BIXLER, PAUL H. Review of Walker's *Frank Norris, American Literature,* V (March 1933), 85–87.

———. "Frank Norris's Literary Reputation," *American Literature,* VI (May 1934), 109–21.

BLANKENSHIP, RUSSELL. *American Literature as an Expression of the National Mind.* New York: Henry Holt and Company, 1931.

BOYESEN, H. H. "Why We Have No Great Novelists," *The Forum,* II (February 1887), 615–22.

BOYNTON, HENRY WALCOTT. Review of *The Octopus, Atlantic Monthly,* LXXXIX (May 1902), 708–9.

BREWSTER, WILLIAM T., ed. *Specimens of Modern English Literary Criticism* (Introduction). New York: The Macmillan Company, 1907.

BRITTEN, FLORENCE HAXTON. " 'Prissy' Frank Norris," *New York Herald Tribune Books,* August 23, 1931, p. 13.

BURGESS, GELETT. "One More Tribute to Frank Norris," *Sunset,* X (January 1903), 246.

CAIRNS, WILLIAM B. *A History of American Literature,* rev. ed. New York: Oxford University Press, 1930.

CALVERTON, V. F. *The Liberation of American Literature.* New York: Charles Scribner's Sons, 1932.

Cambridge History of American Literature. New York: G. P. Putnam's Sons, 1917–21. 4 vols. Bibliography of Norris, Vol. IV, p. 668.

CASSADY, EDWARD E. "Muckraking in the Gilded Age," *American Literature,* XIII (May 1941), 134–41.

CHAMBERLAIN, JOHN. "The 'Prentice Days of Frank Norris," *New York Times Book Review,* May 3, 1931, pp. 2, 10.

CLIFT, DENISON HAILEY. "The Artist in Frank Norris," *Pacific Monthly,* XVII (March 1907), 313–22.

CONRAD, JOSEPH. *The Nigger of the Narcissus* (Preface). Garden City, New York: Doubleday, Page & Company, 1927 [1897].

COOPER, FREDERIC TABER. "Frank Norris's 'The Octopus'," *The Bookman,* XIII (May 1901), 245–47.

———. "Frank Norris," *The Bookman,* XVI (December 1902), 334–35.

———. *Some American Story Tellers.* New York: Henry Holt and Company, 1911.

CRANE, STEPHEN. *War Is Kind, and Other Lines* (*Works,* Vol. VI). New York: Alfred A. Knopf, 1926.

CRAWFORD, FRANCIS MARION. *The Novel: What It Is.* New York: Macmillan and Company, 1893.

Critic, The, XXXVI (April 1900), 352–53. Review of *A Man's Woman.*

DELAND, MARGARET. "The Novel with a Purpose," *The Independent,* LI (April 20, 1899), 1067–69.

DEMILLE, GEORGE E. *Literary Criticism in America: A Preliminary Survey.* New York: Lincoln MacVeagh, 1931.

DREISER, THEODORE. *A Book about Myself.* London: Constable & Co., 1929.

———. Introduction to *McTeague* (*Works of Frank Norris,* Vol. VIII). New York: Doubleday, Doran & Company, 1928.

———. "The Early Adventures of Sister Carrie," *The Colophon,* Part V, March 1931.

EDGETT, EDWIN FRANCIS. "Norris's Posthumous Novel," signed E. F. E., *Boston Evening Transcript,* April 22, 1914, Part Two, p. 8.

EDWARDS, HERBERT. "Zola and the American Critics," *American Literature,* IV (May 1932), 114–29.

EMERSON, RALPH WALDO. *Letters and Social Aims* (Vol. VIII of *Works,* Centenary Edition). Boston: Houghton, Mifflin and Company, 1904.

FIRKINS, OSCAR W. *William Dean Howells: A Study.* Cambridge, Massachusetts: Harvard University Press, 1924.

FLOWER, B. O. "The Trust in Fiction: A Remarkable Social Novel," *The Arena,* XXVII (May 1902), 547–54.

FOSTER, HANNAH WEBSTER. *The Coquette.* New York: Published for The Facsimile Text Society by Columbia University Press, 1939.

"Frank Norris's Werewolf," *Current Opinion,* LVI (June 1914), 455–56.

FREEMAN, JOSEPH. Introduction to *Proletarian Literature in the United States,* ed. by Granville Hicks and others. New York: International Publishers, 1935.

GAER, JOSEPH, ed. *Frank Norris: Bibliography and Biographical Data.* California Literary Research, Monograph No. 3. SERA Project 2-F2-132 (3-F2-197). N.p. (San Francisco?), n.d. (1935?). Mimeographed brochure.

GARLAND, HAMLIN. "The Work of Frank Norris," *The Critic,* XLII (March 1903), 216–18.

———. *Companions on the Trail: A Literary Chronicle.* New York: The Macmillan Company, 1931.

GILDER, JEANETTE. Paragraphs in "The Lounger" department, unsigned, *Putnam's Magazine,* VI (August 1909), 629–33.

GONCOURT, EDMOND AND JULES DE. *Germinie Lacerteux,* nouvelle ed. Paris: G. Charpentier et E. Fasquelle, n.d.

GOODRICH, ARTHUR. "Frank Norris," *Current Literature,* XXXIII (December 1902), 764. Extracted from *Boston Evening Transcript.*

GRATTAN, C. HARTLEY. *Bitter Bierce: A Mystery of American Letters.* New York: Doubleday, Doran & Company, 1929.

———. "Frank Norris," *The Bookman,* LXIX (July 1929), 506–10.

———. Review of *Frank Norris of "The Wave," American Literature,* III (November 1931), 349–50.

———. "Frank Norris," *The Nation,* CXXXV (November 30, 1932), 535–36.

GUÉRARD, ALBERT LÉON. *Literature and Society.* Boston: Lothrop, Lee & Shepard Company, 1935.

HARTWICK, HARRY. "Bibliography of Norris" in Walter Fuller Taylor's *History of American Letters.* New York: American Book Company, 1936. Pp. 564–65.

HATCHER, HARLAN. *Creating the Modern American Novel.* New York: Farrar & Rinehart, 1935.

HAWTHORNE, NATHANIEL. *Mosses from an Old Manse,* Salem Edition. Boston: Houghton, Mifflin and Company, 1893.

HELLMAN, GEOFFREY. "Trail-blazer of Realism," *New York Herald Tribune Books,* December 4, 1932, p. 25.

HEWLETT, MAURICE. *In a Green Shade: A Country Chronicle.* London: G. Bell & Sons, 1920.

HICKS, GRANVILLE. *The Great Tradition.* New York: The Macmillan Company, 1933.

HIGGINSON, THOMAS WENTWORTH, AND BOYNTON, HENRY WALCOTT. *A Reader's History of American Literature.* Boston: Houghton, Mifflin and Company, 1903.

HOWELLS, WILLIAM DEAN. "A Case in Point," *Literature,* n.s. I (March 24, 1899), 241–42.

————. Paragraphs in "The Editor's Easy Chair," *Harper's Monthly Magazine,* CIII (October 1901), 824–25.

————. "Frank Norris," *North American Review,* CLXXV (December 1902), 769–78.

————. *Life in Letters of William Dean Howells,* ed. by Mildred Howells. New York: Doubleday, Doran & Company, 1928. 2 vols.

————. *The Rise of Silas Lapham.* Boston: Houghton Mifflin Company, 1912 [1885].

————. *Criticism and Fiction.* New York: Harper and Brothers, 1891.

————. Review of *Moran of the Lady Letty, Literature,* III (December 17, 1898), 577–78.

HUGO, VICTOR. *Préface de Cromwell and Hernani* (The Lake French Classics). Chicago: Scott, Foresman and Company, [1900].

HUXLEY, THOMAS HENRY. *Evolution and Ethics and Other Essays.* New York: D. Appleton and Company, 1898.

Independent, The, L (October 20, 1898), 1129. Review of *Moran of the Lady Letty.*

————. LI (April 6, 1899), 968. Review of *McTeague.*

————. LV (February 5, 1903), 331–32. Review of *The Pit.*

IRWIN, WILL. Introduction to *The Third Circle.* New York: Dodd, Mead and Company, 1922. (Appears, slightly rewritten, as Introduction to *The Third Circle* in the *Works,* 1928, Vol. IV.)

JOHNSTON, MARY. *To Have and To Hold.* Boston: Houghton, Mifflin and Company, 1900.

Josephson, Matthew. *Zola and His Time.* New York: The Macaulay Co., 1928.

Kipling, Rudyard. *Something of Myself.* New York: Doubleday, Doran & Company, 1937.

Knight, Grant C. *The Novel in English.* New York: Richard R. Smith, 1931.

Kohn, Hans. *Force or Reason.* Cambridge, Massachusetts: Harvard University Press, 1937.

"Last Work of Frank Norris, The," *Harper's Weekly,* XLVII (March 14, 1903), 433.

Levick, Milne B. "Frank Norris," *Overland Monthly,* XLV (June 1905), 504–8.

Lewisohn, Ludwig. *Expression in America.* New York: Harper & Brothers, 1932.

Literary Digest, The, XLVIII (June 20, 1914), 1494–95. Review of *Vandover and the Brute.*

Literary World, The, XXX (April 1, 1899), 99. Review of *McTeague.*

———. XXXIV (March 1903), 54. Review of *The Pit.*

Lummis, Charles F. "Another California Novel" [*McTeague*], *Land of Sunshine,* XI (July 1899), 117.

"M." Review of *Blix, Pacific Monthly,* III (December 1899), 82.

Macy, John. *The Spirit of American Literature.* New York: Doubleday, Page & Company, 1913.

Marcosson, Isaac F. *Adventures in Interviewing.* New York: Dodd, Mead & Co., 1923 [1919].

Martin, Willard E., Jr. "Frank Norris's Reading at Harvard College," *American Literature,* VII (May 1935), 203–4.

Mencken, H. L. *A Book of Prefaces.* New York: Alfred A. Knopf, 1917.

———. *Prejudices: First Series.* New York: Alfred A. Knopf, 1919.

———. Introduction to *Vandover and the Brute* (*Works of Frank Norris,* Vol. V). New York: Doubleday, Doran & Company, 1928.

Millard, Bailey. "A Significant Literary Life," *Out West,* XVIII (January 1903), 49–55.

Millis, Walter. *The Martial Spirit.* Boston: Houghton Mifflin Company, 1931.

Montaigne, Michel de. *Essais,* ed. by Pierre Villey (Vol. I). Paris: Félix Alcan, 1922. 3 vols.

Muzzey, A. L. Review of *The Octopus, The Public,* V (May 3, 1902), 64.

Myers, Gustavus. *History of the Great American Fortunes,* new edition. New York: The Modern Library, 1936.

Nation, The, LXXVII (November 19, 1903), 411–12. Review of *The Responsibilities of the Novelist.*

Norris, Charles G. Foreword to *Vandover and the Brute.* New York: Doubleday, Page & Company, 1914.

———. *Frank Norris, 1870–1902.* New York: D[oubleday], P[age] & Co., [1914]. 28-page pamphlet.

———. Introduction to *Collected Writings Hitherto Unpublished in Book Form (Works of Frank Norris,* Vol. X). New York: Doubleday, Doran & Company, 1928.

———. Foreword to *Frank Norris of "The Wave."* San Francisco: The Westgate Press, 1931.

Norris, Frank. *[Works].* New York: Doubleday, Doran & Company, 1928. 10 vols.

———. *Yvernelle* (with *A Man's Woman* forms Vol. VI of the *Works,* 1928). Originally issued, Philadelphia: J. B. Lippincott & Co., 1891.

———. *Moran of the Lady Letty: A Story of Adventure off the California Coast.* New York: Doubleday & McClure Co., 1898.

———. *McTeague: A Story of San Francisco.* New York: Grossett & Dunlap, n.d. (Originally issued, New York: Doubleday & McClure Co., 1899).

———. *Blix.* New York: Doubleday & McClure Co., 1899.

———. *A Man's Woman.* New York: Doubleday & McClure Co., 1900.

———. *The Octopus: A Story of California.* New York: Doubleday, Page & Co., 1901.

———. *The Pit: A Story of Chicago.* New York: Doubleday, Page & Co., 1903.

———. *A Deal in Wheat, and Other Stories of the New and Old West.* New York: Doubleday, Page & Company, 1903.

———. *The Responsibilities of the Novelist, and Other Literary Essays.* New York: Doubleday, Page & Company, 1903. (Bibliography of Norris' writings, pp. 305–11.)

———. *The Joyous Miracle.* New York: Doubleday, Page & Co., 1906.

———. *The Third Circle.* New York: Dodd, Mead & Company, 1922. (Originally issued, New York: John Lane, 1909.)

Norris, Frank. *Vandover and the Brute.* New York: Doubleday, Page & Company, 1914.

———. *Collected Writings Hitherto Unpublished in Book Form* (Vol. X of the *Works,* 1928).

———. *Frank Norris: Two Poems and "Kim" Reviewed.* San Francisco: Harvey Taylor, 1930.

———. *Frank Norris of "The Wave."* San Francisco: The Westgate Press, 1931.

"Novels of the Month," *Review of Reviews,* XXVIII (December 1903), 753.

"Octopus, The," *The Independent,* LIII (May 16, 1901), 1139–40.

Outlook, The, LXI (March 18, 1899), 646–47. Review of *McTeague.*

———. LXIV (March 3, 1900), 486. Review of *A Man's Woman.*

———. LXVII (April 20, 1901), 923–24. Review of *The Octopus.*

Overland Monthly, The, XXXV (May 1900), 476. Review of *A Man's Woman.*

Paine, Albert Bigelow. Review of *The Pit, The Bookman,* XVI (February 1903), 565–67.

Parrington, Vernon Louis. *The Beginnings of Critical Realism in America, 1860–1920* (Vol. III of *Main Currents in American Thought*). New York: Harcourt, Brace and Co., 1930.

Pattee, Fred Lewis. *A History of American Literature Since 1870.* New York: The Century Co., 1915.

Payne, William Morton. Review of *The Octopus, The Dial,* XXXI (September 1, 1901), 136.

Preston, Harriet Waters. "The Novels of Mr. Norris," *Atlantic Monthly,* XCI (May 1903), 691–92.

Public Opinion, XXVI (March 16, 1899), 347. Review of *McTeague.*

———. XXXIV (January 22, 1903), 121. Review of *The Pit.*

Quinn, Arthur Hobson. *American Fiction: An Historical and Critical Survey.* New York: D. Appleton-Century Company, 1936.

Review of Reviews, XIX (June 1899), 749. Review of *McTeague.*

Roosevelt, Theodore. *The Strenuous Life: Essays and Addresses.* New York: The Century Co., 1901.

Rosny, J. H. *Vamireh: Roman des Temps Primitifs.* Paris: E. Plon, Nourrit et Cie., n.d. (189–?).

Ruskin, John. *Works* (Library Edition), ed. by E. T. Cook and Alexander Wedderburn, Vol. VII. London: George Allen; New York: Longmans, Green, and Co., 1902–12. 39 vols.

SAINTE-BEUVE, CHARLES AUGUSTIN. *Causeries du Lundi,* 3ᵉ ed., tome 13ᵉ. Paris: Garnier Frères, n.d.

SMITH, BERNARD. *Forces in American Criticism: A Study in the History of American Literary Thought.* New York: Harcourt, Brace and Company, 1939.

SOMERVELL, D. C. *English Thought in the Nineteenth Century.* London, Methuen & Co., 1929.

STEVENSON, ROBERT LOUIS. *The Wrecker.* New York: Charles Scribner's Sons, 1898.

TAINE, HIPPOLYTE ADOLPHE. *History of English Literature* (Special Preface to the English translation, and Introduction). Translated by H. Van Laun. New York: Holt & Williams, 1872. 2 vols.

TARKINGTON, BOOTH. *The Two Vanrevels.* New York: McClure, Phillips & Co., 1902.

TAYLOR, HARVEY. Bibliography of Norris in *Frank Norris: Two Poems and "Kim" Reviewed.* San Francisco: Harvey Taylor, 1930.

TAYLOR, WALTER FULLER. "That Gilded Age!" *Sewanee Review,* XLV (January 1937), 41–54.

THAYER, WILLIAM ROSCOE. "The Bases of Fiction," *The Open Court,* IV (July 17, 1890), 2393–98.

THOMPSON, MAURICE. "Tolstoi," *Literary World,* XVIII (August 20, 1887), 265–66.

———. "Breezy Books for Summer," *The Independent,* LII (June 7, 1900), 1387–88.

TOLSTOI, L. N. *What Is Art?* Translated by Aylmer Maud (Vol. XIII of *Works*). New York: Thomas Y. Crowell Co., 1899.

"Trilogy of Wheat, The," *The Bookman,* XIII (May 1901), 212–13.

UNDERWOOD, JOHN CURTIS. *Literature and Insurgency.* New York: Mitchell Kennerley, 1914.

VAN DOREN, CARL. Paragraphs on Norris in *The Cambridge History of American Literature,* Vol. III, pp. 93–94. New York: G. P. Putnam's Sons, 1921.

———. *The American Novel.* New York: The Macmillan Company, 1921; rev. ed., 1940.

VAN DOREN, CARL. *Contemporary American Novelists, 1900–1920.* New York: The Macmillan Company, 1922.

VAN DOREN, CARL, AND VAN DOREN, MARK. *American and British Literature Since 1890.* New York and London: The Century Co., 1925.

VIGNY, ALFRED DE. *Les Destinées* (*Société des Textes Français Modernes*). Paris: Hachette, 1924.

WAGENKNECHT, EDWARD. "Frank Norris in Retrospect," *Virginia Quarterly Review*, VI (April 1930), 313-20.

WALKER, FRANKLIN. *Frank Norris: A Biography*. Garden City, New York: Doubleday, Doran & Company, 1932.

WARDEN, CARL J. *The Emergence of Human Culture*. New York: The Macmillan Company, 1936.

WISTER, OWEN. " 'The Pit—A Story of Chicago'; the Last and Best Novel of the Late Frank Norris," *The World's Work*, V (February 1903), 3133-34.

WRIGHT, H. M. "In Memoriam—Frank Norris," *University of California Chronicle*, V (October 1902), 240-45.

WYATT, EDITH. *Great Companions*. New York and London: D. Appleton and Company, 1917.

ZOLA, ÉMILE. *L'Assomoir*. Paris: François Bernouard, 1928.

———. *La Débâcle*. Paris: François Bernouard, 2 vols., 1927, 1928.

———. *La Faute de l'Abbé Mouret*. Paris: François Bernouard, 1927.

———. *Germinal*. Paris: François Bernouard, 1928.

———. *Nana*. Paris: François Bernouard, 1928.

———. *La Terre*. Paris: François Bernouard, 1929.

———. *Le Roman Expérimental*. Paris: G. Charpentier, 1890.

Index